My Kashmir in Peace and Turbulence

Story of a Native in Exile

B.L. Kaul

PEACOCK BOOKS

Published by
PEACOCK BOOKS
7/22, Ansari Road, Darya Ganj, New Delhi-110002
Phones : +91-11-40775252, 23273880, 23275880, 23280451
Fax : +91-11-23285873
Web : www.atlanticbooks.com
E-mail : orders@atlanticbooks.com

Branch Office
5, Nallathambi Street, Wallajah Road, Chennai-600002
Phones : +91-44-64611085, 32413319
E-mail : chennai@atlanticbooks.com

Peacock Books is an imprint of
Atlantic Publishers and Distributors (P) Ltd.

Printed in India at Nice Printing Press, A-33/3A, Site-IV, Industrial Area, Sahibabad, Ghaziabad, U.P.

Dedicated to

The People of
Jammu, Kashmir and Ladakh

Preface

My Kashmir in Peace and Turbulence (Story of a Native in Exile) is an attempt to recapitulate my eventful life. The idea of writing from my memory occurred to me after reading Dr. A.P.J. Abdul Kalam's *Wings of Fire* a few years ago. Although there is no comparison of the most eventful life of the late President and my life, yet I feel that there are experiences worth sharing with others. I was born when India was still a part of the British Empire and grew up as a citizen of a free yet divided India. The division of the country which resulted in large scale violence was followed by tribal attack of Kashmir. I was still a child then but the turbulent events of those times left lasting memories in my mind.

Kashmir is a unique place in the world. The life and character of Kashmiris has been moulded to a large extent by the river *Vitasta*, also called Jhelum. It has influenced the temperament, character and behaviour of the people living around it. In normal times it flows serenely and is the lifeline of the people of the valley. Its flow amidst them has moulded Kashmiris as calm and gentle people. The same river in turbulence becomes furious and roars like a lion. Likewise, in turbulent situations, the Kashmiris lose their calm and turn violent. To a keen observer it becomes incredible to see the same peace-loving people turn unbelievably violent.

After seeing what happened to Kashmir in 1990, I felt intensely that I should share my experiences that I have lived through peaceful and turbulent times in the valley. It is painful for a Kashmiri brought up in peaceful times to have witnessed phases of violence and consequent untold sufferings of the people of the state during the last over quarter of a century. It was extremely painful to be forced out and to subsequently become an unwelcome person in one's own birthplace. My own family, relatives and friends became refugees in their own land as a consequence of the sudden and unexpected violence quietly hatched by a neighbouring country. Unforeseen violence, murder, rape and loot forced a whole community of peace-loving people to run for their own lives unmindful of leaving behind their homes and hearths. It was indeed unbelievable to find your good friends and neighbours look helpless to protect you from the unleashed violence and some known people turning their heads the other side or even behaving with hostility.

Emperor Jahangir called Kashmir a "Heaven on Earth" when he visited it first in the 17th century. He had a strong reason to describe it so. Had he been alive to witness what hell had broken out in the valley during the last decade of the twentieth century, he would certainly have changed his opinion. Such has been the extent of violence and damage caused to the reputation of Kashmir. As a result, Kashmiris, irrespective of their religion, have suffered during the last 27 years, all due to machinations of an evil-eyed neighbour. Almost the whole population of 4 lakh Kashmiri Pandits were forced out of their homes. Their only fault was that they belonged to a religious minority and their presence in the valley much pre-dated the arrival of Islam in Kashmir in the 14th century.

The Islam that I grew up with was a non-violent and tolerant faith. I grew up in such times when *azan* from a mosque, *aarti* from a temple and *kirtan* from a Gurudwara came at the same time and woke me up in the morning. My story and that of my co-religionists had been one of living with tolerant Muslims as good neighbours and friends. I felt that sweet memories of my childhood and youth spent among Muslims without fear and the economic development that took place from 1947 onwards are worth recording for the posterity. The younger generation need to know that since there was no electricity in villages and small towns children studied under the light of an oil lamp. There was hardly any road connectivity in the rural areas and students had to walk for miles to reach their schools. There were fewer hospitals and no telephones in the rural areas then. Very few people had telephone connections even in the cities and large towns. Accession of the state to India in 1947 changed all that and things started to change at a fast pace. In contrast, the last quarter of a century has been a disaster. The pace of progress has slowed down, and education, health and other services have suffered in a stifling environment of violence.

It is really unfortunate that right from its inception, Pakistan indulged in anti-India activities. Soon after coming into being on 14 August 1947 it conspired and launched an attack on Kashmir in October the same year. Thereafter it attacked India in 1965, 1971 and again in 1999. The 1971 war proved a disaster for them and resulted in separation of East Pakistan, now called Bangladesh. It should have taught Pakistan a lesson, but instead it has indulged in a proxy war against India since 1989. Terrorists are bred, brought up and trained on its soil and infiltrated into Kashmir to cause mayhem. By using subversive tactics Pakistan has neither gained anything nor is there any scope for gaining anything in future.

The only way forward is to talk to India across the table in a spirit of sincerity, give and take and settle all differences once and for all. It should stop worrying about Kashmiris and attend to its own urgent problems at home. Kashmiris will settle their differences with the Government of India on their own. The people of the two neighbours deserve to grow and take care of the teething problems of illiteracy, poverty, health care, environment, energy and economic development. There are lessons to be learnt from others, particularly the Europeans, for development and growth of South Asia. There is an urgent need to move forward for peace and prosperity of the people of the region.

B.L. Kaul

Acknowledgements

In writing a book it is imperative to take help from some fellow travellers and written sources. I have made use of both liberally. I must first and foremost acknowledge that my writing has been greatly influenced by two eminent personalities of the Jammu & Kashmir State, namely Ved Bhasin and Bal Raj Puri. Sadly both of them are no more. They were reputed intellectuals and journalists of the state. I was lucky to have had occasion to interact with them frequently. They knew the ins and outs of politics of the country in general and of the state of Jammu & Kashmir in particular. I confess that I have drawn liberally from their writings and lectures, and express my gratitude to both of them. I also express my thanks to Christopher Snedden for allowing me to quote liberally from his well researched book, *Kashmir: The Unwritten History* (Harper Collins 2013).

I am indebted to Col. (Retd.) Tej K. Tickoo for allowing me to quote from his book, *Kashmir: Its Aborigines and their Exodus* (Lancer Publishers 2012) and to the editors of *Indian Defence Review,* Oct. 26, 2014 for quoting from Col. (Retd.) Tej K. Tickoo's article, "Kashmir: Pandits offered three choices by Radical Islamists".

I am also grateful to Late R.K. Sher, a bureaucrat of the state who had the good fortune of serving under Maharaja Hari

Singh's administration as well as in post-independence state administration. He was a treasure-house of information and a great source of inspiration to me. Despite his honesty, integrity and efficiency, the post-independence state administration treated him unfairly and his juniors were promoted bypassing him.

For writing this book I have received unstinted support of my wife Promila and children. I must thank them for their suggestions and help with editing. I also thank Ms. Sarika Gupta and Mr. Bhanu Pratap Singh who painstakingly typed the manuscript. I also express my gratitude to Prof. A.N. Dhar for his valuable suggestions.

I also express my gratitude to the writers of the publications included in bibliography. Last but not least, acknowledgement is also due to Wikipedia, which is a great source of information on almost everything under the sun and I have definitely benefited from it.

B.L. Kaul

Contents

Chapter 1

Vitasta, the River of Life

The river *Vitasta* also spoken of as *Vyeth* in Kashmiri, Jhelum in Urdu and Hydapses in Greek, finds mention in many ancient books. Nilamata Purana explains why the river is called *Vitasta*: goddess Parvati was requested by the sage Kashyapa to come to Kashmir to ensure purification of the land from the evil Pisachas living there. The goddess Parvati assumed the form of a river in the Nether World. Then Lord Shiva made a stroke with his spear near the abode of Nila (Verinag Spring). With the stroke of the spear goddess Parvati emerged out of the Nether World. Shiva himself named her as *Vitasta* because the ditch excavated with his spear measured one *Vitasti* (distance between the extended thumb and little finger about 9 inches) through which the river—having flowed to the Nether World—had come out; so it was given the name *Vitasta* by him.

The river finds a mention in the Rig Veda as also in the Greek literature. It is mentioned as one of the major rivers in the Rig Veda. According to Srimad Bhagvantum, *Vitasta* is one of the many 'transcendental rivers' flowing through the land of Bharata or ancient India. The river was regarded as a God by the ancient Greeks, as were most mountains and streams; the poet Nonnus in the Dionysiaca makes Hydapses a Titan—descended god, the son of sea-god Thaumas and the cloud goddess Electra. He was the brother of Iris, the goddess of the rainbow and half-brother to the Harpies, the snatching winds. Since the river flows through a country foreign to the ancient Greeks, it is not clear whether they named the river Hydapses or the god was named after the river. Alexander the great and his army crossed *Vitasta* at a time when in spate in 326 B.C. at the battle of Hydapses river where he is believed to have defeated the King Porus.

Vitasta rises from Verinag spring at the foot of Pir Panjal in the south-east of Kashmir valley. It winds its snake-like course through the valley of Kashmir passing through the towns of Anantnag, Khanabal, Bijbehara, Awantipur, Kakapur, Pampur, Srinagar and Sumbal before joining the Wular Lake. Then it flows through Sopore and Baramulla towns before entering Pakistan-occupied Kashmir through a deep gorge. Enroute it is joined by the tributaries Arpat, Bringhi and Sadrina at Khanabal; Lidder at village Gur, Veshav and Rambiara at Sangam; Roomsh at Kakapur, Mahuri, Dudh Ganga and Tchoonth Kohl at Srinagar: stream Sindh at Shadipur; Sukhnag stream and Ferozpur nallah at Trikulabal; Ningalat at Ningal village; Erin and Madhumati at Bandipur, Pohru stream at village Doabgah near Sopore town. Near Domel Muzaffarabad (in Pakistan-occupied Kashmir) *Vitasta* is joined by the tributaries Kishan Ganga (also called Neelam river) and Kunhar river before flowing into the Mangla Dam reservoir created after partition by drowning Mirpur town.

From Khanabal to Khadanyar the river *Vitasta* flows calmly and is therefore navigable. The lives of the people of the Kashmir valley, particularly those of Srinagar city and other towns situated on the banks of *Vitasta* have been greatly influenced by the river for centuries. Upto the beginning of the twentieth century, the river was the sole source of drinking water for the Kashmiris. The services of water fetchers called mashkis were utilized by those citizens who could afford to pay them; otherwise it was women folk generally who filled pitchers of water and carried them home. It is no wonder than that water-borne diseases such as cholera often erupted as epidemics and took a high toll of lives. Potable water supply to the Srinagar city was commissioned during the rule of Dogras with the help of British engineers. They helped create a reservoir at Harwan and laid C.I. and G.I. pipes throughout the city. Most citizens could not afford to get private connections and the state-run taps provided water to the public in general. One could see long ques of women filling their pitchers of water on the streets of Srinagar even in forties and fifties of the last century. The redeeming feature, however, was that the public taps provided water for twenty-four hours a day, except in certain areas such as Zaindar Mohalla, Tankipora and parts of Rainawari where water pressure was low due to their higher location. People of the city had a great relief once clean potable water was made available to them and thus the incidence of cholera epidemics almost came to an end.

Vitasta continued to be the chief bathing and washing place for majority of the people living in Dongas (house boats) and in the houses located on the banks, especially during the summer months. Special bathing ghats on both sides of the river were built for the convenience of the people. At some bathing ghats facilities for covering women folk of the boatmen and others were provided.

In addition to utilizing the banks of the *Vitasta* for construction of beautiful and majestic houses the river provided sufficient space for the boatmen to anchor their small and large transport boats and the roofed boats (dongas) used for residential purposes. Small boats were also available on ghats to ferry people across the river as well as to carry them to various destinations in the city. Connected as the *Vitasta* was with Dal Lake and other water bodies boats provided an easy, though time consuming, means of transport.

The Katta Kohl a tributary originating from *Vitasta* at Tankipora near the old palace, passes through various parts of the city and joins the river again at Chhatabal in the down town. It was also used for transport as it passes through Tankipora, Zaindar Mohalla, Kani Kadal, Syed Mansoor, SMGS Hospital, Navpur and Danish Kadal before joining *Vitasta* again. Dal Lake was also connected through Tchoonth Kohl as also through channels like Nalla Mar (later filled up and converted into a road with disastrous consequences for the lake) which all finally joined *Vitasta*. All these provided additional waterways for transport of passengers and materials.

Besides the small and large houses, there were beautiful majestic temples and mosques on the banks of *Vitasta* all along its course, especially at Srinagar, among them mentionable being Hanuman temple, Shergarhi temple, Ganesh temple, Raghunath temple and Shah-e-Hamdan mosque, that added to its grace. The reflection of these buildings in the crystal clear slow moving water created images of elegance in the minds of the viewers. Often large logs of timber tied together to form rafts moved down the river craftily driven midstream by men holding long poles to keep them away from the boats and dongas anchored on the river banks.

Once in a while a large house boat with a white foreign couple sitting under a canopy on the top, sipping tea or coffee and watching the splendor of the surrounding buildings of the city, pulled by a motor boat upstream could also be seen. Children watched them from the banks and from the bridges with awe and uttered tunefully, "mem sahib, salam pata pata golam" (salute to the gentleman and the lady attended by a servant). Picnic and marriage parties entertained by a group of singers and dancers inside dongas rowing up and down *Vitasta* caught attention of the residents on both sides especially in the calm of the night with lights of gas lamps shimmering in water. The slow movements of the oars created pleasing sounds and ripples in water and shimmering lights danced. Such scenes were a feast to the eyes and ears.

Dongas were actually precursors of house boats which were built in the later part of the nineteenth century by a Britisher. Inspired, a Kashmiri Pandit enterpeneur named Naranjoo (nick named Navanaran—Narayan the boatman) joined the business and owned most of the house boats in the Dal Lake. Dongas were anchored on the banks of the river and formed residential quarters of most boatmen. At times, these were rented to picnickers to earn a living. Khochas (transport boats) and small ferry boats occupied a part of the banks of river *Vitasta*.

On the ghats, boatmen waited to ferry passengers across the river. Since there were only seven bridge located wide apart across the river at Srinagar persons in a hurry preferred to cross the river in a boat rather than walk a long distance. On some festivals the citizens especially Hindus lighted earthen lamps and placed them on rings made of dry grass and floated them on slow moving water of the river. It gave a beautiful look to the river with lamps scattering dancing lights in the slow moving down stream current.

During heavy rains *Vitasta* got flooded and threatened the citizen's lives especially those living in the Dongas and Khochas. The poor fellows spent sleepess nights keeping vigil and watching the rising level of water in order to anchor their boats safely. The fury of the river was discernible with trees, logs of wood and carcasses of dead animals and froth flowing down threateningly. Muddy water rose up the steps of the ghats and threatened the lives of the citizens like the enraged bull elephant in heat. The government machinery became alert and sand bags were used to close breaches in the banks. When the level of water rose to dangerous levels the government ordered cutting of embankments upstream at Kandizal near Kakapur village to let flood water flow to low lying areas often resulting in inundation of large areas of agricultural land and villages to save the Srinagar city from getting flooded, of course at the cost of poor villagers. The agricultural lands got silted but villagers benefitted in the long-term from the rich minerals present in the silt. A flood channel got built by the Dogra rulers at Ikhrajpura on the left bank of the river also took large quantities of flood water to save the city. The channel later joins the Wullar Lake. I remember the flood of September 1950 when river Jhelum flooded and engulfed large areas. The National Highway from Bijbehara to Awantipura was immersed in flood waters. Traffic stopped for several days. Badami Bagh cantonement and the surrounding areas close to the river also were immersed in water. The Srinagar city, however, was saved from getting flooded. The flood left 100 people dead. A devastating flood was recorded in 1903 which converted Srinagar city into a lake and 7000 houses went down including 773 on the Dal Lake.

It is recorded in History how an engineer 'Soya' solved the flood problem several centuries ago by persuading the King of the time to do as he was advised. Gold and Silver coins were thrown into the river and divers dived down with baskets and brought up silt along with coins. They were advised to dump the silt away from the river and keep the coins. In this way major portions of the river were desilted and thus the floods were averted for a long-time. The present town of Sopore (Soyapur) was named after this genius. During the tenure of Bakshi Ghulam Mohammed as Prime Minister of J&K desilting of the river *Vitasta* was undertaken on a large scale. Huge dredging machines were used for the purpose to desilt long stretches of the river from Baramulla upwards and enormous quantities of silt were removed in the process and dumped away. The river having thus been deepened it solved the frequent flooding of the *Vitasta* for a long-time.

As mentioned earlier *Vitasta* being connected with lakes such as the Dal, Nageen and Anchar in the vicinity of Srinagar city water transport was used to ferry men and materials. As children we used to be taken on picnics to Mughal Gardens, by our schools, using dongas and boats through these water ways. People in general also used to visit places of pilgrimage such as Tulla Mulla (Khir Bhawani), Pokhribal, Zeshta Devi, Ishbar, Hazratbal Shrine and Shah-e-Hamdan mosque using water transport.

Vitasta and her tributaries irrigate the agricultural fields, orchards and vegetable gardens in the valley. Fish from the river, her tributaries and lakes provide a rich source of proteins to the Kashmiris who are fond of and relish eating them. Special feasts at which fish and rice are served are organized especially during winter season to withstand the cold. The river and her tributatries also light up houses of Kashmiris by the electricity produced in the power houses run by water.

Vitasta has always remained closely connected with the lives of Kashmiris. It is in fact a part and parcel of their existence. The river revered by the people of all faiths is affectionaly referred to as Vyeth because it has always served them like a benevolent mother. It facilitates their existence in many ways. My own life has been shaped and influenced by the river like many others who loved and adored it for the sheer benevolence showered by it.

Alas the river that smiled on her children was forced to cry and wail by the same people whom she nurtured and nourished like a mother. It all started years ago when municipal drains were constructed in all towns and cities to carry waste water into the river. The clean water which was earlier used for drinking and cooking was polluted as a result. As if it was not enough the municipal workers started dumping solid wastes into the river from the bridges, to avoid carrying the same to dumping grounds wherefrom it was to be lifted by lorries to landfill sites outside the city. It polluted the river to such an extent that bathing on the ghats became virtually impossible.

The last nail in the coffin was driven when militancy erupted in the valley in 1989-90. Bleeding bodies of innocent people killed in cold blood were dumped into the *Vitasta* turning her water red and foul. *Vitasta* the mother cried like a mother does on the death of her children. There was no one to console her. People, out of fear of the killers, spoke in whispers. No one had the courage to face the ire of the gun wielding militants. The river that Alexander the great and his generals feared and hesitated to cross was reduced to a wailing grave. Her purity was spoilt. Will the future generations forgive those who desecrated the holy *Vitasta* praised by rishis and worshipped by the inhabitants whose lands it irrigated, whose food was cooked in its water, whose houses it helped to build, and whom it nourished like a mother does? Is there a way to ask for forgiveness and wipe tears from the eyes of a wailing mother?

A mother never wishes her children ill even if they treat her shabbily. But nature does not forgive. *Vitasta* which was a river full of life and vigour was reduced to a shallow stream. Such was the curse of Nature that limited snow fall and scanty rains dried up the sources of water during the peak years of militancy. Her tributaries and *Vitasta* had a low discharge of water. It threatened the very existence of the people by reducing agricultural and horticultural production. The wails of the river could be heard by the natives who loved her and were forced out of the valley, but not by those whose vision had been blurred and who had turned deaf with the sounds of gun fire and grenades. Nature finally retaliated in September 2014 and the calm river turned into a furious one and devastated the whole valley of Kashmir. A full chapter is devoted to it.

Chapter 2

Zaindar Mohalla

Among the many Mohallas (clusters of houses) on the banks of the *Vitasta* at Srinagar one that stands out is Zaindar Mohalla, where I was born on Hora Ashtami in the month of Phalgun according to Hindu calendar. It is situated between the left bank of the river and right bank of Katta Kohl, a tributary of the *Vitasta*. It lies between Sher garhi/Tankipora Mohalla (on south) and Habbakadal (on north). It had a mixed population of Hindus and Muslims living in peace and amity. While the Hindus were mostly middle and lower rung officials in the government and small traders, the Muslims were mostly craftsman, tailors, washermen, skilled and unskilled workers and preachers. The two religious communities respected each other's traditions, religious beliefs and culture. Communal harmony prevailed in the valley then. They lived together in peace and harmony.

The Pandits living at Zaindar Mohalla belonged to different gotras (clans). But they had also different surnames. Some of the surnames sounded funny for example Monda Kath (wagabonds), Kokar (roosters), Gagger (rats), Kaw (house crows), Braru (cats), Khar (donkeys), Khachar (mules), Jawansher (young tigers), Thalatsur (plate lifters), Thapal (snatchers), Duloo (urns), Kachroo (red haired), Shangloos (six digited); funny nick names (like those of the Britishers) given to some individuals casting aspersions on them in a neighbourhood that stuck to their families for generations. Some surnames were given after profession like Kander (bakers), Bazaz (cloth merchants), Waza (cooks), Peer (preachers), Sadh (ascetics), Malas (boatmen), Dass (servers) etc. Some other surnames were of unknown origin like Chogtus, Magazines, Chickens, Fotedars, Saprus, Safayas, Misris and Thusoos. Many surnames were after the names of their original villages or towns like Kakapuris, Badgamis, Soporis, Kashkaris (from Kashgar), etc. and were understandable. The common surnames like Pandits, Bhats, Kauls, Dhars, Razdans of course formed the majority. Muslims were mostly Sunnis and carried the common surnames like Khans, Dhobis, Wazas, Gilkars, Bhats, Gujris, Sheikhs, Dars and Pandits, etc. Some recent Muslim converts had retained their Hindu surnames like Bhat, Kaul and Pandit.

In spring and summer the mud roofs presented a beautiful look with yellow flowering Sisymbrium irio plants shining in bright sunlight. These roof top gardens of flowers compensated for the lack of any in the compounds. The whole city of Srinagar looked like a beautiful garden with most roofs dressed in yellow. Some houses with G.I. sheets and wood shingle roofs in between looked irrelevant in this scenario. These flowering plants called "London rocket" in English and "tchari lachhij" in Kashmiri are known to have medicinal properties.

A motorable road passed through the middle of the mohalla connecting it to Tankipora and Habbakadal. The lanes inside the mohalla were narrow. Houses were in rows, some large, some small but mostly pucca. Most house roof tops were covered with mud laid over planks of wood covered with bark of birch (bhojpatra). Some houses had wooden shingled roof tops but very few were covered with G.I. sheets. Most houses had small compounds but hardly any had trees except those on the banks of Katta Kohl and *Vitasta*. Such was the condition of Zaindar Mohalla where I was born. Situated as it was on of the banks of the *Vitasta*, my memories of childhood and youth have a deep relationship with this river.

The earliest memories of my childhood relate to my ancestral house at Zaindar Mohalla. It was a four storey house with a cobbled compound. There was also an outhouse which was used for housing our cows and storing fodder for them. We had a domestic help Habib whom I remember as a cleanly dressed kind and humble man. He helped my mother and other members in running the house. I also have a faint memory of an elder unmarried uncle Raghu Nath who had a benign appearance despite his position as a sergeant in the police department. There is also a faint memory of two elderly persons—Gojamam and his sister Yemberzal. The former was the father-in-law of my eldest late uncle Lalla Kaul whose third wife the only daughter of Gojamam too was dead. She had borne three children my cousins Batni, Nathji and Triloki Nath. His first two wives had died childless. Batni was already married to a fine gentlemen Prem Nath Kakroo when I was born. Nathji was employed in Srinagar Municipality and he was married in 1945 when I was about 4 and have a faint idea about it. The third cousin Triloki Nath was disabled having suffered from Polio as a child. Lalla Kaul had been a very influential person and held a responsible position in Srinagar Municipality prior to his sudden death due to stroke in 1938. Gojamam also died sometime in 1945 after which his sister Yemberzal shifted to her own house in the city.

Another elder brother of my father Nand Lal was an Inspector in police. He had a daughter Shyama from his first wife who had died due to tuberculosis and he had taken a second wife Kamlawati. He had died suddenly of heart failure in 1937 a year before the death of Lalla Kaul. The youngest uncle Gobind ji had died a month before I was born on 8th February 1942 to my father Maheshwar Nath and mother Somawati, their fourth child. Gobind ji had died of tuberculosis (for which there was no treatment then) leaving behind a young childless widow Shobawati while my father was hospitalized due to some ailment. I was later given in adoption to Shobawati by my parents as per eldest aunt Zaparded's wishes.

Raghu Nath was immediately older to my father. He was not married. After the death of their mother, leaving behind two young kids, i.e. my father and uncle Gobind ji aged five and two respectively he had taken it upon himself to look after them. I remember him as a very affectionate person who looked after four of us—two older sisters an elder brother and myself—so affectionately. Unfortunately his death in 1945 due to stroke left my father a broken man. He was left alone to look after besides his own wife and children, two widowed sisters-in-law and two nephews. One orphaned niece Shyama was married while Raghu Nath was still alive but Nathji's, marriage was arranged single handedly by my father Babuji.

Babuji had two sisters older to all the five brothers. The oldest Zaparded was an affectionate old lady who lived upto a ripe age and died in December 1963. She was married to Shivjee Peer of Habbakadal, who was a saintly person and Maharaja Pratap Singh revered him. They had two sons and two daughters. Another sister of my father was married in the family of landlords at village Nillora in Pulwama district. I never saw her because of her death before I was born. She had a daughter and three sons. I often visited Nillora village during summer vacations in company of my cousin Nil Kanth an employee of Srinagar Municipality. It was a typical Kashmir Village with a small brook passing by and plenty of chinar, willow and poplar trees. The main occupation of the people was agriculture and horticulture. I loved the place for its greenery, peace and tranquility. During the summer vacations I enjoyed to watch birds, most of them migratory, insects, butterflies, fish, tadpoles and frogs. There was plenty of space to play with the children of my cousins and children of their neighbours. Sometimes their older cousins, Mohan Lal and Chaman Lal from nearby Bijbehara town would also come and life was all fun. There was a Chinar Shaded flat area in the village where the elders would play cards and smoke cigarettes in their spare time while we played hide and seek and other games. It was all fun and carefree life away from the madding crowd of Srinagar and I loved it.

As I said earlier my father was a broken man after all his brothers had died in the Zaindar Mohalla house. Nand Lal had died at 45, followed by Lalla Kaul at 48, Gobindji at 28 and Raghu Nath at 50. One feature that characterized our family was tall and robust physique. All of them including my father were tall, handsome and well built people but suffered from hypertension and perhaps also diabetes. I suspect that they were unaware of their ailments with the exception of my father and died prematurely. Another killer disease prevailing those days was tuberculosis. It killed lots of people due to lack of proper sanitation, poor ventilation and lack of treatment. Beside my uncle Gobind ji, Nand Lal's first wife Lilawati, Zaparded's one daughter and Lalla Kaul's daughter Batni and one of my mother's sisters all had died of tuberculosis. As is well-known Pandit Jawaharlal Nehru's wife Kamla also died of tuberculosis as no treatment for it was available those days. Now the situation has changed and very effective drugs for treatment of patients suffering from tuberculosis even at advanced stages are cured. The discovery of B.C.G. vaccine was a great boon to mankind and brought down the incidence of tuberculosis in Kashmir and else where in the world drastically. It is a matter of concern that tuberculosis cases are still reported due to of resistance developed by some strains of the Bacillus causing the disease. B.C.G. vaccine has now become as important element of immunity development programme. My elder brother, sisters, myself and younger brothers and other kids received B.C.G. vaccines in the schools from forties of the last century. It had been made mandatory to give this vaccine to school going and all other children and we benefitted from it.

Zaindar Mohalla has also been important in our lives because but for two of our younger siblings Prediman and Bal Krishan we were born there. Our schooling also started from there. While our elder sisters Mohini and Kamta were initially admitted to Kathlishor Girls School, my brother Pushkar and myself were admitted to C.M.S. Primary School Habbakadal, which was under the administrative control of Christian Missionaries. The first such school was started by Tyndale Biscoe at Fatehkadal and he is rightly called the father of modern education in Kashmir.

A very vivid memory of Zaindar Mohalla that I have in my mind is the marriage of cousin Nath ji in summer of 1945. I remember him as a well dressed bridegroom wearing a saffron coloured turban and profusely garlanded. He was seated in the front seat of a chauffeur driven car and the back seat was occupied by my father, a Pandit ji and my brother Pushkar (6) and myself (3) seated in between the two. Rest of the marriage party were seated in a bus. The marriage party had to go to Rainawari. The bride Shanta's family seemed affluent and all

I can recall is that I fell asleep after a hearty meal. Rest I do not remember any other thing connected with the marriage ceremony. However, I do remember birth of Roshan Lal the first child of Nathji and Shanta, in the summer of 1946 when I was over four year old.

Our family was one of the well to do families of Zaindar Mohalla but misfortune had struck it with the death of my four uncles and some of their wives and children in a row. My parents were left alone to look after a large family including my two widowed aunts and three cousins. My memory also takes me back to the day when I was just over four years old. I was neatly dressed by my mother in the morning and my father took me for enrolment in the Christian Missionary Primary School at Habbakadal. The initial enthusiasm vanished the moment my father left the school after admission procedure was over. I cried and wanted to go back home. As my wailing continued my elder brother, reading in class three was summoned. Seeing him I felt reassured and stopped crying. The Kindergarten teacher was an affectionate bearded old man named Naba Saheb. His kindness, warmth and love must certainly have contributed to my interest and continuation in the school.

Our next door neighbour Abdul Salam was a tailor master by profession. He was a close friend of my father and the two of them had grown up together. He was also a political activist having a close link with the National Conference. We called him "uncle" and he treated us like his own nephews and nieces. His elder son Ali Mohammed was the same age as our eldest sister Mohini. The bond continued even after we had left Zaindar Mohalla and bought a new house at Nai Sarak.

My memories of Pahalgam are also linked in a way with Zaindar Mohalla. Being an important tourist spot Pahalgam with its own charm and beauty used to be hub of activity especially during Amarnath Yatra time. So the Government Hospital at Pahalgam was given additional staff for six summer months (May to October). My father was a qualified Pharmacist and due to tourist rush he used to be deputed for this period to Pahalgam. Thus our residence shifted to Pahalgam from Zaindar Mohalla during these months. The hospital and the staff quarters were located half a kilometer away from the market in the midst of a dense conifer forest. It was a beautiful location. I still remember the two bed hut allotted to my father. It was a small timber hut, with a kitchen and bath. Each of the staff hut had an open drain pipe with a fall bringing in crystal clear water from a nearby spring. However, G.I. water pipes were laid in the town, the market and hotels. The town used to be a favorite destination of the Indian tourists compared to Gulmarg which was preferred by the whites. The few whites who visited Pahalgam preferred to stay in tents away from the din of the town and engaged themselves in golfing and angling for trout fish found aplenty in the Lidder stream.

Pahalgam used to be a scene of hustle and bustle especially during Amarnath Yatra in July-August and the market was full of tourists and shopkeepers made good business during the period. There were not sufficient number of hotels and dharmshalas (inns) to accomodate the yatris. So tents were put up in the open spaces on both sides of the Lidder stream and in the adjacent meadows. Sadhus dressed in saffron clothes wearing long hair and flowing beards added color and mystique to the whole landscape. One Kanth Ram nursing aid in the hospital also helped my mother in household chores. He used to accompany us on visits, to the market. Being the youngest he used to carry me on his shoulders through the market filled with people wearing colorful clothes. I enjoyed this ride and often fell asleep in the process. The temple in the main market was lit with bright oil lamps at night and the fragrance of incense created a strange halo about the place as the devotees chanted hymns accompanied by musical instruments in the praise of lord Shiva.

Another busy place at Pahalgam used to be the "officers club" located in what was called "island". This was a piece of land surrounded on all sides by the roaring Lidder stream having its source at Seshnag on way to Amarnath. It had all facilities of a club including a swimming pool with ice-cold water. Pahalgam's beauty is mainly due to Lidder stream surrounded on both sides with wooded mountains and meadows. The "island" was linked with the town by a wooden bridge. In the sixties of the last century a devastating cloud burst destroyed many buildings, hotels, old hospital as well as the 'officer's club" which was then relocated to another location on the left bank of the Lidder.

Pahalgam will always remain in my memory for its sheer beauty and attraction. I remember that across the Lidder there used to be a small ancient temple called "Mamleshwar". It was situated at a higher location where from one could view the whole town. A small town especially at yatra time looked like a busy place with people, horses, carriages and buses moving about. When I grew up Pahalgam continued as a favourite place for my visits. I always made it a point during my visits to pay obeisance at "Mamleshwar temple" for it gave me a strange feeling of peace and tranquility. The roaring Lidder, the meadows, tall pines and the singing cicads and birds give a special character to Pahalgam. It looks like a veritable tiny heaven in summer. Strange coincidence though it may appear a small sleepy area of Srinagar called Zaindar Mohalla where I was born and grew up as a child and by contrast Pahalgam a thing of beauty and a place of great attraction, both hold a special place in my heart.

Chapter 3

The Tribal Attack

Circumstances had forced my father to sell our ancestral house at Zaindar Mohalla in 1946. Loss of his four brothers, some of their wives and children in that house in a short span of time from 1935-45 had affected him physically as well as mentally. He was thus advised by his spiritual preceptor Swami Nand Lal of Badgam to change residence immediately. My aunt Zaparded his only living sibling offered a part of her house as a temporary residence. Nathji, my cousin, who had by that time a son took his and brother Triloki Nath's share of the sale procceds and bought a small house at Sathu Barbarshah. So my parents along with four children and two widows shifted to aunt Zaparded's (whom we called Ded—revered mother) large house at Rishi Peer Mohalla Habbakadal. Ded was indeed like our grandmother (she must have been more than twenty years older to my father), very affectionate and loving. Her family was small. Her elder son Radha Krishen, an intelligent and efficient teacher, had died leaving behind his wife Prabhawati and son Makhan Lal. Her another son Amar Nath was unmarried. He was the sole bread winner. With her also lived that time her orphaned grandsons Chaman Lal and Nathji from a deceased daughter. They, however, shifted to their own house at Drabiyar a year later when Chaman Lal got married. By now Pushkar (my elder brother) and myself were attending C.M.S. Primary School, located at a stone's throw and sisters Mohini and Kanta had been transferred to Kashapa Girls Middle School Drabiyar. Zaparded's granddaughter Durga (Jiga) who was almost my age and lived at Nawakadal used to occasionally visit with her mother Devki Jigri. She played with me and Pushkar and we developed a strong lifelong bond.

Shifting house indeed helped my parents to overcome the pain and trauma that they had gone through the previous decade. But what followed in less than a year proved no less traumatic and disturbing. India gained her independence but at a heavy price. The country was divided into two independent countries—India and Pakistan which resulted in bloodshed and violent death of an estimated million people on both sides of the religious divide. Kashmir suffered too for on 22nd October 1947 tribals from North Western Frontier province of Pakistan backed and supported by Pakistan Army regulars attacked the state. Maharaja Hari Singh's inadequate but brave small number of forces posted at Muzaffarabad, Mirpur, Kotli and Kohala put up resistance but were outnumbered by the hordes of marauders. The helpless citizens were raped, killed and brutalized. The few officials and their families who survived and were later repatriated had horrendous tales to tell. The Maharaja's force would not have been defeated but for the fact that the Muslim soldiers deserted him and joined the raiders and Pakistan army. The raiders had been told that Kashmir was rich in gold and the women there were beautiful. The raiders took brass utensils of the Hindus for gold and started looting these besides gold ornaments. They also raped women and killed men and children. These activities slowed down their march towards Srinagar. At Baramulla town they entered St. Joseph Hospital and killed two patients an English man and his wife and raped white missionary nuns. One brave nationalist named Maqbool Sherwani misled them when they asked about route to Srinagar. This too slowed down their movement and allowed time to many Hindus and Sikhs to march to Srinagar on foot. When the attackers realized that Sherwani had misled them they brutally martyred him. A memorial built in his honour at Baramulla reminds of the sacrifice of this brave nationlist to this day.

The news of raiders attack and atrocities reached Srinagar and Maharaja Hari Singh feeling helpless had to leave for Jammu at night. I vividly remember the turbulence that the attack of raiders created in the valley of Kashmir in that October of 1947. Our own lives were thrown out of gear. On a cold day in early November 1947 my adopted mother Shobawati who had gone to her parental house at Rohama, in Rafiabed near Baramulla before the raid, returned accompanied by her brothers and their families without any belongings and literally in tatters. Their village like many other neighbouring villages had been attacked by the rapists, looters and arsonists. Many of their relatives had been killed and women raped but they were sheltered and saved by the influential Mir family of the village with whom they had close relations. The Mir family hid them in the attic of their house, gave them their own clothes to wear and provided rations to cook their own food. However, some people from other villages who had taken shelter in their house were brought out into the compound, lined up and shot dead. One of the victims was mother of Parmeshwari Devi a young lady teacher from Muzaffarabad posted at Baramulla. The daughter was taken along by my mother's family to Mir's house and she escaped death. Her mother, however, was gunned down along with others. Parmeshwari Devi later married Prithvi Nath one of the brothers of my mother Shobawati. There were numerous instances of Muslim neighbours sheltering Hindu families in their homes to protect them from the tribal attackers.

Baramulla town bore the brunt of the brutalities of the tribal attack as it was the first major town of the valley. Besides attacking the officials and the civilians they did not spare even patients and their attendants in hospitals. The looters spread out in the villages and towns and targeted Hindus and Sikhs besides those Muslims who opposed them and had sheltered their neighbours. They looted and burnt houses, raped women, sodamized young boys and killed men. When I visited Baramulla with my mother in 1949 the signs of loot and arson were still visible in the once flourishing town. It took quite sometime to rebuild the town. My maternal uncles had shifted from Rohama in the aftermath of the attack. While Prem Nath, a teacher by profession, had moved to Baramulla, Gobind Ram and Prithvi Nath had moved to Sopore and Srinagar respectively.

After things had settled down Prem Nath returned to his home at Rohama. I usually accompanied my mother to visit her paternal home during summer vacations walking on foot a hilly terrain from Baramulla. It used to be quite tiring but once there I used to enjoy the rich food and company of cousins Rattan Lal and Ashok both of my own age. The village located in the lap of a Karewa was rich in greenery and fruit trees especially those of cherries, apples and walnuts. Drinking water was scarce and had to be brought from a nearby streamlet. Due to lack of irrigation facility the villagers grew maize and pulses as the main crops on the rainfed dry land. There was a narrow kucha tanga road which connected the village with Baramulla.

The brutal attack by the tribals backed by Pakistan regulars could have been avoided had the ruler of Jammu and Kashmir Maharaja Hari Singh not dithered. Under the Cabinet Mission Plan the Constituent Assembly of India had started functioning in December 1946. The Maharaja did not join the Constituent Assembly and ignored Gandhiji's and Jawaharlal Nehru's advice. He wanted Jammu and Kashmir to remain independent and have relations with both—India and Pakistan. He was misled by a vociferous section of Jammu Hindus namely All Jammu and Kashmir Rajya Hindu Sabha and All Jammu and Kashmir Muslim Conference leaders to declare Kashmir as an independent country and establish a separate Constituent Assembly (Balraj Puri, 1993). This was in line with Mohammed Ali Jinnah's declared stand that the Indian states were free to join India or Pakistan or remain independent if they chose to do so. Maharaja Hari Singh did not see writing on the wall. In July 1947, Lord Mountbatten visited Srinagar and tried to persuade him to accede to either of the two dominions before 15 August 1947, but the Maharaja remained unmoved. Mountbatten had envisaged that dithering to join either India or Pakistan would bring trouble (Pyare Lal, *Mahatma Gandhi the Last Phase*, Vol. II, Navjivan, Ahmadabad, 1958, p. 32). On August 1, 1947 Gandhiji visited Kashmir to persuade Hari Singh to join the secular Indian State. While Hari Singh remained unmoved the people of Jammu and Kashmir returned the Mahatma's affection by welcoming him wherever he went. He paid a tribute to the people of the state by declaring that Kashmir was the only part where he saw a ray of light in the otherwise communally surcharged Indian subcontinent. Perhaps one of the reasons that made the Maharaja complacent was his belief that the state Muslim Conference supported him in his plans of an independent Jammu and Kashmir. Another reason could be the assurance given by Mr. Jinnah's personal secretary Khurshid Ahmed in July 1947 at Srinagar that Pakistan would not touch a hair of his head and take away an iota of his power.

Pakistan came into being on 14 August 1947. On 15 August 1947, Maharaja Hari Singh chose to sign a Standstill agreement with Government of Pakistan. Under this agreement the Pakistan flags fluttered over the offices of the Posts and Telegraph Department throughout the state of Jammu & Kashmir. No such agreement was made with the Government of India. While the Maharaja fully trusted Pakistan Governments' commitment Prime Minister Jawaharlal Nehru smelt a rat. He felt that Pakistan was waiting for the winter when Kashmir remains isolated. Then it would infiltrate and take some action. In his letter to the Home Minister Sardar Patel he expressed the view that the best course available to the Maharaja was to seek cooperation of National Conference and accede to India (Balraj Puri, *Kashmir Towards Insurgency*, 1993). This would make it difficult for Pakistan to invade Kashmir officially or unofficially and avoid confrontation with India. Had the Maharaja heeded this advice, there would have been no Kashmir Problem today.

Under pressure from different quarters Maharaja Hari Singh ordered release of Sheikh Mohammed Abdullah on 29 September 1947. On his release Sheikh Abdullah declared that primary issue concerning Kashmir was that of freedom from autocratic rule and need to form a responsible government to decide the issue of accession. He expressed his secular views and ideological affinity with Nehru and Gandhi. But as Pakistan had come into existence he was willing to negotiate with the governments of both the countries to secure interests of the people of Jammu and Kashmir.

Government of Pakistan thus deputed two emissaries Dr. Tasir and Sheikh Sadiq to Srinagar. According to Sheikh

Abdullah they tried to persuade him to accede to Pakistan and warned that otherwise Pakistan would use other means. Not deterred by such tactics Sheikhs Abdullah sent his colleagues, Bakshi Ghulam Mohammed and Ghulam Mohammed Sadiq to talk to Pakistan leaders. Neither the Governor General Mr. Jinnah nor the Prime Minister Liaqat Ali Khan met them. Instead they sent tribal raiders supported by Pakistan Army to invade the state on 22 October 1947 in order to create mayhem. It was a desperate attempt on the part of Government of Pakistan to grab Jammu and Kashmir by force.

Margaret-Bourke-White was a correspondent and photographer of the American Magazine *Life* and she covered tribal invasion of Kashmir in 1947-48. Her reportage on Kashmir—"Democracy in the Himalayas" and "Struggle for Kashmir" form part of her book on India *Halfway to Freedom* (New York 1949). The "Struggle for Kashmir" deals specifically with 'Raider invasion'. According to her, "taxi companies (in Rawalpindi) were donating twenty or ten or a couple of trucks each, the number I suppose depending on the intensity with which the owner believed the Muslims in Kashmir needed 'rescuing'. The trucks and buses would at times return within a day or two bursting with loot, only to return with more tribesmen to repeat terrorizing the Hindus, Sikhs and Muslims alike". She debunked the myths that arms for the invasion came from tribesmen themselves. In an eye witness account about the delivery of arms she writes, "in Pakistan towns close to the border, arms were handed out before daylight to tribesmen directly from the front steps of the Muslim League headquarters". She further revealed, "from Pakistan's capital a train loaded with medical supplies and volunteer personnel left every Wednesday morning for the Kashmir frontier. Some of the 'Azad Kashmir' soldiers taken as POWs by the Indian army, were found to have pay books of the Pakistan Army in their pockets".

She further writes, "for nine days Baramulla witnessed reign of terror under the forces of occupation". About the situation in the convent she records, "the nuns, their hospital patients, and a few stray towns people who had taken shelter at the mission were herded into a single dormitory and kept under rifle guard. On one occasion one of these days, after an air attack from the Indian army had left the tribesmen in a particularly excited and nervous mood, six of the nuns were brought out and lined up to be shot. It was by accident that one of them had a conspicuous gold tooth that saved the sisters. One of the riflemen wanted to get that tooth, before his colleagues had a chance at it. In the scuffle that followed, one of their chiefs arrived; he had enough vision to realize that shooting nuns was not the thing to do, even in an invasion, and the nuns were saved".

Margaret-Bourke-White visited Baramulla soon after its liberation by Indian forces. She records, "the once lovely town, straddling the Jhelum River at gateway to the valley, was as heaped with rubble and blackened with fire as those battered Jewels of Italian towns through which many of us moved during our war in Italy...the deserted convent on the hill was badly defaced and littered...we made our way into the ravaged chapel, wading through the mass of torn hymnbooks and broken sacred statuary. The altar was deep in rubble." She also gives an account of how martyr Maqbool Sherwani was killed by Pakistanis. Bourke-White met Sherwani's father and brother. On seeing Sherwani's photograph she notes, "even the soft-focus effect of the fuzzy studio portrait could not erase the intensity of the eyes and the look of strength in the high forehead."

Despite the claims made then by the Government of Pakistan that she had nothing to do with the invasion and it was raiders religious zeal to liberate Kashmir, facts came to fore soon after as is clear from Margaret-Bourke-White's account. It is now well-known that the attack was conducted under command of Major General Mohammed Akbar Khan who was in active service in Pakistan in 1947. He commanded the raiders under the pseudonym. "General Tariq". In his interview published in *Defense Journal* (Karachi June-July 1985) he said. "A few weeks after partition, I was asked by Mian Iftikharuddin on behalf of Liaqat Ali Khan (Prime Minister of Pakistan) to prepare a plan for action in Kashmir. I found that the Army was holding 4000 rifles for the civil police. If these could be given to the locals an armed uprising in Kashmir could be organized at suitable places. I wrote plan on this basis and gave it to Mian Iftikharuddin. I was called to a meeting with Liaqat Ali Khan at Lahore where the plan was adopted, responsibilities allotted and orders issued. Everything was to be kept a secret. In September the 4000 rifles were issued at various places and the first shots were exchanged with the Maharaja's troops and the movement gathered weight".

General Khan further revealed, "Khurshid Anwar had joined the Muslim League and he had been appointed commander of Muslim League National Guards. In September 1947, when the P.M. launched the movement Kashmir 'struggle' Khurshid was appointed commander of the Northern Sector. He then went to Peshawar and with the apparent help of Khan Qayyum Khan raised the Lashkar which assembled at Abbotabad.... Thereafter Qayyum Khan continued to take active interest in Kashmir and helped with the tribal Lashkars through the Kashmir operation. It was part of the agreement with Major Khurshid Anwar of Muslim League National Guards who was their leader that they would loot non-muslims. They had no other remuneration."

The raiders overran defences of the Dogra Army consisting of just 100 or so men led by Brigadier Rajinder Singh and reached the out skirts of Srinagar. The brave men led by Brig. Rajinder Singh fought valiantly up to the last man and last round. Had they not delayed the advance of the raiders and Pakistan forces the Srinagar city would have fallen and the citizens suffered immensely at their hands. This angered the peace loving Kashmiris and they united to face the onslaught of the raiders and defend Srinagar city. I remember as a five year old how young and old, men and women came out with sticks, axes and whatever they could lay their hands on the streets of Srinagar shouting, "Hamlavar Khabardar Hum Kashmiri Hain Tyar" (Beware the raiders we Kashmiris are ready to face).

The tribal raid left no option open to the Maharaja and Kashmiri leadership but to turn to India. When the Governor General of India Lord Mountbatten refused assistance, the Maharaja flew Mehar Chand Mahajan to Delhi on October 26, 1947 to convey his willingness to accede to India. The demand of the Maharaja through his emissary to fly troops the same day otherwise he would negotiate with Jinah enraged Nehru and he asked Mahajan to 'get out'. Sheikh Abdullah sitting in the adjoining room intervened and calmed down Jawaharlal and his attitude softened. The Instrument of Accession was signed by Maharaja and accepted by the Governor General of India on 26 October 1947. The India Army personnel were flown to Srinagar by special sorties on 27 October 1947 to clear the state of the invaders (Balraj Puri 1993, *Kashmir Towards Insurgency.* Orient Longman; Lt. Gen. (Retd). S.K. Sinha—News Point Dec. 6, 2010). The people of Kashmir heaved a sigh of relief on their arrival and welcomed them as defenders. Some tribal invaders were caught by the people, paraded through streets and handed over to the police.

The accession by the Maharaja had popular backing. This was vividly demonstrated when the invaders were repelled by the people of Kashmir led by Sheri-Kashmir Sheikh Mohammed Abdullah, towering leader of the National Conference. The wishes of the people were also ascertained when the Instrument of Accession was finally approved by the duly elected J&K Constituent Assembly. The elections to the J&K Assembly held subsequently have confirmed that the State is an integral part of the Indian Union. The Article 370 of the Indian Constitution gives a special status to J&K state and safeguards interests and aspirations of her people.

Serious doubts have been expressed in Pakistan academic and strategic circles about the wisdom behind 1947-48 tribal invasion on Jammu and Kashmir. Mohammed Ali Jinnah's role in the events leading up to the invasion has also come in for scrutiny, notably for its cursed legacy. It might come as a surprise to many that a section of scholars and experts in Pakistan are of the opinion that the 1947 invasion was a folly because it had precipitated Kashmir's accession to India even while Maharaja Hari Singh was inclined to opt for an independent Jammu and Kashmir. Pakistan and Kashmiris are seen as the end-losers (Mohammed Sayed Malik, *Kashmir Times* April 4, 2010).

With this misadventure, without any provocation from the Maharaja, Pakistan inflicted wounds on Kashmiris and destroyed their peaceful life. The two Nation Theory, which was a creation of communal politics of Indian Muslim League had not only resulted in the division of India but also in large-scale violence and killings on religious lines. The communal divide and killings destroyed the age-old communal harmony of united India. The scars resulting from mass killings resulted in lasting hatred between Muslims and non-Muslims of the subcontinent.

It was well-known then that both the Maharaja of Kashmir and Sheikh Abdullah were eager to negotiate with Pakistan Government, but had delayed the decision for accession for their own reasons. There are indication that both the Maharaja and Sheikh might have settled for independence had the Pakistan Government guaranteed it. Instead the Pakistan Government was in a hurry to grab the state by force. Had there been no armed invasion of Kashmir resulting in loot, arson and rape the course of history of the subcontinent might have been totally different from what we see today?

The residents of Srinagar were unaware of what was happening at their door steps. The raiders had reached the out skirts of the city at Parimpore and were firing gun shots. Marriages continued to be solemnized by the unsuspecting citizens who had seen a hundred years of peace in the valley. When a lady at Safakadal asked her husband in the middle of the night to find out what sort of noise was coming from somewhere in the neighbourhood. He admonished her and said that the noise must be coming from the neighbour's house who were probably dusting their carpets for the forthcoming marriage of their daughter. Such was the innocence and simplicity of the populace. While the division of the country resulted in a blood bath in the Punjab, Sindh and Bengal provinces of the British India there was calm and peace in the State of Jammu and Kashmir. That large-scale violence would erupt in the State forty-two years later in the valley, in particular, must have never occurred to any one then.

My father, unfortunately, had his right knee plastered during the tribal raid. He had been on sick leave for almost six weeks when the raiders reached the out skirts of Srinagar. It was on 26 October 1947 that the Instrument of Accession had been signed between the Maharaja and Government of India. On 27th October forces were flown by air to Kashmir. Major Som Nath Sharma of the Indian army was amongst the first to land at Srinagar airport along with his men and took a position on the Karewa of Budgam. He and his men were surrounded on all sides by the raiders and Pakistani regulars. The brave soldiers kept the enemy at bay for several days and saved the Srinagar Airport. Since it took time for more troops to arrive by air and road, the valiant soldiers kept on fighting the enemy till their last man and attained martyrdom. The engagement of the enemy by our brave soldiers stopped the raiders to spread in the surrounding villages and cause harm to the civilians who got sufficient time to escape to the safety of the city. Major Som Nath Sharma who laid down his life was the first soldier of Independent India to be awarded 'Parmvir Chakra' posthumously for his bravery and sacrifice for the country.

During this crucial period my brother Pushkar and myself in the company of our aunt Kamlavati were visiting our relatives at village Nilora in South Kashmir. The news of the attack by raiders in North Kashmir and their progress towards Srinagar was trickling through occasional arrival of a vernicular newspaper reaching the village and through word of mouth by those who were returning from the city. There was, however, no panic. Radio sets and electricity were unknown things in villages those days. These luxuries were available only in the city of Srinagar and some towns like Baramulla, Sopore, Pattan and Anantnag. There was only one small hydroelectric power station at Uri which was the first target of attack by the raiders and the whole valley was thrown into darkness. It may appear odd to young Kashmiris today but it is a fact. In Jammu also there was one small hydroelectric power plant located at the canal which generated electricity hardly sufficient for the Jammu city. All other towns and villages of Jammu were without electricity and homes were lit at night with oil lamps throughout Jammu and Kashmir.

In 1947, there were no means of entertainment except three cinema halls in Srinagar one at Baramulla and one at Jammu. Later on a cinema hall at Anantnag and another one at Sopore were built in fiftees. People in those days slept early and woke up only after the sunrise. There were very few hospitals and dispensaries. These were available besides the cities of Jammu and Srinagar only in major towns, i.e. tehsil and district headquarters of Kashmir, Jammu and Ladakh. For example, the nearest hospitals available to my relatives at Nilora village were at Pulwama and Bijbehara. People generally got their common ailments treated by Hakims and Vaids who used herbs and medicinal plants for treatment of their patients. There was no immunization programme in vogue at that time. It was only after independence that immunization against tuberculosis and small pox was made compulsory.

In villages, there were small shops which kept common commodities like tea, sugar, salt, condiments, edible oil, cigarettes, shaving blades, match boxes, cloth, etc. One of my cousins Ved Lal owned a small shop in his village. It was there that I saw for the first time how barter system worked. People were generally poor and hardly possessed cash. So ladies would come with paddy in baskets to buy whatever they needed. My cousin bartered goods and items with his customers depending upon the quantity of paddy they had brought. He stored the paddy thus collected in a part of his shop. Sometimes the customers brought eggs to barter them against their requirements. He used to sell the paddy to owners of watermills who husked it and sold rice in the cities. He would also visit Srinagar city to buy commodities from wholesalers mostly on credit and pay them in instalments. From his standard of living, I guess he did not make much profit. Most of my cousin's requirements of rice, cereals, vegetables, fruits, pulses and edible oil came from their own fields which one of the three brothers Darshan Lal ploughed with the help of farm hands. Their elderly uncle Tika Lal supervised the agricultural activities. Another cousin Nila Kanth was employed in Srinagar Municipality.

Village Nilora had no school. The nearest primary school was at another neighbouring village Achhan some three miles away. A middle school was available at another village Tahab and a high school at Pulwama, five and ten miles away respectively. My relatives had three daughters Kanta, Ratni and

Sheela but none of them was sent to school. They had four sons Som Nath, Omkar Nath, Moti Lal and Shiban Krishan and they were sent to the primary school at Achhan. A group of children from the village including those of neighbours—both Hindus and Muslims—would leave home after breakfast in the morning and return home in the afternoon. The school was a single teacher school and the roll must have been around fifty students. After appearing in 8th class examination my cousin Nila Kanth took me along to visit Nilora. During that period I had an occasion to accompany my relatives to their primary school. I found that the single teacher (a muslim gentleman) was a dedicated person and managed five classes efficiently. Som Nath and Omkar Nath did very well in their studies later, I am sure, because of the sound foundation laid in their primary classes by that noble teacher. They later rose to the position of Heads of their respective departments of Soil Conservation and Sheep Husbandry in Kashmir. The other two brothers also joined government service after graduation.

A child's formative years are very important both from the physical and mental point of view. Good nutritive food rich in proteins helps build a healthy body and a fertile brain. A good teacher in the early formative years of a child lays the foundation of his future. My brother Pushkar and myself and many of our friends like Brij Krishan Dass (who later become a noted educationist), Bushal Lal Tickoo and Bansi Lal Kashkari were lucky to have had our early education at C.M.S. School Habba Kadal. It was an excellent school run by Christian Missionaries from Newzealand, England and Scotland. In fact, Kashmiris owe a lot to Rev. Canon C.E. Tyndale Biscoe the pioneer of modern education in Kashmir. He started a chain of schools in Kashmir where in addition to teaching, sports, games, swimming, trekking, etc. formed an essential part of the school activities. It is no wonder that most luminaries of Kashmir were educated in these schools.

I vividly remember how during the tribal raid all village elders at Nilora assembled in a flat plot of common land covered with large majestic chinar trees called "Boni Dragur", and shared the incoming news and discussed the fall out of the raider's attack. Occasionally some guest would arrive from Srinagar or Anantnag with a newspaper and the news would be read aloud to those present. There was an air of uncertainty and fear especially in view of atrocities committed by the raiders. Kashmiris being peace loving people they did not own or keep fire arms. When the instrument of accession was signed troops started coming through Banihal Cart road. The villagers would gather in the "Boni Dragur" at night and watch the lights of the caravans of Trucks which passed through the serpentine Banihal cart road in the Pir Panchal mountains.

With the arrival of the Indian troops there was a sense of relief. At Tatoo ground and Badami Bagh in the outskirts of Srinagar camps of troops came up. The raiders who had reached the outskirts of Srinagar were engaged and killed and only a few managed to escape death. Air force was used to bombard the enemy camps. Ultimately the enemy was decimated and the people of the valley heaved a sigh of relief. It is a different matter that the troops did not cross the Kohala Bridge and take over Muzaffarabad. The troops also took much longer time to reach Poonch and Rajouri where the enemy played havoc and massacred thousands of innocent people. The people of Mirpur and Kotli were the greatest sufferers and hardly four thousand souls were able to reach Jammu in an emaciated condition and in tatters.

When there was some semblance of normalcy in Srinagar our aunt Kamlawati decided to return home with Pushkar and myself. By then, I suppose a month or so had already passed. Early one morning we set out on foot accompanied by cousin Darshan Lal. Our first stop was Jagan Nath Temple at Achhan. Set in beautiful surroundings the temple consisted of a spring and images of Lord Krishna and other deities. After breakfast in the house of a relative living nearby we left again. They gave us some packed food—rice and vegetables to consume enroute. We reached Pulwama at about noon and boarded a tanga (horse driven cart) which took us to Kakapora. There was a change over to another tanga for Pampore. By the time we reached there it was about 5 p.m. Finally one more change over at Pampore for Srinagar took place. We reached Srinagar when it was dark.

The troops had repaired the Uri Power house and at Srinagar Residency road and Amira Kadal were well lit. A tanga station was located at Lal Chowk those days and it used to be a hub of activity. I have no idea why we had to travel by tanga from Pulwama to Srinagar. Possibly there was shortage of petrol those days as Pakistan had stopped supplies even before the tribal attack. There was definitely bus connectivity between Srinagar, Pulwama and Shopian. As I write this Kakapora happens to be a rail stop for the Banihal-Baramulla railway line. In 1947, it would not have occurred even to our angels that Kashmir valley would one day have a railway service. Progress is on to connect Katra with Banihal with a railway line. Once this railway line is completed, Jammu and Srinagar will be reachable in just six hours. The Jammu-Srinagar railway line is an engineering marvel as it passes through long tunnels and tall bridges one of which over Chenab river will be the tallest in the world. The Jammu-Srinagar National Highway is being four-laned and tunnels at Chenani and Banihal will not only cut distance but also travelling time. These are indeed great achievements and will boost tourism and generate employment in Kashmir.

Chapter 4

Sheikh Abdullah's Naya Kashmir

Post independence, Kashmir was one of hope and fulfillment of aspirations of the people. Sheikh Mohammed Abdullah's slogan of 'Naya Kashmir' was on every one's lips. The wounds inflicted by the tribal invasion had started to heal and life was coming to near normalcy. The departure of the English from the country and Hari Singh from the state had drastically changed the political scenario and hope of a new era had kindled the hearts and souls of the people.

A new line had been drawn on the political map of India as a result of the tribal raid. Kashmir was divided into the so-called "Azad Kashmir", the part held by Pakistan and the Indian Kashmir. A vast territory of non-Kashmiri speaking people and of Ladakh was usurped by Pakistan and ironically given the name of "Azad Kashmir". This part has right from the start been held as a fiefdom by the rulers of Pakistan who even went to the extent of gifting a part of northern territories to China. Gilgit and adjoining areas are being directly administered by the Pakistan Government.

Soon after the accession of the truncated Jammu and Kashmir state a new administrative set up came into being. However, the people of the valley felt the impact of the division of the state immediately after the tribal attack was over. The closure of Jhelum Valley road which connected the valley with Muzaffarabad and Pakistani Punjab resulted in shortage of essential commodities in the winter months and even later. The Pakistan Government had stopped supply of rock salt, sugar, petrol, etc. even before the Indian Army took control and the meagre stocks available were withheld by the unscrupulous profiteers. To top it all the insufficient produce of local paddy crop made things even more difficult for the people. The winter season of 1947-48 was a very difficult one for the poor people of the valley in particular. Supplies of essential commodities, started pouring in from the Indian Punjab through Banihal Cart road but early snowfall closed the road. I remember that when my younger brother Prediman was born in February 1948 there was not a grain of salt in the house. I accompanied a relative to a shopkeeper who secretly agreed to sell 50 gms of salt for Rupees five (in normal times 800 gms cost one quarter of a rupee). In the absence of availability of rice, people started eating chapatis made from wheat or maize flour. When even these were not available people had to consume boiled potatoes and dried beans. The spring and summer of 1948 was very difficult and full of hardships for the people of the valley. It was only after Government of India started supplying rice imported from Burma that the food situation in Kashmir improved.

Initially Sheikh Abdullah had taken over as head of the Emergency Administration on 27 October 1947. Maharaja's administration had almost completely broken down and Sheikh's National Conference party filled the administrative vacuum. The N.C. workers not only manned the 23 member Emergency Council, but were also appointed as government officials. The state was still governed by the J&K constitution Act of 1933 which had no provision of emergency. The Abdullah administration acted arbitrarily without any defined powers. The party workers assumed de facto authority to arrest and punish whosoever they held guilty. With unchecked political power and controlled administration Abdullah was able to further regiment all aspects of Kashmiri life (Balraj Puri 1993). This was, however, before March 1948 when Maharaja Hari Singh appointed a Council of Ministers.

On 5 March 1948, Maharaja Hari Singh appointed a council headed by Sheikh Abdullah. The council of ministers started working in the right earnest and the people of the state had a sigh of relief. Accession of the state to India meant dawn of democracy for the people of the State. However, it also meant transfer of power from a Jammu based ruler to a Kashmir-based leadership. The Kashmiri leadership did not make any effort to understand the mind of its people—both Hindus and Muslims. As a matter of fact the Kashmiri leadership ignored the basic aspirations of the people of Jammu and there was a simmering discontent among the already alienated feudal class and the people of Jammu in general (Balraj Puri 1993).

Jammu and Kashmir state was the first state in the country which legislated agrarian reforms. With one stroke the government ended the feudal system in the state. It created a furore in the state but at the same time liberated poor farmers from the bond of working for the landlords. "Land to the tiller," overnight made a large majority of landless people owners of the land that they tilled. It brought a new dawn in the lives of the landless farmers. They became owners of the land that they had been tilling for landlords for generations and it changed their lives forever. With these reforms the already popular Sheikh Abdullah became a messiah—a liberator. His popularity among the rural poor in Kashmir touched the sky. It however, alienated the influential landlord class many of whom in the valley were non-muslims, but included muslim landlords also. They felt that their livelihood had been snatched without compensation. In Jammu also the reforms were not popular among the feudal class. Later these very people actively supported the Praja Parishad movement in Jammu with not so good consequences.

There was a simmering discontent among the already alienated feudal class and the people of Jammu. To it was added fuel by the loose talk by some National Conference leaders who openly declared that they were in favour of reversing the 100 years of "Dogra Raj". Although Jammu region represented 45 per cent of the population against 53 per cent of the valley, yet in 1952 there was only one representative in a cabinet of 5 from Jammu region. The ruling party did not include even a single important office bearer in its hierarchy from Jammu region. The inclusion of Article 370 in the Indian Constitution, at the behest of Sheikh Abdullah, and the possibility of holding a plebiscite and Muslim majority of Kashmir voting against India created doubts and fear in the minds of the Jammu people. All these things led to the launching of an agitation in Jammu by Praja Parishad, Jana Sangh, Hindu Maha Sabha and Ram Rajya Parishad. Thus seeds of the beginning of the end of Kashmir's emotional relation with the rest of India were sown. It hit the Kashmir psyche as it threatened their identity as Kashmiris who had openly opposed a two Nation Theory and fought against their co-religionists in Pakistan and had opted for India. It was an unfortunate development for which the leaders of Jammu were responsible (Balraj Puri 1993).

In constituent Assembly in 1951 N.C. won all the seats. The nomination papers of Praja Parished candidates were rejected on flimsy grounds. It set a trend to be followed in subsequent elections as is now universally recognized that the elections in the state were usually manipulated especially during Bakshi Ghulam Mohammed's regime. Sheikh Abdullah had made Bakshi his Deputy P.M. resulting in Mohi-ud-din Karra parting ways. He formed a Pro-Pak "Political Front" in 1948 and in December 1963 Mr. Karra led an agitation after disappearance of the holy relic of Prophet Mohammed PBUH from Hazratbal shrine.

While all the political change was happening, changes in educational system were also taking place. My Primary School at Habba Kadal was housed in a private rented building with a large compound owned by the rich Mir family. The School had besides moderately large classrooms, a big hall connected with the ground by an emergency fire-pole, Principal's room, a staffroom, a sports room and a tuck shop. There used to be a morning assembly in the open compound on dry days and in the hall on the second floor on wet days. A Padri (priest) used to come on Thursdays and we used to assemble in the hall and sing a melodious hymn of which I remember just one line. "Mera hoga Khudawand gadariya". This was followed by a sermon by the south Indian Priest which I hardly understood except for the part concerning life of the Christ.

Our teachers were mostly Kashmiri Pandits. I remember names of two Janki Nath Krandu and Shamboo Nath Durani both of whom hailed from Rainawari and wore turban. Earlier there was a tall and smart Headmaster named Radha Krishan but later he was replaced by Gobind Razdan who also used to wear a turban. Janki Nath was my form teacher in class 3. He was an affectionate and good humoured person. Pupils loved him. Shamboo Nath was form teacher of class 5. He was a sportsman as well and quite popular with senior students.

I remember an incident when I was in class 3. It related to two of my friends and class mates Brij Lal and Girdhari Lal both of whom lived at Purshyar. Brij used to call Girdhari by the nick name "goor" (milkman). I too sometimes used to tease Girdhari by calling him by that nick name. One day after the school closed Girdhari invited me to visit his home. I happily agreed and accompanied him. His house was situated on the bank of the river Jhelum. It was a grand house considering its location and construction. I was warmly received by Girdhari's grandfather an affectionate old man. He made me sit comfortably and asked about my parents while my friend went away to change. The old man then called somebody, perhaps their domestic help and asked him to get some fruit for me. A sliced apple was bought on a plate and placed before me. In the meanwhile Girdhari also returned and sat near me. I hesitated but the old man persuaded me to take a slice of the apple.

The old man told me that he knew my father well. I smiled when he said so, obviously pleased. Then he asked me whether I had seen any cows in their compound to which I replied in negative. Then he asked me so why did I call Girdhari as "goor"—a milkman. I blushed and fumbled to say that Brij was calling him so. The kind old man reassured me and said that he did not mean to admonish me but it was a bad habit among Kashmiris to call people names. Indeed their ancestors used to own milch cows for religious sentiments and also for the sake of having pure milk for personal consumption and not for sale. So they were not milkmen in reality, but the neighbours and others started calling them by that name and it had stuck. The old man had succeeded in bringing home to me that it was not a good habit to call others names. He had also succeeded in making me learn a lesson. It was obvious to me that the old man had asked his grandson to invite me to meet him.

For some reason the C.M.S. School at Habba Kadal was closed down by the management. I suspect that for the missionaries it had become a financial burden. By then I had been promoted to class 4 and my brother Pushkar had passed class 5 a year ago and had joined another school. The students were given a choice to take a school leaving certificate or to move to C.M.S. High School at Feteh Kadal or C.M.S. High School at Sheikh Bagh. My father chose to take my discharge certificate and admit me in Model Public School Magharmal Bagh where my elder brother was enrolled earlier and Babuji's friend Mr. B.N. Chhatoo was Headmaster. The school was an experimental school directly under the control of Teachers Training College.

It was the year 1951 and we had already moved to our new house at Nai Sarak a year ago. Here I had found new friends in Bej Kishan Waza and Kakaji Trisal. While Kakaji was about my age Bej Kishan was a year younger. Nai Sarak area was less congested than Zaindar Mohalla and Habba Kadal. There was a large open space surrounded by a marsh and open water body called "Kashram Demb". The marsh was full of Coots and Moorhen. In the summer wild ducks mostly mallards would also arrive in the wet land. Milkmen Haji Gafar Joo and Shahban Joo also lived nearby. Besides their homes they also owned open land where they accumulated cow dung in big heaps. Later they dried cow dung as cakes which was sold for use as fuel during winter months along with wood in chulahs in all homes. The children of the area played hide and seek between these heaps of dung.

Haji Gafar Joo was highly revered by all for his piousness and having performed pilgrimage to Mecca. His wife Khadija Bee was a kind lady and whenever children were sent by their elders to buy milk or yogurt from her shop she would offer a little yogurt on their palms to taste. So children were too pleased when sent by elders to buy yogurt or milk from her shop. The eldest son of Gafar Joo, Qadir Joo was a noble and hardworking person but he was hard of hearing. He did most of the work involved in feeding, looking after and milching of cows and was helped in this by his wife. His another brother Rehman did other connected errends like fetching fresh grass, fodder and also cleaning and removing cow dung from the sheds. Their only sister Daulat was already married when we moved.

Bej Kishan and Kakaji had befriended a Muslim boy Rashid, rendered blind by small pox. He was the only son of a poor couple working as municipal workers. He was older to all the three of us and more mature and wise. Besides being soft spoken he was well mannered. His parents always kept him clean and well dressed. We liked his company for his wit and wisdom. While other kids, both muslim and non-muslim, distanced themselves from him we loved his company. Unfortunately the poor fellow suddenly fell sick and soon after died of some unknown disease which shattered his parents completely and deeply saddened all three of us and we cried inconsolably when he was buried. We had another muslim friend Ashraf Khan. Occasionally his younger sister named Tota would accompany him when we played in the large compound of Wallis in the neighbourhood.

The Central Model School was in fact an experimental school and new methods of teaching were adopted there. Besides normal teaching, arts and crafts were also taught. I developed a taste for drawing which later helped me as a student of science in higher classes. Since the school was under the control of Teachers Training College, pupil teachers would deliver lessons, once in a while, using teaching aids like charts and models. Some pupil teachers were really good; they used humour, anecdotes and interesting tales to catch our attention. Sometimes we were taken to the Teachers Traning College, situated just at a stone's throw for assessing our learning capabilities. Mr. Chhatoo, the Headmaster was in complete control and it was indeed a Model School.

Those days exams were really stiff in the schools and some students were not promoted to the next class if they did not perform well. I remember when one of my class fellows Shafi was declared unsuccessful in class 5 his father Tailor Master Ghulam Rasool approached the Headmaster to know as to why his son was not promoted. The Headmaster asked him to meet the second master who was also the Examination Incharge and at that time busy teaching our class. The teacher asked the father and son to enter the classroom and wait. He then went out to bring the English answer sheet of the student. On his return the teacher handed over the answer sheet to Shafi and asked him to read his essay on cow that he had written. Here I reproduce what Shafi had written:

> Cow
> Cow is my mother.
> Cow is my father.
> Cow is my titter (sister).
> Cow is my brother.
> Cow eats deen dass (green grass).
> Cow gives L.

When he had completed reading the whole class burst into laughter. The second master asked father of the boy, "now tell me sir, is your son fit for promotion? How can a cow be father, mother, sister and brother all at the same time? What does he mean by 'titter', 'deen dass' and 'L'? At this point father of the boy intervened to say that his son had a problem with his speech. By 'titter' he meant 'sister' and 'deen dass' meant 'green grass'. The teacher then asked Shafi what did he mean by the letter 'L'. Shafi blurted out "sir 'lober' (Kashmiri for cow dung). I left it there because I did not know the spellings". The teacher asked the father of the boy whether he still felt that his son should be promoted to the next class "Certainly not sir," said Ghulam Rasool and left.

Soon after my promotion to the next class in the spring of 1952 transfer orders of our father as senior Pharmacist at Government Hospital Pulwama were issued. After joining at Pulwama he decided that Pushkar and myself should accompany him and got us admitted in the High School at Pulwama. Dr. Padam Nath Ganjoo a man of literary taste and a close friend of the famous Kashmiri poet Abdul Ahad Azad was the Medical officer at that time. His son Bushan Lal was my age and we became good friends. Pulwama then was a Tehsil Headquarter. It is the District Headquarter now. Situated 20 miles from Srinagar, Pulwama was then a small sleepy town with a stream passing through. The main bazaar consisted of shops on both sides of a road leading from Srinagar to Shopian. There was a small open area by the stream which served as a bus stand. There was also a tonga stand nearby. The Tehsildar's office, police station and treasury were situated behind the row of shops on the eastern side. The hospital was well located in a three acre elevated piece of land with staff quarters and a small brook passing by. The town was full of activity during the day but after 5 P.M. all was quiet. There was no electricity and we used kerosene lamps at night. A battery operated radio blurted out music and news from a room of the Information Department also located in the main bazaar. People would gather to listen to news broadcast from Radio Kashmir Srinagar and All India Radio, New Delhi.

A few buses plied daily between Srinagar, Pulwana and Shopian towns. The buses those days were small meant for seating 20 passangers beside the driver and conductor (called cleaner). Those buses were just the size of mini buses that ply in our cities today. The front seat by the side of the driver was always reserved for a V.I.P., viz. some government official or a political leader.

The Government High School at Pulwama to which my brother and myself were admitted in classes 7 and 5 respectively, by contrast to the schools attended by us at Srinagar, was poor in infrastructure. The school building was a private rented house in the main market. There were a few classrooms with inadequate equipment but well qualified staff made up for these deficiencies. Nearby there was a large open area partly covered by Chinar trees which on most part served as our classroom and playground on dry days. The Headmaster Mr. Ghulam Mohammed Hakim used to sit in a chair with a table in front under these majestic trees keeping a watchful eye on the open room teaching activities. Blackboards were portable ones and we were made to sit on coir matting. Initially we felt uncomfortable having been used to sitting on desks at Srinagar and complained to our father about it. He listened to our complaint and then cited the example of Vishwa Bharati University started in open by Rabindra Nath Tagore at Calcutta. Weather permitting examinations were also held in the open. As I said earlier the teaching staff was good. I especially remember second master

Mr. Gopi Nath Moglu. Other teachers included Shamboo Nath Chaloo, Dwarika Nath, Makhan Lal, Mohan Lal, Maulvi Rashid Sahib, Akbar Jaipuri and a jolly good arts teacher whose name I am unable to recall. Mr. G.N. Moglu's sons Kashmiri Lal and Tej Krishan became my best friends. There were other class fellows like Mohd. Akram Hajam, Jawaharlal Bhat, Girdhari Lal and Triloki Nath who became my good friends. All of them later did well in their careers. While as Akram went into administration, Girdhari and Jawahar became college professors and Triloki join the prestigious C.M.S. Tyndale Biscoe School at Srinagar as a teacher.

Every morning there used to be an assembly where after singing patriotic songs, the Headmaster would address the students. It was during these morning assembly sessions that he would inform us about the latest developments in the state and the country. I vividly remember when he informed us about Karan Singh, son of Maharaja Hari Singh becoming Sadre-Riyasat (now called Governor) of Jammu and Kashmir. Similarly, it was again he who informed us about Edmund Hillary and Tensing Norgay conquering the Mount Everest on 29 May 1953.

Maulvi Rashid taught us Urdu. Besides teaching he used to inculcate good manners and habits among his pupils. It was he who educated us about importance of cleanliness and good personal hygiene. He always asked his students whether they had washed their hands after visiting a toilet. I remember how he used practical methods to educate us. Once he asked a student to get some drinking water for him. The boy returned with a metal tumbler containing water. The teacher returned the tumbler and told him to get it in a glass tumbler. When the boy returned with a glass tumbler full of water the teacher just kept it on the table. Later he lifted the glass tumbler containing water and explained why he had refused to accept the metal tumbler. He said as he could not see through the metal tumbler whether it contained clean water that is why he did not accept it. Then he continued and said that before we drink water we must look whether it is pure and clean. If it is not clean we should not drink it. We should, if necessary, let it stand and allow sediment to settle down before having a few sips. Those days potable water was not available in the towns and villages and people used water from springs, brooks or streams for drinking and cooking. Even in the hospital there was no tap water available then. We used water from a spring in the premises for drinking and cooking.

Another teacher, Mohan Lal who taught us science took our class to a nearby watermill where corn, wheat and rice were grounded to flour and explained to us how a water fall was used to turn a turbine which in turn helped convert cereals to flour. Similar method, he explained was used to let water fall from a height to turn turbines which in turn generated electricity with the help of large magnets. So even in the absence of a laboratory he would explain things to us. For example, he would take us to a field and show how to observe insects, snails, tadpoles, birds, flowers and other forms of life. This laid a sound foundation of science temper in his students.

Sometimes, we ventured out of the town on our own into the country side where men and women worked in the fields transplanting rice seedlings, deweeding and applying manure etc. For miles and miles one could see green rice fields. When autumn arrived the rice fields, changed colour to golden yellow and the whole countryside gave a beautiful look. This was followed by harvesting and other activities. A city boy but for such an exposure would otherwise never have an opportunity to have a practical knowledge of village life and farming practices.

I remember an incident while I was still a student at Pulwama. During July 1953, there were a few holidays and to utilize this time in fun and frolic, I requested my father to let me pay a visit to our relatives at village Nilora. All other family members had gone to Srinagar so I was feeling lonely. My father was reluctant to let me walk eight miles to the village alone but on my insistence he allowed me to go. It was a cloudy day and I left home happily after breakfast. After walking about two miles it started to drizzle and I thought it might be better to return rather than get drenched all the way. I stopped under a tree and was still thinking when I saw two men coming from Pulwama one of them was in police uniform and his companion was a rather dark and sturdy man. When they reached the tree under which I had taken shelter they also stopped. The police officer asked me, "is your name Bansi Lal?" I was surprised and said, "yes sir, but how do you know?" "Doctor Sahib met me by chance outside the hospital and he asked me where I was going. When I said that I was going to Achhan he told me that you too are going that side and I should take care of you. He told me that your name is Bansi Lal and you are eleven year old".

Soon after drizzling stopped and all the three of us continued our journey. The first village that we passed was "Trisal". A streamlet passed through the village and we had to remove shoes and wade through ankle deep water. The tall and lean police officer involved me in conversation while walking. He asked me questions about my school and the class in which I was, the subjects I read and the teachers who taught me. He also told me about his own sons who also studied in the same school and about their progress in studies to make the journey pleasant. He had already told me that his name was Abdul Hamid and he knew my father very well. The name of his companion was Majid, he had told me. The next village that we reached was Tahab. A canal built by the government to irrigate fields of the nearby "Koil Karewa" passed through the village and there was a small bridge over it. Although lot of money had been spent on construction of the canal, it was widely believed that it had failed to bring water to irrigate the fields of the Karewa. There was also a stream passing through the village at a lower level than the canal. It was full of water. Although I was reluctant, yet Abdul Hamid asked his companion to carry me on his back to cross the stream. The water touched his waist. The strong man then crossed back and carried Abdul Hamid also on his back.

After crossing the stream we rested for a while and the police officer sent his companion to buy a packet of cigarettes for him from a nearby shop. When Majid was away he told me that he himself was a police sergeant and the man who had carried me across the stream on his back was a notorious criminal serving a jail term. He had been released on parole to see his ailing mother and that he was escorting him to his home in Achhan village. "So today you have taken a ride on the back of a criminal", said Abdul Hamid laughingly. Sensing that I was scared about it, he continued, "but don't worry he dare not harm you".

As we continued our journey the next village we passed through was Tamulahall. Here I had to part ways with my companions. While they proceeded to Achhan on the right side I took the path on the left to a village named Gadbug. I had visited both the villages on a previous occasion. The beauty of rural Kashmir is breathtaking. Strewn with streams & streamlets and covered with trees mostly willows, poplars, mulberry trees, and majestic Chinars besides the orchards of apple, pear, almond, walnut, plum, peach and apricot the landscape is green and beautiful. The houses those days mostly had thatched roofs. Rice straw was used for thatching roofs and changed after every couple of years. Gadbug or for that matter any village in Kashmir looked alike with a slight variation here and there. The next two villages through which I passed were Lavaypur and Hajidarpur. Whereas Gadbug was a predominantly Hindu village, other neighbouring villages were inhabited by Muslims. At Lavaypur, there was a watermill which I had visited during an earlier visit. At Achhan there was also a rice husking mill run by a water fall. When I reached Nilora my relations were surprised that I had come alone. As I told them that I was accompanied by a police officer named Abdul Hamid up to Tamulahall and that I had a ride on a criminal's back at Tahab they had a hearty laugh.

In September 1953, my sisters Mohini and Kamta were married to Jia Lal Rawal a school teacher and Prem Nath Shangloo a pharmacist respectively. Four of us Pushkar (14), myself (11), Prediman (6) and Bal Krishan (2) were also given a holy thread at a yagneopavit ceremony. The yagneopavit ceremony among Pandits lasts a whole day; besides a havan it also involves tonsuring your head, bathing and wearing saffron coloured clothes. Pushkar and myself were made to beg from our relatives and friends for the Pandit ji who performed the Puja and havan. The proceeds received from our begging (bikhsha) were recorded in a notebook and at the end total was made and all the money went to the family priest (purohit also called Guruji or Panditji). At the end of this ceremony a vegetarian feast consisting of Rice, Dal, Dam-aloo and many other vegetables was served to the guests, relatives, friends and of course the neighbours. Partaking meals after a havan ceremony is considered by most Kashmiri Pandit men and women as auspicious even today.

The years from 1947 to 1953 were full of turmoil and change in the history of Jammu and Kashmir state. In August 1947, India became Independent and the country was divided into two and a new country Pakistan came into existence. Jammu and Kashmir state which was ruled by Maharaja Hari Singh had the choice of either joining India or Pakistan. Before the Maharaja Hari Singh could take a decision Pukhtoon tribals supported by Pakistan regulars attacked the state. The Maharaja was left with no choice except to accede to India with the consent and whole hearted support of the most popular leader of Kashmiris Sheikh Mohammed Abdullah. With this came to an end the autocratic Dogra rule in the state and opened a new chapter namely "Naya Kashmir" in the life of the people. It was the beginning of a new era of peace and progress in the history of Jammu and Kashmir. The dream that our tall and popular leader Sheikh Mohammed Abdullah had seen for his people was coming true. He was later deposed and arrested on charges that could not be proved in a court of law. Sheikh's arrest marks an unfortunate departure from otherwise shining history of Independent democratic India. It later led to unforeseen and unfortunate consequences for the state and the country.

Chapter 5

Transformative S.P. School

The year 1953 has left an imprint on my mind for many reasons. One of the reasons being the large-scale turmoil associated with the arrest of Sheikh Mohammed Abdullah on 9 August 1953. Early in the morning on that fateful day word spread that Sheikh Saheb had been deposed as Prime Minister by the Sadr-e-Riyast Karan Singh and arrested. The news spread like wild fire. All of us except Babuji were at Srinagar in connection with the forthcoming marriage of my sisters in September. He was at Pulwama attending to his official duties. People immediately started collecting in groups on roads discussing the matter. Curious children, of course I was one among them, also gathered near these groups trying to understand what had happened and hardly making out anything. Our peer group including Bej Krishan, Kakajee Trisal, Ashraf Khan and myself started moving with the group of adults toward Pratap Park where a large group of agitators had assembled and police and army troops were patrolling the main streets on both sides of the park. An elderly neighbour Shivji Trisal who worked in a cinema hall situated near the park admonished and asked us to return home as a dangerous situation was brewing up and anything could happen. Thereafter we immediately returned to the safety of our homes.

The same day crowds of protestors in large number passed through the streets of Srinagar shouting slogans in favour of Sheikh Saheb and condemning the action of the Indian Government. As we learnt later there were protests throughout the valley that day. These protests and agitations continued for several days and mobs turned violent. Police and military had to resort to firing to stop the spreading violence and resulted in many deaths and injuries. At village Nilora a group of agitators started moving towards the house of our relative Ved Lal to attack him for allegedly having spoken against the Sheikh some time back for enacting "land to the tiller" Act. Timely escape from his house on the advice of a Muslim friend saved his life and he stayed in our Srinagar house till normalcy returned.

As a matter of fact "Land to the tiller Act" no doubt benefitted the landless but it also hurt those landlords who did not have large holdings. Some landowners were having hand to mouth existence like their farm hands because of poor agricultural yield. In addition to giving a share to the tillers the land owners had also to part with some of the yield called "lagaan" or "mujwaza"—a sort of tax in kind—to the government for distribution to the city and town dwellers through a public distribution department. For this the small as well as big land owners detested the Sheikh but the landless loved him. His deposition and arrest was thus widely resented by his urban supporters and rural masses of the valley.

The same day Bakshi Ghulam Mohammed a minister in Sheikh's cabinet was sworn in as the Prime Minister (under the constitution of Jammu & Kashmir Chief Minister was designated Prime Minister). He retained all the Ministers of the Previous government with the exception of Mirza Mohammed Afzal Beg who was also arrested. Some bureaucrats known to be close to Sheikh including his son-in-law Ghulam Mohammed Shah were also arrested.

After taking over as P.M. Bakshi Ghulam Mohammed a couple of days later spoke to a small gathering of people including curious young boys (and I was one of them) in the polo ground. Standing on an open Land rover, he spoke for about 15 minutes and an eleven year old that I was then understood not much of what he said. Slogans like "Bakshi Ghulam Mohammed Zindabad" rent the air. The same evening he addressed the people from Radio Kashmir Srinagar and announced a few popular measures. He announced that education from school to postgraduate level would be made free, ration distributed through P.D.S. would be substantially subsidized and treatment in government hospitals would be provided free of cost to all. The compulsory parting of paddy called "lagaan" or "mujwaza" was also scrapped. He also announced that cheap transport would be provided to the people. One important measure was the introduction of a City Bus Service at Srinagar and Jammu cities at just one 'Anna' (1/16 of a rupee) as fare. The Bus service became an instant success since it was fast and cheap and earned the nick name 'Ponda bus' (pond meaning one anna)—to keep with the penchant that Kashmiris have for nick naming everything and everybody. Later during Sadiq Saheb's regime when tongas were replaced by three—wheeler 'tempos' these were called 'woon woon motor' for the sound they made and similarly auto-rickshaws were called, 'teela keom' for their black colour and fast speed like the insect of the same Kashmiri name.

In the Autumn of 1954 Babuji qualified as a Licensed Medical Practitioner and was posted as In-Charge Medical officer of Govt. Hospital at Gurez—a far flung area of Baramulla District. Gurez remained cut off from the valley almost for six months of the year. Most people refused to accept such difficult postings but Babuji had always acted like a soldier in the matter of his postings and never refused even difficult ones like the one in 1938 at Sharda, an important pilgrimage center of Pandits (now in Pakistan Occupied Kashmir). During his tenure at Gurez Babuji upgraded the facilities available at the small hospital and became very popular among the local populace. Following Babu Ji's tranfer Pushkar was admitted in Govt. High School Bagh-e-Dilwar Khan and I was admitted in Govt. Sri Pratap High School. These two government school were then headed by well-known educationists Mr. Abdul Aziz and Mr. Ghulam Rasool Dar respectively. Mr. Abdul Aziz later rose to become Registrar of Kashmir University and Mr. G.R. Dar rose to the rank of Director of Education in Kashmir. During Babuji's posting at Gurez my maternal uncles Raghu Nath, Radha Krishen and Jia Lal Miskeen were a great support to our mother. They used to visit us regularly and enquire about progress in studies of Pushkar and myself.

My schooling at S.P. School, one of the premier institutions of Srinagar, was transformative and memorable. I developed friendships of a life time there. The Principal Mr. Dar was a good administrator and a disciplinarian. The Vice Principal Mr. Tulsi Nath was a good teacher. He was a noble and God—fearing man. The infrastructure and academic atmosphere of the school was quite good and we had some exceptionally good teachers. Mr. G.L. Labroo was my form teacher. He taught Maths and English. He combined teaching with humour and made lessons very interesting. Mr. Mohi-ud-din (Khazar Magrabhi) a humorous Kashmiri poet taught us History and Urdu. His rendering of anecdotes related to the history subject made it very interesting. Occasionally when he felt that the class was getting bored he would recite his humorous poetry and make us laugh. These two teachers left a deep imprint on my mind. Mr. Labroo later did postgraduation and doctorate in English and was appointed as lecturer in Regional Engineering College at Srinagar. He retired as a Professor and Head. Mr. Mohi-ud-din was promoted as an Education Officer.

In the 9th and 10th class I was taught English and Maths by Mr. Nilakanth Kaul and Mr. Kashi Nath Tickoo; and science by Mr. Gopi Nath Ganjoo and Mr. Pran Nath Miya. The School had a good Science laboratory and our science teachers took pains to demonstrate experiments. Mr. Ganjoo rose to become Chief Education Officer and Mr. Miya after postgraduation in Botany became a College lecturer and Principal. There were a large art & crafts room and a music room. Mr. Prem Nath Sopori taught music and some of his students later became good singers and musicians. My close friend Pran Nath too became a good singer. In keeping with Kashmiri tradition he was nicknamed 'Prana Music' by fellow students but he did not mind it. Mr. Sopori later became a lecturer in music at Womens College Maulana Azad road and among his notable students were Ms. Kailash Mehra and Ms. Shamima Dev Azad. His own son Bhajan Sopori continued the tradition of his father and became an eminent musician and maestro. My niece Girija Shangloo Kashkari was also his student. She did her Master's in music and became a music teacher in Kendriya Vidyalaya Sangathan.

Although smoking in the school was strictly prohibited, yet some of the students and teachers managed to smoke during the break. While the students used the lavatory for the purpose the teachers smoked on a hubble bubble (hookah) in a room located at the end of the garden allotted to the agriculture teacher. The non-smoker Principal knew about the teachers, as told to me by Ghulam Jaelani, his son and my friend, but granted this little concession to them. But he was very strict with students. Those who were caught smoking were punished and had to pay a fine.

S.P. School days were lively and full of fun and frolic. Adolescence they say is a very sensitive period of transformation from childhood to boyhood and girlhood. The hormonal changes that take place in the body make an impact which is both physical and mental/psychological. The physical changes are so obvious and there is also a change in the attitude and behaviour. An adolescent thinks that he or she is no more a child (which is true) and resents being treated as one. Parents need to be understanding and vigilant about their adolescents. As a matter of fact adolescents start taking interest in the opposite sex and this is the period when we need to educate them about sex. Generally adolescents talk about sex among their peer groups and often read porn literature or see porn videos which are misleading and dangerous. It is therefore important for parents to keep a track of their children's activities and for teachers in schools to educate adolescents about sex in a healthy manner.

In our school, there were some boys who came from wealthy house-boat owner families. These boys used to have pockets full of money to spend and would sometimes offer us chocolates and cookies. One of the boys Aziz who sat next to me in the 10th class was married at that young age. The teachers did not approve of it but all of us felt excited and asked him uncomfortable questions which, of course, he was wise enough to evade. The result of Aziz's getting married at a young age was that he failed in the 10th class examination. I lost touch with him and never knew whether he ever matriculated. The custom of early marriage of boys and girls among both Muslims and Hindus was very common in earlier decades but was not so common in fiftees and sixtees of the last century.

A major distraction from studies was the cinema. There were just three cinema halls in the city two of them Amresh and Regal cinema halls were very close to S.P. School. A new film would arrive every Friday that is when the ticket blackers made a quick buck. Some films ran for several weeks, but most would hardly last for more than a week. One of hit films I remember was *Nagin*. It was a big hit and ran for several weeks. Some boys would bunk classes to see a new film on Fridays. Since money was hard to come by the boys would go for the cheapest tickets which cost seven and half annas (little less than half a rupee). That was the era of black and white films and the colour films came much later. On one occasion my namesake friend and myself bunked school. We somehow managed two cheap tickets but by the time we entered the hall all the benches were full and we had to sit on the floor closer to the screen to watch the new film of which I do not even remember the name now. As the first film show used to end at 4 p.m. coinciding with our school timing no one at home suspected our cheating.

I vividly remember an incident related to watching a film. During one of the days a relative named Mohan Lal from Bijbehara who was older to me came on a visit. When I was about to leave for my school next morning he suggested that I accompany him to watch a film. It was a tempting proposition. He said that he would wait outside my school at lunch time for the first show. I agreed and bunked school at lunch time (1 p.m.). There used to be a watchman at the school gate but I managed to give him a slip. I still remember the title of the film *Surang* (tunnel) in which Dileep Kumar, a very popular actor those days, was in the lead role. The film at Amresh cinema went on well for an hour and then there was power break down. The cinema did not have a backup generator. The spectators raised hue and cry. After waiting for half an hour the cinema manager came into the hall and announced that there was no hope of immediate restoration of power so we would be issued passes valid for the second show or any show on subsequent days for a week. We took our passes and I suggested to my relative that we return home and watch the film next day. My relation did not like the idea as he was returning home the very next day.

Reluctantly, I agreed to watch the second show which started at 4 p.m. forgetting that my mother would feel worried if I did not return home from school. When I returned home at 7.30 p.m. all hell broke loose and my mother was furious. Feeling terribly guilty Mohan Lal then explained to her that he had actually taken me along from school to help him to do some shopping, for which he was sorry. I never ever repeated such a mistake even when I went to the university. My mother would always be informed of my whereabouts.

One of my passions during school days was cycling. I had achieved some degree of expertise in cycling stealthily using my father's or some visiting relation's or friend's bicycle. Since I was small for the large adult size bicycle I rested my left foot on the left paddle and crossed my right leg across the gap and rest the right foot on the right paddle after giving a push and then half paddle. Full paddle I could manage only later. In the process, I fell down and hurt myself several times. Small size bicycles were available on rent for quarter of a rupees an hour and I would occasionally enjoy a ride sitting on the saddle. I was quite popular with my friends for training them free of cost but they would have to pay the hire. My namesake friend avoided to learn for fear of hurting himself. Surprisingly on one holiday, Bansi Lal came to my home and expressed his desire to learn cycling. I was too happy to help. So we went to the nearest bicycle hiring shop owned by the one Pandit Tikka Lal at Badiyar. We decided that our school lane would be free of traffic on that day and thus suitable for his learning. I helped him sit on the small saddle and keep his feet on the paddles then I balanced him and asked him to apply force on the paddles. He followed my instructions and the bicycle started to move. All went well as long I did not let the bicycle go. When I felt that he could balance on his own I let the bicycle go. For some distance he did so well but then lost control and struck against a wall. Luckily despite a fall he did not sustain an injury. Unfortunately, however, the axle of the bicycle broke down and the front wheel came off the handle.

The situation seemed serious and both of us felt perplexed and sat down on the side of the road to think. What would it cost to get the bicycle repaired? I knew that Tikka Lal was a strict man and expected that he would demand a hefty amount as damages which would be beyond us. Taking courage in our hands one of us picked up the detached front wheel while the other took the handle and balanced on the rare wheel and started to move towards Tikka Lals's shop 1 km. away. Luckily for us there was a carpenter's shop enroute. The shop owner understood our predicament when we approached him for help. He agreed to attach the detached wheel with the handle, if we paid him one rupee. We bargained for 1/2 rupee but he refused. Finally, he agreed for 3/4 of a rupee and agreed to do the job. He took out a piece of wood from his shop and sharpened it on two ends to fit one end into the handle rod and the other into the hollow of the rod of the fork of front wheel. With one push with a hammer on the top of the handle the piece of wood was miraculously in place. Then he demonstrated to us that the job was done perfectly. He took his wages but cautioned not to ride the bicycle again for the measure was just a temporary one. With great caution I wheeled the bicycle to its destination—Tikka Lal's shop, mounted it on its stand and showed it to him. He looked up the watch and said we were twenty minutes late. I lied that we had no money on us and would pay the next time. He relented and we hurried back home never to hire a bicycle from him again! Later he had discovered the mischief and complained to my father about it who in turn reprimanded me. I doubt if Bansi Lal Kar ever learnt to drive a bicycle but he did manage to become a qualified veterinarian. It is pertinent to mention here that Tikka Lal's son, a good friend of my brother, Krishan Langoo distinguished himself as a composer and music director.

In our Primary School Swimming was taught at the pool of the Christian Missionary High School at Sheikh Bagh. Pushkar had learnt it by the time he passed 5th class. Since the school closed down when I was in class 4, I did not get an opportunity to learn swimming. In 1955, I was reading in class 9 at S.P. School. On a particularly hot day during summer break I took it into my head to have a dip in the river Jhelum at Ganpatyar Ghat. Many boys were having a bath in the river. Some were even swimming. First I gave my four year old brother Bal Krishan

(Nanaji) a bath and then rested him on a step of the ghat and then ventured into water step after step, to have a dip, but soon realized that I had gone into deeper water. I felt that I was going to drown and by some quirk of luck I decided to hold one of my arms up. Some elderly person standing on the ghat saw my hand and thought that I was going to drown. He shouted and a boatman caught hold of my hair and brought me out. He rebuked me for the foolish venture. I never ventured into water again till the age of sixty when my son Anil encouraged me to learn swimming along with my six year old grandson Ahan at Liverpool, England. But that is a different story. After that incident I returned home thanking my stars for the save. Jhelum the river of life had really taken pity on me and given me a lease. Many people mostly young boys used to drown in the river every year during the hot summer days because they did not know swimming. As I learnt later, man is a natural swimmer. He drowns because he panics in water and does not move his hands and feet to keep afloat.

Schooling does not mean just learning to read and write. It is an all-round process of development. A school should include many other activities which prepare a child to live a full life as he or she grows. The Revd. Cannon C.E. Tyndale Biscoe the pioneer of education in Kashmir in the days of his active service used to lead parties of boys over the mountains and through the valleys and thus inculcated love of nature in them. These outings were continued by the Revd. F.E. Lucey, the Revd. and Mrs. Dugdale, the Revd. R.D. Thompson, Mrs. and Mr. E.D. Tyndale Biscoe, Mr. F. Jacob and Mr. John Ray at C.M.S. School (Now Tyndale-Biscoe Memorial School). Swimming and boating formed an important part of the activities besides sports at C.M.S. School. Although at S.P. School many sports formed a part of school activities, yet swimming was not one of them.

Swimming and boating regattas inculcated spirit of competition among the pupils. The British missionaries who ran schools made it a point to develop an overall healthy approach to life among their students. My father used to tell us that the British Administrators preferred candidates with good sports certificates in the matter of appointment in their offices. It was a common joke in Kashmir that when a certain young man approached a white officer with an application for a job, he asked him, "What Pass?" the young man replied, "Sir Wular cross". Impressed the white officer appointed him as a clerk even though he had not cleared matriculation examination. My uncle Lalla Kaul a student of C.M.S. School Fateh Kadel was appointed as an assistant in Srinagar Municipality in preference to another equally qualified candidate because of producing a certificate by Tyndale-Biscoe of having successfully crossed Wular Lake, the largest lake in Asia, in a competition. He was equally successful in his service career at the Srinagar Municipality and rose to the level of head of the office before he suddenly died of heart attack in 1938.

In the spring of 1956 when results of 9th class Exams were declared by the School I had done well to deserve a place in the Golden section of the 10th class. This section had been created for above average boys so that they could be made to work harder in a competitive manner. I recall that some of my classmates were brilliant such as Ghulam Jealani, Sohan Lal Razdan, and Omkar Nath. Our form teacher's style of teaching improved my Maths and English. Compared to Maths my interest lay in Science subjects both Physical, and Biological. Since my father was a practitioner of medicine my interest in Science was natural. I also had an interest in History and Geography perhaps because my teacher Mr. Mohi-ud-din made it very interesting.

By autumn the students were expected to complete their course of study and were given a qualifying test to fill up forms for 10th class examination to be held in March by the University of Jammu and Kashmir. Those who did not qualify the test were 'detained' and had to put in another year in the school. This policy, however, was scrapped later for good reason and all those who had attended school regularly were allowed to fill up the forms and appear in the examination. Earlier many of those who were not allowed to take the examination lost interest in studies and dropped out.

Schools in Kashmir used to close in the last week of December up to end of February for winter break. So syllabi were completed, sometimes in a hurry, before the beginning of the break. Matriculation examination used to be held in the second week of March and the results were declared a couple of months later. Matriculation examination used to be a major test those days and gave a lot of stress not only to the students but to their parents as well. The winter break period was utilized by the studious type of students to revise the syllabi in order to get through. Those who could afford went for private tuition. I, for some unknown reason, did not approve of going for private tuition and obstinately refused when my parents suggested it. When examination approached my mother showed my birth chart to some astrologer who predicted that some evil stars might come in the way and obstruct my success! My mother naturally felt perturbed and asked him if there was a solution to ward off the evil effect of bad stars. So I was subjected to a small puja on every examination day before leaving home. I didn't like to perform the ritual but agreed lest my mother felt offended. Thanks to the puja the evil effect of bad stars had been removed and I did pass my matriculation examination when results were declared to the joy of my mother!

India had been free for about ten years by the time I matriculated. The middle class which had enthusiastically taken part in the freedom movement wanted to surge ahead and expected the government to create opportunities for their progress. The Central Government under the leadership of Jawaharlal Nehru was also keen that the country should move ahead on the road of progress and development. It was understood well that to realize this dream education, science and technology should be given priority. Maulana Abul Kalam Azad was the first Education Minister of India and he was given a free hand to give shape to the educational policy and planning. To meet the aspirations of the people new schools, colleges, technical institutions and universities were opened. All classes of the population wanted to surge ahead and sent their wards to schools and colleges. This opened new vistas and opportunities for employment. Thus all sections of the society started to benefit from the education of their children. The Government of Jammu and Kashmir had made education free in 1953 and more and more people benefitted from it and sent their wards to schools and colleges.

With the support of my family and my own efforts I had secured good marks in my matriculation examination which facilitated my admission to S.P. College Srinagar in July 1957. In their eagerness to gain popularity among the majority, the Government of Jammu and Kashmir after independence had devised a policy of admission in government run schools, colleges, and technical institutions based on religion. The policy provided that the distribution of seats for admission should be 70% to the majority community and 30% to the minority communities. This policy was obviously devised to encourage the majority community to enroll their wards and help them receive the benefit of education, but compromised with merit. Since, most members of the majority community were 1st or 2nd generation learners they got admission easily under this policy. To enable the wards of minority communities to receive education some well meaning leaders of the Kashmiri Pandit community like Pandit Jia Lal Kilam, Badri Nath Parimoo and poet Dina Nath Nadim had opened private schools and colleges. This step did compensate educationally members of the minority communities but they had to pay for their education and could not benefit from the free education in the government run educational institutions. These private institutions, however, were provided grant-in-aid by the government on applying for the same.

The policy of discriminatory admission was carried on even for nomination to technical institutions outside the state. When Medical and Engineering colleges were opened in the state the same policy was adopted for admissions. Merit was given a go by and this created a situation, where lesser merit holders of one community were admitted in preference to those belonging to the minority community. The policy was also carried on to appointments and promotions in services as well. This policy was changed decades later during the return of Sheikh Mohammed Abdullah to power under the directions of the Supreme Court of India which disapproved of denial of admissions, appointments and promotions on the basis of religion.

When I took admission in S.P. College Srinagar in 1957 there were just three more colleges, viz. Amar Singh College, Govt. College for Woman Maulana Azad Road and Gandhi Memorial College. There was one private college, viz. St. Joseph College at Baramulla and two more government colleges, one at Sopore and another one at Anantnag. While degree courses were available in the city colleges the colleges at Sopore and Anantnag were intermediate colleges. At Jammu, there were two colleges for boys, viz. G.G.M. Science (Erstwhile Prince of Wales) College and M.A.M. College and one college for girls located at Parade Ground. At the district level there were four colleges located at Bhaderwah, Poonch, Udhampur and Kathua. But for the Poonch and Baramulla, other District level colleges were recent creations. There were two colleges for teachers training, one at Srinagar and another at Jammu. A Polytechnical College (earlier started as a technical school during Maharaja's time) at Srinagar imparted diploma courses in civil, mechanical and electrical engineering besides draftsmanship. St. Joseph College Baramulla run by Christian Missionaries was later taken over by the government. The missionaries who contributed greatly to education in the state still continue to run schools such as Tyndale Biscoe Memorial and Burnhall Schools at Srinagar and Convent Schools for girls at Jammu, Srinagar and Baramulla.

Although opportunities for higher education were widened after independence, yet these were still inadequate for a growing population. Since the number of seats available (intake capacity) in science subjects were limited many desirous students had to change stream to arts, viz. social sciences, languages, etc. As there were no postgraduate courses available except those recently started in English and Math at Srinagar and Economics and Political Science at Jammu in college campuses most aspirants had to seek admission in the colleges and universities outside the state.

From the year 1953 to 1963 Bakshi Ghulam Mohammed ruled the state of Jammu and Kashmir like a benevolent ruler. He was able to get funds liberally from the Central Government and the state made progress in all fields including education. He was tough with opponents and pro-Pakistan elements and put them behind the bars. The people could see the progress as it became visible everywhere in the form of new buildings, roads, bridges, schools, colleges and hospitals and a large number of people found employment. Those ten years were indeed memorable. But as happens with most rulers they become complacent with passage of time and get surrounded by sycophants. They are not able to see the simmering discontent all-around and writing on the wall. That ultimately results in their fall. This is what exactly happened to Bakshi Ghulam Mohammed despite the good work that he painstakingly did for the progress of the State. When he was moving towards height of his power I matriculated from S.P. High School.

Chapter 6

Unforgettable College Days

The S.P. College Srinagar where I had got enrolled as a student in 1957 with English, Physics, Chemistry, Biology and Urdu was one of the premier institutions of the state in terms of reputation, infrastructure and staff. Founded in 1905, it is the oldest college in Kashmir. The main building built in the first decade of twentieth century had the aura and grandeur of an institution of higher learning. The classrooms were spacious, laboratories were well equipped and library well stocked with books, magazines and journals. The lawns and the playgrounds were well maintained and added beauty to the landscape. The staff of the college included men of great learning some of whom later joined the postgraduate departments of the erstwhile University of Jammu and Kashmir. Some of them like M.R. Puri, Sat Bhushan, Shakeel-ur-Rehman and A.H. Himidi later became Vice-Chancellors. Shakeel-ur-Rehman had a stint as a Minister in the Central Government as well.

A change over from school to a college entails change in attitude and mannerism. S.P. College and Amar Singh College at Srinagar and G.G.M. Science College (Prince of Wales College) were comparable to many good colleges of the country and enrolment to any one of them automatically gave one a sense of achievement and a degree of pride as well. Going down the memory lane I remember the feeling of excitement on the first day at the college. I was excited because entry into an institution held in high esteem in the society at that point of time gave me a sense of achievement. While I was still in the school in the years 1954-56, a grand festival was held in the college, which included sports tournaments and numerous other activities which I could watch along with other schoolmates across the low wall separating the school and the college playgrounds. The sight of big boys in white shirts and pants playing cricket in the sprawling college ground was worth watching. The college grounds were used besides the cricket tournaments for hockey and football tournaments as well. Football tournaments were particularly popular with people and large number of supporters of the competing teams came to watch them mostly held in the evenings.

On my first day in the college I was accosted along with other new comers by senior students. They were nice and decent guys and just asked about my name and the school from which I had come. It gave a moral boost to speak to senior students some of whom later rose to high positions in the government. Mufti Mohammad Sayeed was one of them and he rose to became Home Minister at the center and Chief Minister of state twice.

In 1958, Maulana Abul Kalam Azad the first Education Minister in the Central Government led by Pt. Jawaharlal Nehru passed away. A series of lectures were organized in the college hall for a few days. Among those who attended were Bakshi Ghulam Mohammed the Prime Minister on the inaugural function. Besides Ghulam Mohammed Sadiq Education Minister, D.P. Dhar, other Ministers, many vice chancellors and scholars from various universities and many other dignitaries also attended. It gave a great opportunity to the students to be a part of the audience and listen to an array of scholars and politicians who spoke about the life and work of the great departed leader. I recall an incident wherein the speaker a vice chancellor compared Abul Kalam Azad to Swami Vivekananda. Later during question-answer session Prof. Hassan Shah who taught history in the college objected to the comparison and said that Vivekananda was a Hindu communalist. In his reply the learned speaker spoke at length and pointed out that Prof. Hassan was ignorant about the import of writings of Swami Vivekananda and that he should go deeper into his works. Showing grace Prof. Hassan on the intervention of the president of the session apologized to the speaker.

Another occasion that I remember was the visit of Pandit Sham Lal Saraf, Minister accompanied by Director of Education. They entered along with the Principal S.L. Raina into the junior Chemistry laboratory where our group was busy performing an experiment. The Hon'ble Minister asked us to explain to a layman like him as to what experiment we were performing and what it meant. As no student could answer the teacher Incharge Mr. Deva then explained to the Minister and others that the experiment involved calculation of the amount of a substance (say for example common salt) dissolved in a litre of water by mixing a measured amount of it with another chemical (alkali/acid) in a flask and adding a drop of reagent called phenolphthalein and then go on shaking till a change of colour occurs. Then you stop and calculate from the amounts of two liquids used in the experiment the amount of the given salt dissolved in a litre of water. This is called acid-base titration method of calculation. The Minister and others accompanying him had left apparently satisfied with Mr. Deva's explanation. However, Mr. Deva was visibly upset and annoyed with us for our failure to explain what the experiment was all about.

The problem actually is that a teacher is required to use the simplest possible words and means to explain what the science experiment is about before proceeding to demonstrate it. The practicals are the soul of science education. Without practicals science education is meaningless. As a teacher fifteen years later, I attended a Summer School in Biology at Kashmir University organized by the University Grants Commission. There were two American Professors who demonstrated more by experiments than delivery of classroom lectures in contrast to the Indian Professors who simply delivered lectures. It was a very useful course which helped me in improving my teaching skills. At the end of the course Prof. Kachroo Director of the Course asked the participants to give their impressions. A Sikh lecturer Manjit Singh from Punjab had this to say, "as a fresher I was assigned a class to teach morphology of lower plants to my students. After having taught my students morphology and Biology of a liverwort plant a student got up and told me that he had not been able to make out as to what did the plant look like and how big it was. I felt shocked by his statement but also realized that had I taken with me a specimen of the plant in a glass jar and shown it to my students before embarking on lecturing for a week the student would not have got the doubts in his mind. The mistake was mine. I expressed regrets and next day took a specimen of the plant which is a small flat leaf-like plant growing on moist soil. I realized that the student had taught me a lesson."

As a teacher of Biology I know that field studies are more important than classroom lectures. Students learn more in the field than in the classroom. The chalk and talk method of teaching has lost its relevance today. The revolution in educational technology has helped to make basic principles of science easier to explain. With the aid of modern educational gadgets classroom teaching has become easier and exciting both for the teacher and the learner.

I studied at S.P. College for four years (1957-61). The first two years of study called Intermediate those days was equivalent of today's 10+2. After passing this examination one qualified for going for some technical course, viz. medicine, engineering, veterinary, dentistry, etc. available those days. Accordingly I applied for admission for undergoing medical training. The year I passed intermediate examination (1959) a Medical College was established at Srinagar and like many other aspirants I had also applied for admission. An interview was held and I answered all the question to the best of my ability.

It was the month of August and annual pilgrimage to Amarnath cave was about to start. My older brother Pushkar had joined service as an assistant in the medical department. He later gave up that job and joined private sector in Bombay. He was deputed by his department to assist Dr. S.N. Ghasi the incharge of medical contingent in the yatra. Pushkar suggested that I accompany him. I felt it was a godsend opportunity and readily agreed. He had to leave a day earlier to set up a base camp at Pahalgam. When I met him at Pahalgam the next day he introduced me to Dr. Ghasi who welcomed me with a smile. My brother suggested that he will hire a horse for me for the pilgrimage but I refused. I preferred to perform the pilgrimage on foot. A neighbour and friend of my brother Prithvi Nath Braroo also arrived at Pahalgam on way to Amarnath and stayed with us in the same tent for the night. Next day after breakfast we joined the yatra led by Chief Priest Mahant Giri Sahab who carried the Silver Mace called "Chhari Mubarak" among the chants in the praise of Lord Shiva. The holy mace is believed to be Shiva's protecting symbol for the pilgrims. Actually the yatra consisting of Sadhus commences from Srinagar ten days before the final day of yatra culminating at Amarnath cave on Shravan Poornamashi. It reaches Pahalgam after six days on foot. After performing Puja at Dashnami Akhara at Srinagar the yatra passes through Pampore, Awantipur, Bijbehara, Mattan and Aishmuqam before arriving at Pahalgam base camp.

From the base camp Pahalgam the yatra travels to the first stage at Chandanwari. According to J.N. Ganhar, "Amar Nath Pilgrimage is the most exhilarating mountain trek which combines piety and pleasure. The journey to the cave lies through some of the most picturesque scenery in the world". Personally Pahalgam has always fascinated me because of having spent some earlier summers of my childhood there. The roaring sound of the Lidder at night and the pleasing sound and aroma produced by the pine needles at the slightest breeze are indeed enchanting. The singing of Cicadas and birds on the pine trees adds to the enchantment.

Chandanwari is 16 kms. away from Pahalgam lying at a height of about 2900 meters above the sea. It is a picnic spot famous for its snow bridge, the first in the route of Amarnath. Now a jeepable road connects Pahalgam with Chandanwari. Devout pilgrims prefer to walk all the way to the cave despite the availability of horses. The trek to Chandanwari involves a gradual ascent, mostly along the bank of the stream coming down from Sheshnag. Incidentally mention must be made of the fact that Chandanwari is a pent-up opening among the hills where streams coming from Sheshnag and Astanmarg meet. Prithvi Nath and myself trekked the distance and enjoyed it to the fullest possible. There was a little drizzle enroute but it stopped soon after. Weather is unpredictable during the yatra as it is monsoon time and the pilgrims carry raincoats, umbrellas, etc. to protect themselves. Sometimes, rains can take a nasty turn and pose a threat to the lives of the pilgrims.

In 1928 nearly 500 pilgrims and about as many ponies are reported to have perished due to heavy rains and floods. Again twelve pilgrims and 12 ponies lost their lives in August 1970. In the year 2012 although there were no rains yet more than a hundred yatris died due to health related reasons. The government ordered an enquiry and one of the main recommendations made was to make it mandatory for yatris to get a medical check up done before proceeding for the arduous yatra.

The ascent to the next stage namely Sheshnag through steep Pissu ghati (hill) is really very tough. The tree line ends before reaching the top of the Pissu hill. The last visible trees are the "Bhojpatra" (Birch) trees. Once the ascent is over, one has to trudge along a spur of about 5 kms. to reach the great mountain lake Sheshnag. The Pilgrimage Camp at Wavjan, a windswept camping site 13 kms. from Chandanwari which overlooks the beautiful and awesome Sheshnag lake set against a massive triple peaked glacier strewn mountain has no parallel in the world. The three peaks represents the Hindu trinity—Brahma, Vishnu and Mahesh. Wavjan is 3700 m. above the sea level and commands a fascinating view of Sheshnag and the surrounding snow covered mountains. Unlike the previous night spent at Chandanwari, the one at Wavjan was frightening as the howling winds blew throughout the night. The name Wavjan (Wav-wind, Jin-demon) is derived from the fact that fierce winds always blow at that site. However, the chanting of songs in the praise of Lord Shiva by the Sadhus and pilgrims reduced the effect of the howling winds to some extent. While my companion in the tent Prithvi slept like a log and snored all through I could hardly manage a wink of sleep and when I did feel sleepy in the morning it was time to start yet another ascent.

Panchtarni is about 13 kms. from Wavjan. The ascent to the top of Mahagunus pass at 4,300 m. involves a stiff climb. Except for flowering herbs nothing grows right from Wavjan onwards. The climb is exhausting but once you have reached the pass the route winds down to the plain of Panchtarni lying at 3650 metres. It is a small valley lying in the lap of mountains and crossed by five streams coming from glaciers on the mountains in the east. The name Panchtarni is derived from the panch (five) streams that a pilgrim has to cross. The valley is inhabited by Himalayan Marmot whose shrill cries can be heard all over. I enjoyed the peace and tranquility of Panchtarni—the meadow of five streams—and had a sound sleep after having an early dinner under the light of a kerosene lantern. The various stages of the yatra turn alive at night and buzz with activities under the dim light of kerosene lamps. Now I learn that diesel generators are used to bring alive the various stages of the yatra by the "Amar Nath Shrine Board". The Chants of Mantras, songs and bhajans by the devotees convert the whole area into a celestial one.

Early next morning, I was awakananed by my brother Pushkar to get ready for the last lap of the yatra to have darshan of the Ice Lingam. The yatra started early and a whole township, as if it were, came to life again. The trek from Panchtarni to cave is 6 kms. The first half of the route is uphill and the second half is plain but partly covered with frozen snow over which the pilgrims have to walk cautiously. The view of the holy cave from a distance brings thrill and ecstasy to the pilgrims and the whole area echoes with their shouts of "Har Har Mahadev". Before entering the cave for darshan we had a bath in the ice cold water of the sacred Amravati, a tiny stream which issues from the snow on the adjoining mountains and the cave. After the bath my fingers became so numb that Prithvi had to help me to button up my shirt. Before entering the cave we, like all other pilgrims, smeared our faces with a chalky clay taken from bed of Amravati stream or from the sides of the troughs at the back of the cave.

The volunteers at the entrance to the cave guided us to the place where the ice lingam stood. I felt blessed instantly by the sight of it and went into a trance and tears of joy rolled down my checks. The joy was enhanced by the water drops that fell from the roof of the cave and sight of a pair of pigeons roosting in the roof of the cave. After having the darshan the volunteers led us out of cave and we trekked back to Panchtarni. By noon all of us—my brother, his friend Prithvi and other colleagues including doctors, assistants and helpers had returned to the Panchtarni camp after the darshan. Some devotees started to leave Panchtarni for Sheshnag the same day but most of them stayed back to enjoy stay of yet another night. Some devotees after darshan took the short but risky Saskut route to reach Chandanwari the same day bypassing Wavjan and Sheshnag altogether.

Nowadays a short route from Baltal on the Sonamarg side is also used by pilgrims to have darshan. It involves only one day from Baltal to cave and back. Helicopters are also available now on yatra days, which start more than a month earlier, from Baltal and Pahalgam to the helipad built near the cave and involve a very short walk. However, traditional route from Pahalgam is still popular and yatris use horses and palanquins to reach the cave. Horses and palanquins are available from Baltal side as well. But most devotees on both the routes prefer to walk.

The medical officer in charge of the medical contingent camp Dr. Ghasi was a kind and gentle person. He knew that I was son of a fellow doctor and throughout the yatra he enquired about my welfare. On way back from Panchtarni to Pahalgam he offered me a horse ride, which I politely declined.

Back at home in Srinagar a couple of days after performing the yatra I received the bad news that my name did not figure in the list of candidates selected for admission to the Srinagar Medical College. It upset me because many of those selected had lower merit than myself. I was greatly hurt and disappointed because boys and girls from the majority community lower in merit had been selected. Out of 75 seats only one Kashmiri Hindu girl had found a place in the list. What hurt the most was the discrimination on the basis of religion. In fact, this policy had been in place right from the day administration went into the hands of the National Conference leaders. Apparently we lived in a democracy but the policy of reservations & pick and choose had been followed even by the Central Government. The policy of reservations which was originally meant for a short period to encourage and help disadvantaged sections of the society continues even today. It has given rise to a peculiar situation. The son of a highly placed affluent government official from a S.C./S.T. or backward community is entitled to reservation over the meritorious son of a poor man from the so-called upper caste. This policy has been perpetuated by the politicians for creating vote banks for themselves. It has also created a vested interest among those influential people who have benefitted from this policy from generation to generation and they will never like any government to discontinue the policy. An affluent S.C./S.T. or backward class person's son or daughter has a definite edge over the son or daughter of a poor man from their own class and community. The policy of reservations needs a relook in view of the fact that even well off sections of the society like Patels of Gujarat and Jats of Haryana and so on also want reservations.

Having been denied admission to the medical college I enrolled myself in S.P. College Srinagar for two year B.Sc. course with English, Chemistry, Botany and Zoology as my subjects and soon settled down to serious study. On a certain day a close relative visited us and expressed dismay about denial of a seat to me in the medical college. He said that the Prime Minister Bakshi Ghulam Mohammed was a benevolent person and I should meet him to express my grievance. His suggestion appealed since the denial of my due had upset me. He informed me that Mr. Bakshi was meeting people at his residence on Friday mornings. I considered the suggestion with skepticism and did not act for some time. On one particular Friday, however, our Chemistry practical class finished earlier than usual in the forenoon. Since there was sufficient time left to attend the next theory class I scribbled a few lines on a sheet of paper and strolled to the private office of the P.M. which was just five minutes walk from the Chemistry department. A large crowd had assembled outside waiting to meet Mr. Bakshi. The security people outside were letting people in one by one. Being in a hurry to attend my classes I requested one of the staff to let me in and he asked me to wait and allowed me in when he found an opportunity.

On entering the big hall I found Bakshi Sahab sitting imperiously on a chair with a small table in front and I wished him with a bow. There was a big gathering of people in the hall sitting on chairs. I could not make out who these people were. Between the Prime Minister and these people there was at least a distance of ten feet with a low wooden fence in between. May be it was a sort of a darbar going on. I have never been really able to figure out. I approached Bakshi Sahab with all humility and respect and handed over my representation to him. He took it from me and without reading or asking me what did I want he simply flung it on the floor. I felt perplexed and did not quite understand what mistake I had committed. The image of a kind, patient and benevolent leader simply melted in front of me. Before I could say anything two security men caught hold of me and pushed me out of the hall. By the time I returned to my college in shock and disbelief I had resolved in my mind never to approach anybody in future for my admission or career. I had also resolved to say good bye to a career in medicine because I did not have any recommendation, which was order of the day, and thus concentrate on my studies at S.P. College instead.

The academic atmosphere at S.P. College was conducive to attain scholarship. Prof. S.K. Raina was the Principal and looked very graceful in his office. There were some excellent teachers in the college like Prof. J.N. Kaul, Prof. R.N. Kaul, Prof. J.N. Sharma, Prof. A.H. Hamidi (English); Prof. R.K. Zutshi, Prof. N.L. Wazir, Prof. Naqash, Prof. Mir (Chemistry); Prof. S.K. Kaul, Prof. T.N. Dhar, Prof. K.L. Razdan, Prof. Qazi Mubarak, Prof. B.N. Kaul, Prof. Shafi-ud-din, Prof. S.N. Tickoo, Prof. D.P. Zutshi (Botany), Prof. B.L. Kaw, Prof. D.N. Fotedar, Prof. J.N. Wattal, Prof. G.Q. Bhat, Prof. M.K. Munshi, Prof. S.P. Vohra, Prof. P.L. Bakshi, Prof. Sumair Singh, Prof. J.L. Kaul (Zoology); Prof. A.S. Dhar, Prof. Mohd. Yusuf, Prof. J.N. Durani (Physics) and many more in other subjects including languages. Prof. Mohi-ud-din Hajni of Arabic was a well-known scholar of Kashmiri language and Prof. Shams-ud-din had achieved scholarship in Persian language and Prof. K.N. Dhar was a scholar of Sanskrit. Prof. Khazir Mohammed, Prof. B.L. Trakru (Mathematics), Prof. Peerzada Hassan Shah, Dr. Mohammed Iqbal (History) and Prof. G.A. Bhat (Economics) and Prof. Maqbool Fazili

(Persian) also enjoyed good reputation as teachers. The college was a co-educational institution at undergraduate level for science subjects. The female students were treated with respect by their male classmates. I enjoyed to learn from dedicated teachers. It was here that I was influenced by my teachers Dr. B.L. Kaw, Prof. D.N. Fotedar, Prof. B.N. Kaul and Prof. K.L. Razdan to take a keen interest in Natural History. They were the main source of my inspiration to choose Zoology at the postgraduate level after I completed undergraduate studies.

Beside academics, sports and literary activities were encouraged. There was also a company of N.C.C. (National Cadet Corps). There was a literary club in English under the charge of Prof. J.N. Sharma and another in Urdu called Bazam-e-Adab, under the charge of Prof. A.H. Hamidi. I attended both the clubs and took a keen interest in their activities like reading essays, discussing and reviewing books and listening to poems written by students. I had an interest in Urdu literature and used to show my pieces to Prof. Hamidi who corrected and published them in Urdu section of the college magazine *Pratap*, Similarly, Prof. Sharma also corrected my essays and book reviews in English and included them in the English section of the college magazine. Prof. Hamidi was a soft spoken and nice person who encouraged students for creative writing. He himself wrote short stories which were published in *Beeswi Sadi* an Urdu magazine published from Delhi. Krishan Chander, Pushkar Nath, Thakur Punchhi and many well-known short story writers also published their pieces in this magazine. As a student I sent some of my short stories in Urdu to *Beeswi Sadi* but they were rejected which dejected me and I stopped writing short stories. I regret it, in hindsight. Initially short stories or articles even by great writers were also rejected. There was a lot of scope for writing in my own mother tongue—Kashmiri. I will always regret this fact. My friends in Bazm-e-adab like Farooq Nazki and Shafi Shaida earned a name as poets and writers. It is, however, a matter of satisfaction for me that the taste for writing that I developed under the guidance of Prof. J.N. Sharma helped me in developing writing skills in the English language.

Prof. J.N. Sharma had the advantage of having studied Sanskrit literature beside English. He possessed M.A. degrees in both these languages. In our regular classes Prof. Sharma taught us for three days a week the text, *India Rediscovered.* It was an abridged form of *Discovery of India* by Pandit Jawaharlal Nehru. Prof. Sharma's knowledge of Sanskrit and ancient Indian culture made it easier for him to interpret and explain Nehru's assessment of ancient and modern India at the same time. Another teacher of English Prof. J.N. Kaul taught us another textbook *Eminent Victorians* by Lytton Strachey for three days a week. He created word pictures of the events of the Victorian era as described in the text relating to lives of eminent personalities of those times. When I visited England, Scotland and Wales later in my life I found that the word pictures created by eminent English writers and poets were so close to the reality.

I must also say something about other teachers who taught me Chemistry, Botany and Zoology. Prof. R.K. Zutshi, a man of few words but a good administrator was the Head of Chemistry Department. He taught us Physical Chemistry. He was so strict that you had to be in the class on time. Late comers were refused entry. He taught well but hardly smiled and kept a distance with the students. On the other hand, another teacher Prof. Naqash was of a jovial nature. His delivery of the English language was shorn of grammar but his knowledge of Chemistry that he taught us was impeccable. He was nice and approachable. Another teacher Prof. N.L. Wazir taught us Inorganic Chemistry. He too would occasionally humour up the class. There were other good teachers who instructed us in the conduct of practicals like Nazir Ahmed Rather, Waheed-ud-Zaman and Babuji Salman.

Profs. Shiban Krishan Kaul, T.N. Dhar and Qazi Mubarak taught us Botany theory and practicals were conducted by Profs. B.N. Kaul, K.L. Razdan, Shafi-ud-din and S.N. Tickoo. Zoology theory was taught by Profs. B.L Kaw, D.N. Fotedar and J.N. Wattal. Junior classes were taught by Profs. M.K. Munshi, G.Q. Bhat and practicals were conducted by Profs. S.P. Vohra, P.L. Bakshi, Sumair Singh Bali and J.L. Kaul. I was lucky to have been taught Biosciences by stalwarts like Profs. B.L. Kaw, S.K. Kaul, D.N. Fotedar, K.L. Razdan, B.N. Kaul, Shafi-ud-din and others who inculcated love for nature and natural history in their students.

Principal S.K. Raina was replaced by Prof. Noor-ud-din but he stayed in that position for a brief period. He was then replaced by Prof. Abdul Aziz. While Prof. S.K. Raina retired as Deputy Director of Education, Noor-ud-din finally rose to the position of Vice Chancellor and Abdul Aziz became Registrar of Kashmir University. I must make mention of an incident while Prof. Abdul Aziz was the Principal. During the final year of B.Sc. (1960-61) I had become an active member of the youth wing of Democratic National Conference of which I have made a mention earlier. In December 1960 a Youth Congress meet was taking place at New Delhi and members of Youth D.N.C. were invited to attend. Many of my colleagues and myself also decided to attend. While others did not feel the need to take permission of the Principal I felt that I should do so. When I approached Principal Aziz for permission he did not say 'no' but advised that since I was in the final year and syllabi were being completed it would be unwise, in his opinion, to miss my lectures especially as the college was soon closing for the winter vacation and I would lose touch with my teachers. I took his advice seriously and did not go and those who did had to return soon for the meet was postponed for some unknown reason.

College days are important for two reason: one you are passing through a period of changes in the body brought about by entry into youth; two you are trying hard to understand the world around you and what lies in store for you. You are not really sure of what you are going to do next. Also you develop comaraderie and lasting friendships during this period. Among my college friends I must mention Bansi Lal Bhan, Ashok Raina, Kulbushan Razdan, Rattan Lal Khosa, Autar Krishan Malla, Jawahar Lal Thusoo, Rafiq Ali, Som Nath Razdan, Som Nath Pandita, Santosh Dhar, Mohammed Shafi, Deedar Singh, P.K. Hak, Autar Wali, Mohd. Abdulla Dhobi, Atul Bhan and Anil Bidani. All of them thrived and did very well in their careers. Special mention must be made of some of my close friends. Ashok Raina who later settled in U.S.A. earned a name as a scientist and Agricultural Entomologist of repute.

Bansi Lal Bhan specialized in Urology and established a good practice first in Kashmir and later in New Delhi. Kulbhushan Razdan had a flair for English Literature. After B.Sc., he changed stream and did M.A., Ph.D. in English. He took to teaching and rose to become Head of English Department in Jammu University. Som Nath Pandita also did postgraduation in Botany and joined Higher Education Dept. as a Lecturer. Santosh Dhar was an ace cricketer and college team captain and later became a Scientist in Pharmacology at I.I.M. Jammu. Rafiq Ali Joined Higher Education Department like myself and became a popular teacher of Zoology. Mohd. Abdullah Dhobi, P.K. Hak and Deedar Singh studied medicine after B.Sc. and became doctors of repute. Mohd. Shafi did postgraduation in Biochemistry from Aligarh Muslim University and later taught at the Srinagar Medical College. Atul and Anil too went for medicine but I lost touch with them.

As I have mentional earlier S.P. College was a co educational institution for science students at B.Sc. level. Those days boys and girls (or should I call them men and women) did not mingle much. The interaction was limited to classroom and laboratory activities only. Though there were at least twenty female students in my class I recall the names of only a few of them like Shibani Daftri, Vijay Choudhary, Bimla Kaul, Janak Dulari, Shama Fotedar, Jaiki Kaul, Neena Bambroo, Parveen Jabeen, Akhter Banu and Parveen Kour. Most of these ladies also did very well in their careers in teaching and medicine. Like most of my male classmates I have lost touch with them. Even Facebook has not been of much help despite putting on it a group photograph of B.Sc. Final year (1959-61 Batch) which thankfully Santosh Dhar had preserved. He gave me a copy of it at Jammu some years ago. I must also add here that my maternal cousin Roshan Mattoo was one year junior to me in the college. He and his friend Autar Mattoo often interacted with me to remove their academic doubts. While Roshan went on to become a noted biochemist, Autar made a mark as a microbiologist in the United States. The four years from 1957 to 1961 spent at S.P. College are among the most memorable period of my life.

Chapter 7

Hazratbal Campus

Jammu and Kashmir went through a lot of change educationally as well as in other spheres of life from 1957 onwards. Opening of postgraduate departments in the erstwhile University of Jammu and Kashmir made it possible for many graduates to seek admission in postgraduate courses for which earlier they had to go outside the state. Since majority of graduates who wanted to go for postgraduation could not afford it they sought employment. In 1961 several postgraduate departments in science subjects were started by the university, some at Srinagar and others at Jammu. Since I had graduated I too sought admission in the newly opened Botany and Zoology departments. I was selected in Zoology.

University campus at Hazratbal for which Dr. Karan Singh the Chancellor had donated his own sprawling orchard was still in the process of development and P.G. classes in Botany and Zoology were initially started at S.P. College where infrastructure already existed. With a little extra input by way of materials, chemicals and books postgraduate courses were started with the staff appointed by the university. It was only after one year that the building housing P.G. departments of Zoology and Botany was completed. By that time we had nearly completed 1st year of the two year course.

Initially there were four teaching staff members provided to P.G. departments of Zoology and Botany each. The Zoology department had Prof. S.M. Das as Head, Prof. D.N. Fotedar as Reader and Prof. Y.R. Malhotra and Prof. P.L. Duda as lecturers. Professor Das was a well-known Zoologist and Prof. Fotedar had been my teacher during four years at S.P. College. Prof. Malhotra and Prof. Duda had been teaching in different Government Colleges before joining the university. The teaching staff were supported by clerical and laboratory staff. Only seventeen students were admitted in the 1st batch which included ten males and seven females. In my batch there were four school teachers—three males from Kashmir and one female from Jammu. It was a good step to include serving teachers for postgraduation so that the standard of education could be improved in the schools when they went back to their jobs. I believe this practice was followed earlier in admissions to arts subjects as well. The classes went on smoothly for most part of first year at S.P. College and it was only towards the start of the examinations that the departments of Botany and Zoology shifted to the campus. When results were declared two students—a male student from Kashmir and a female student from Jammu had failed all others had passed. Perhaps to overcome the sadness of her failure the female student got married and lived a happy life thereafter! The male student, however, was not disheartened. He appeared privately next year and passed. He then joined the regular class and passed final year meritoriously.

Our final year course of M.Sc. started in good earnest in the sprawling Campus of the University at Hazratbal. There were already a number of postgraduate departments in arts, languages and humanities running in the campus when we moved in. That year two more science departments—Chemistry and Physics were added. There was also a large hostel for boys. The campus as I mentioned earlier, was actually a sprawling orchard of fruit trees donated by Dr. Karan Singh. The fruit trees were auctioned by the university authorities to some contractor who had appointed guards. A constant conflict existed between the students (who plucked the fruit from the trees) and the guards. Such conflicts were generally restricted to verbal duals but sometimes took ugly turn when some student received a thrashing from the guards while caught stealing red handed. Ultimately these conflicts were resolved amicably but apples continued to be plucked stealthily by the hostlers during night!

The postgraduate departments of Zoology and Botany were accommodated in the ground and 1st floors of the same building respectively. The accommodations was quite adequate and would suffice for at least ten years. Later when the number of students and specialties increased the building was extended on both sides adding more accommodation. The holy Shrine of Hazratbal housing the relic of Prophet Mohammed PBUH added to the halo and serenity of the campus. Nearness of the campus to the Dal Lake with Zabarwan hills in the background further added to its charm and beauty. I have no hesitation in saying that Kashmir University Campus is definitely one of the most beautiful campuses in the country. Students would go to enjoy rides on Shikaras (boats) to visit Sona Lank Island in the lake whenever an opportunity arose. For the muslim students nearness of the holy shrine provided an opportunity to offer prayers on Fridays. For the students of Botany and Zoology the lake provided sufficient material for experiments on fish, plankton (microscopic plants and animals) and water plants. It is no wonder then that nearness of Dal Lake to the campus provided an impetus to a large number of students of the two departments to choose to do research in limnology.

When our classes started in the campus in August 1962, there were already a few languages and social science departments functioning there. Since the student population was low a single cafétaria in the arts block existed to cater to them. As the number of students was less there was naturally greater interaction and bonhomie between arts and science students. Most of the students came from the Srinagar city but there were also those who came from suburbs and towns of Jammu, Kashmir and Ladakh.

Although a department of sports then existed at the campus, yet there was not much sports activity going on because the playgrounds were not ready. Most of the inter college tournaments were still being organized in the good playgrounds of S.P. College and Amar Singh College. The central library was housed in one wing of the main administrative building. Since most students came to attend from the city there was not much activity after 4 p.m. when the departments closed.

However, hostellers took full advantage of the library which remained open till late in the evening. Later a bus was kept at the disposal of the library for the staff and those city students who chose to stay late to use the facility. Many years later when I was engaged in research I used to stay in the library till it would close. One day Governor Bhagwan Sahai, who was the Chancellor of the University dropped in. On finding very few students in the library he remarked that academic atmosphere had not yet picked up in the valley. "Despite a bus being made available to the students to commute back to the city most of them are not making use of the facility", he said with some disappointment. He cited his own example from student days at Lucknow University. He said that the library there used to remain open for 24 hours 7 days a week and students made full use of it using bicycles as their mode of transport. Those of us present just listened to him quietly. Initially the university did not own transport and students, teachers and other staff commuted in chartered private buses. The university acquired a fleet of buses later after I had already completed my P.G. course and joined service as a lecturer.

The academic atmosphere in the Zoology department started to pick up soon after it had shifted to the campus. Two lecturers Prof. Malhotra and Prof. Duda were enrolled for Ph.D. under the supervision of Prof. S.M. Das. Prior to it research activity in the campus did not exist at all. Only teaching work was done. So credit goes to Prof. Das for initiating the process of research. It was at his initiative that rules for conducting research and granting research degrees were framed by the Academic Council of the University. The department of Botany followed suit with Prof. T.N. Khashu, a geneticist of repute, registering some scholars for Ph.D. under him. Thereafter more and more departments started to register students for Ph.D. Prof. Das also started a research journal titled, *Kashmir Science* in which research work mostly done by the local scholars was published. It is unfortunate that the journal stopped publication soon after the retirement of Prof. Das in 1973.

In the final year of our course we had to take up a special paper. In the Zoology department, there were only two options available at that time, viz. Ichthyology (fish and fisheries) and Helminthology (Study of helminth parasites). The first was with Prof. Das and second with Prof. Fotedar. Prof. Das was a well-known scholar who had published research work in national and international journals. His fields of specialization included Fisheries, Protozoology and General Zoology. Prof. Das had guided research at Lucknow University and many of his students had been awarded Ph.D. degree. Prof. Fotedar on the other hand had not yet earned a Ph.D. degree for which he was registered with the University of London, but he had many research publications to his credit. The choice of awarding the special paper to the students was kept by Prof. Das to himself. Accordingly I was assigned Ichthyology (fisheries) as my special paper which set the course of my future research work.

At the beginning of winter break in December 1962 the department organized a "Zoological Tour" to Bombay (now Mumbai). Most of us had, not ventured out of the valley till then so it was a good opportunity to see rest of the country. I had, however, soon after appearing in the first year of M.Sc. in Oct. 1962 travalled down to South India where my brother Pushkar had taken up a job as the manager of a small industrial unit at Samalkot in East Godhavari district of Andhra Pradesh. That trip had been a memorable experience which I will describe elsewhere. The tour party headed by Prof. Das himself included Prof. Duda and fifteen students (9 male and 6 female) from both first year and final year classes. The party left in a tourist bus early in the morning for Jammu where our stay had been booked in advance in the Tourist Reception Centre at fashionable Residency road. The next day another bus took us from Jammu to Pathankot a distance of 110 kms. Those days railway line terminated at Pathankot and was extended to Jammu only after a decade or so later. Earlier Jammu was connected by rail to Sialkot (now in Pakistan) in the pre-partition days.

The railway journey which started at evening in the Kashmir Mail an express train lasted forty hours or so. I remember how excited all of us were on reaching busy Victoria Terminus Station at Bombay the dream city. A short distance away at Dhobighat arrangements for our stay in a hotel had already been made. We stayed for seven days at Bombay and during this period Prof. Das took us to the maximum possible number of places to make it literally a study tour. We went out into the sea in a boat provided by the fisheries department of Bombay to have a first hand knowledge of life in the open sea. We were also taken to Khar, Juhu and Elephanta Caves to study ecology and biology of marine life near the shores. Visits to Malabar hills, Elephanta caves, Taraporewalla aquarium, Bombay Zoo, Marine drive and Chowpati were really great experiences. To add entertainment to the trip he also took us to the famous Maratha Mandir Cinema hall where the film *Professor* with Shami Kapoor in the lead was showing. On our way back we stopped at New Delhi to visit the Zoological Park in addition to visiting other places of interest there.

Needless to say that educational tours are very useful as they provide an opportunity to see to believe. What we study from books and in the classrooms is not sufficient to gain true knowledge. India is a vast country with diversity in geography, ecology, wild life, culture, languages, religions, food habits, architecture, dresses and so on. Again the country is rich in heritage sites and places of historical value. Educational tours add by way of experiencing India first hand. In Biological science and Earth sciences field trips are essential. In our case, for example, our group belonged to Jammu and Kashmir which is thousands of miles away from the sea. A visit to Bombay gave us the first hand knowledge and insight into of the sea and marine life which no textbook or classroom lecture could give. It is a different matter now though, as television has made it possible to see visual images of not only the world but even beyond it.

Professor Das believed in setting high standards and saw to it that we received the best possible facilities. He also invited the well-known Zoologists as our examiners. In the first year of M.Sc. we were examined by Prof. G.P. Sharma, Head of Zoology Department at Punjab University Chandigarh. In the final year Prof. M.D.L. Srivastava, Prof. G.S. Thapper and Prof. Bose were our practical examiners. With the exception of one of our batch mates all of us passed scoring high marks.

Prof. Das also exposed us to interaction with eminent scientists. I remember that he once invited Dr. Kashi Nath Kaul, the Director of Botanical Garden Lucknow, to deliver us a lecture on snakes. Although Dr. Kaul was an eminent Botanist he had also made a deep study of snakes and knew how to identify and catch them alive. His lecture was a memorable one for the fact that he tried to remove many common misconceptions that people have about snakes. He told us that only about 10% of over 200 species of snakes in India are poisonous. The students freely asked him questions on snakes (both poisonous and non-poisonous) which he answered with great ease.

After passing M.Sc. Final examination the next problem was to find a job. Those of my classmates who had been deputed by the school education department for improvement of qualifications had joined back soon after the exams were over. The rest including myself started looking for a job after the results were declared rather late in September 1963. An advertisement by the State Public Service Commission appeared sometime in the month of October for recruitment of lecturers in the newly opened colleges at district level. So I applied along with others and was advised to wait for an interview. In the meanwhile, I applied on a plain paper for an 'Adhoc' appointment and personally met Mr. Pushkar Nath Kaul, Education Secretary for the purpose. He said that as offices were closing for annual Darbar move to Jammu he would consider applications received for 'Adhoc' appointments at Jammu. Mr. Kaul was a thorough gentleman and kept his word. He issued some 'Adhoc' appointment orders for a period of six months and I was posted at Government College Sopore. Accordingly I joined the college on 2nd December 1963.

Mr. Shamsuddin had taken over as the Prime Minister of Jammu and Kashmir some time ago, after Bakshi Sahab's resignation. Bakshi Ghulam Mohammed administered the state for over ten years. His period will always be remembered for the process of development that he initiated in all walks of life. He was a man of ideas and action at the same time. Building activity—roads, buildings and bridges had picked up. At Srinagar a Medical College and a Regional Engineering College were opened; besides two colleges of Indian system of Medicine, Ayurveda at Jammu and Unani Medical College at Srinagar also came into being. The University of Jammu and Kashmir started campus at Hazratbal Srinagar and at Canal road Jammu for postgraduate courses. Some postgraduate departments were started at Srinagar and some at Jammu. There was a fast growth of transport and more buses and trucks started plying on the roads. Cheap transport became available to the public. More schools and colleges were opened to bring education at all levels to the doorsteps of the people. The progress made during Bakshi Sahab's period was visible. Tourist industry also witnessed growth. Industrial estates were opened though most of them flopped. A new tunnel named Jawahar Tunnel was opened in the Pir Panchal mountains which shortened distance and reduced travel time between Srinagar and Jammu. It also made possible to run traffic on Banihal cart road for most part of the year.

It is rightly said that power corrupts and absolute power corrupts absolutely. The period of Bakshi's rule will also be remembered for the corrupt practices that gained ground during that period. Bakshi was surrounded by sycophants who made him believe that he was indispensable. Some of his policies and methods had already made him unpopular and there was discontent growing among the members of his party. A group led by Ghulam Mohammed Sadiq parted company. The group included D.P. Dhar and Mir Qasim and they formed a new party named "Democratic National Conference". I was a student of S.P. College then and a member of the youth wing of the new party. Feeling the danger to his rule he soon made a compromise with these leaders and they returned to the fold of National Conference. This step of the D.N.C. leaders disillusioned the youth including myself.

The central leadership led by Jawaharlal Nehru was aware of the discontent, corruption and the growing unpopularity of Bakshi among the people of Jammu and Kashmir. In Punjab too Partap Singh Kairon despite many progressive programmes initiated by him had become unpopular. It was difficult to remove these powerful men. Thus came the "Kamraj Plan" under which some Chief Ministers including Kamraj Nadar, Chief Minister of Tamil Nadu himself would voluntarily step down and take up party work. G.M. Bakshi like Partap Singh Kairon and many others stepped down, though unwillingly, to make room for others. Bakshi was supposed to propose the name of G.M. Sadiq in the Assembly to replace him but he surprised everybody by proposing the name of less known Shams-ud-din instead. Thus Shams-ud-din took over the mantle of Prime Ministership from Bakshi. This was done ostensibly to retain power by Bakshi himself but circumstances took a turn and Shams-ud-din's rule could last only for a few months. He had to step down in favour of G.M. Sadiq on March 1, 1964.

Chapter 8

Train Journey to Samalkot

In the second week of December 1963 I received a letter from J&K Public Service Commission to appear in an interview for the post of lecturer in Zoology at Jammu on 30th Dec. 1963. On 22nd December the colleges in the valley closed for winter break. I along with my friends who too were invited to appear for the interview decided to leave for Jammu on 25th December. My cousin Mohanlal Miskeen was also travelling to Jammu along with his wife and six month old son Anil in the same tourist bus. My plan was to proceed to Samalkot in Andhra Pradesh after appearing in the interview to see my brother and his wife expecting their first baby.

It was a good decision to leave for Jammu on 25th December 1963 because the same night the valley experienced heavy snow fall and all roads and Banihal tunnel were blocked by snow. As destiny would have it my aunt "Ded" who was like a grandmother died on 24th December in the evening. My father was posted at Drugmulla at that time and he had to be informed. Those days telephone services were very limited and the only telephone available at Drugmulla was at the Post office which was closed at that time. So I sent a telegram which I hoped my father would receive in the morning next day.

I came to know on my return after two months that the telegram was not delivered to him as expected and in the mean while all roads were blocked by snow and he could reach Srinagar only after three days. I am writing this to give the young readers an idea about the poor communication system that existed then. A heavy snowfall would generally break all means of communication. Jammu and Srinagar remained cut off after heavy rains and snow fall for days together. The only means of communication then left was air service. There was a single Indian Airlines flight between Jammu and Srinagar every day. This was also suspended if weather did not permit. Twenty-eight seater Dakota and Foker Friendship turbo planes alone flew in the Indian skies those days. The bigger jetplanes arrived much later.

My travel to Jammu on 25th proved timely for another reason also. On 27th of Dec. 1963, it was reported that the holy relic of Prophet Mohammed PBUH had been stolen from Hazratbal Shrine. It outraged all Kashmiris and resulted in a peaceful upsurge in the valley in which Hindus and Sikhs joined the Muslims. The Central Government directed the P.M. Shams-ud-din to leave no stone unturned to recover the holy relic. Jawaharlal Nehru deputed the then minister without portfolio Lal Bahadur Shastri to Srinagar to help in the recovery of the holy relic. On 4th January 1964 to the relief of all, the government announced that the holy relic had been found. There was jubilation after the news of the recovery came. Mr. Lal Bahadur Shastri used his skill and wisdom in the early recovery of the relic in which he was helped by Mr. Shams-ud-din using utmost restraint and care. It was alleged that ISI of Pakistan was involved in the theft to cause uprising in Kashmir. Having failed in their design and seeing the mood of the Kashmiri people the stolen holy relic was silently put back from where it had been stolen by those involved in the heinous crime.

My interview was held on the scheduled date, i.e. 30th Dec. 1963 in the J&K Public Service office then located in the Old Palace premises at Mubarakh Mandi. The interview Committee consisted of the Chairman Mr. Durani two other members Mr. Mehra I.G.P. (Retd.), Col. (Retd.) Sambyal and the subject expert Prof. S.M. Das. Luckily for me I was able to answer all the questions put to me by the expert and all other members. My answers to two particular questions put to me seemed to impress the members. One question pertained to spread of Malaria. As I told them it was spread by *Anopheles* type of mosquito, one member wanted to know as to how can a layman identify it. Thereafter, I sought permission to make a demonstration which was granted to me. I went straight to a wall in the room and demonstrated with my hand how the body of a malaria causing mosquito makes an angle while sitting on it. On the other hand, the body of the mosquito which does not spread malaria rests parallel to the wall. As simple as that. The subject expert smiled and nodded in approval. Another question asked was about the names of the Indian Cricket team announced that morning. Two surnames in the team coincided with those of two members of the selection committee, and the chairman wanted to know it from me perhaps to test my general knowledge. Luckily for me while I was leaving the hotel in Raghu Nath Bazar radio in the manager's room was beaming morning news. I stopped to listen to the news and thus came to know about the names of the team announced by B.C.C.I. The surnames of two players coincided with those of the members—Durani and Mehra. My reply to this last question put to me seemed to please all the members and a "thank you" from the chairman indicated that my interview was over.

After my interview, I wished well to those friends who were waiting for their turn and went straight to the hotel to collect my suitcase. My cousin Mohan Lal had decided to drop his wife and child with his relatives at Jammu and accompany me to see my brother, a childhood friend of his, at Samalkot. He was waiting for me at the hotel. We went to the bus stand which was located then at Parade ground and boarded a bus for Pathankot. The weather was pleasant and within three hours we reached Pathankot. The train to Delhi had to depart at 8.30 p.m. So we moved around the Pathankot railway station to while away time and had dinner at a dhaba before boarding the train to Delhi. This was my third journey by train from Pathankot station.

*****

The first journey from Pathankot that I had undertaken earlier was in the 1st week of October 1962, on way to meet my brother Pushkar at a town in Andhra called Samalkot. That journey will ever remain etched in my memory. I had just finished my examination papers of M.Sc. Part 1st and was waiting for results. My brother suggested that I go down south and meet him. It was a good idea and my parents gave me enough money to undertaken the journey. I left Srinagar with eight other co-passengers in a van owned by N.D. Radha Krishan and Company at 7 in the morning. The journey was smooth and pleasant especially because by the end of September monsoon is over and the weather becomes good. We reached Pathankot Station at 6 p.m. I immediately purchased a general class ticket for Delhi which cost me ₹ 10 (not a small amount those days). The train had to leave at 10 p.m. so I waited at the platform after taking dinner in the railway restaurant. Sensing that I was an stranger a porter (cooli) approached me and asked if I would like to sleep for the night. Those days there were no sleeper coaches but only general coaches. Sleeping berths were available for travelers of 2nd and 1st class only. It was much later that the term 3rd class was abolished and replaced by 2nd class by the Indian Railways.

To sleep for the night instead of just sit and doze off was a nice proposition and I replied in affirmative to the porter. He agreed to provide a nice place to sleep if I paid him ₹ 5 which was rather too much so I declined. After a while he returned and came down to ₹ 4. As I again declined he then suggested ₹ 3 and I agreed. The deal done I started to wonder how he could arrange a sleeping place for me. I had never before seen how a rail coach looked from inside. Ten minutes before the arrival of the train the porter again approached me and explained that he was going to occupy a berth in a coach for which I should give him a sheet to spread on it. I had a bed sheet inside my bed roll but felt reluctant to trust a stranger. He felt my unease and said, "alright I will spread my own sheet on the berth but be vigilant and watch out for my signal when the train rolls on the platform". As the train approached the platform I could see his figure from a distance waving at me and he asked me to follow till the train comes to a stop. As I entered the coach, he spread my bed roll on the berth on which he had spread a piece of red cloth. Then he put my suitcase on the berth and also helped me to mount on it. The job done I paid him the promised dues. Actually as I understood now the berth was meant for baggage of the sitting passengers, but clever ones occupied these to sleep during night travel. It was a case of "might is right". The berth opposite mine was also occupied for another young passenger by a different porter.

Next morning, I woke to the hustle and bustle of New Delhi Railway Station. I had to meet my sister-in-law in Old Delhi before proceeding to Samalkot so I deposited my baggage in a cloak room. After having a shower in the waiting room I moved out of the station and walked towards Pahargunj. I was feeling hungry and looked out for an eating place. There were a number of dhabas in a row and I chose one serving vegetarian food. It was almost lunch time and I was offered a plate of rice with vegetable and Dal for an unbelievable price of six annas (about 40 p). It is the cheapest meal I have ever had in my life.

My sister-in-law Pushpa was doing some short course at Delhi at that time and was residing with her elder sister and her family at Rana Pratap Bagh. The family had left Kashmir in 1947 after the tribal invasion when many pandit families too had left and settled in Delhi. I had planned just to say hello to my sister-in-law before proceeding to Samalkot where her husband Pushkar was living alone at that time. However, the head of the family Mr. Prem Nath Dhar insisted that I should spend a night with them before continuing my journey. In the evening, he took me around the place. R.P. Bagh was a middle-class settlement and rather calm and quiet compared to what Delhi is now. Delhi of those days and of today are totally different with enormous expansion and development having taken place in the last fifty years.

The journey from New Delhi Railway Station to Vijayawada in Andhra Pradesh on way to Samalkot is the most memorable one and I would like to share my experience with the readers. When I purchased a ticket for Samalkot the clerk at the booking counter told me that there were two trains leaving for Madras (now called Chennai), viz. Deluxe Express leaving at 5 p.m. and G.T. Express leaving at 5:30 p.m. My ticket would be valid for both in the general class. He instructed me to get down at Vijayawada and take a connecting train to Samalkot from there. I purchased a ticket and looked for a Cooli and found an elderly one. He took me to Deluxe Express in which there was only one general coach that too was full with passengers standing even in the doorway. I told my porter to take me to the G.T. Express as it had many general coaches. His advice was that the Deluxe Express would be a better option as many passengers whom I had seen standing were daily commuters who would get down at stations up to Agra and thereafter I would be able to get a seat. It would have been wise to listen to his advice but being inexperienced, I insisted that he take me to G.T. Express. On boarding a general coach I was shell shocked. The coach was an old model and looked like a hall, like of which, I never saw in my life again. It did not have the usual compartments as I had seen in the coach in which I had travelled from Pathankot to New Delhi. Instead the coach was a single compartment with four long rows of benches—one along each side with windows and two back to back in the middle. All the benches as well as the racks above meant for baggage were occupied with unrolled beds on which passengers were lying in sleeping posture. Most of the passengers were Sikhs from Punjab. Later I leant during my journey of two nights and one day that they drove taxis in Madras. I somehow managed a small space to sit near a window and thanked my stars for it.

The train powered by two steam engines, one in front and one at the back pulled out of the station on time and gathered speed pretty fast. Soon soot and pungent smoke started entering the coach through the windows. It passed through many stations but stopped only at a couple of them including Agra at about 9 p.m. I spent the night waking and dozing off alternately while all other passengers slept like logs either on the seats or racks and even on the floor. The night seemed unending and the train passed through totally unlit areas for hundreds of kilometers. The only lights that I saw were on the railway platforms and the main towns where the train stopped. India of fifty years ago was not the India of today. The next morning, I had a refreshing cup of tea and snacks at some railway station. A kind passenger who had slept on the rack above me came down and offered his space to me for having some sleep, I gratefully accepted and went to deep sleep immediately after lying down.

When I woke up it was already mid-day. Actually my sleep was broken by shrill voice of hawkers on the platform of some big town, whose name I am unable to recall. I got down and felt fresh after sprinkling water from a drinking water tap on my face. By now I felt hungry and found hawkers selling south Indian food—Vada and Idli with sambar (Dal). These food items I had seen for the first time and selected Idli as these looked like rice cakes but were actually made of some other stuff. Anyway I relished taking them with sambar to overcome my hunger. Later during my stay of over a fort night at Samalkot I found that south Indian foods are rich in taste and variety. At another station I heard a hawker shouting something like "Daksh". It sounded like "Dachh". Out of interest I called out for the hawker and he approached my window. He was indeed selling grapes (Dachh in Kashmiri) and I bought some. From co-passengers I learnt that the train was now passing through Andhra. South Indian languages like Kashmiri are rich in Sanskrit; grapes in Sanskrit are called "Daksh". The black seedless Andhra grapes tasted well. Later I learnt that Andhra is also a big producer of Mangoes.

I had to spend one more sleepless night till the train came to a halt at Vijayawada Station. The people there pronounce it as "Bijwada". If you take a look on the names of places in different parts of the country there is a likeness and resemblance. For example "Nilore" in Andhra has a similar village "Nilora" in Pulwama District. Srinageri in Mysore, Srinagar in Garhwal and Srinagar in Kashmir is another example. The terms Nagar, Pur, Kot, Abad are commonly used all over the country which gives one the feeling that India is indeed one country. There is definitely "Unity in Diversity" in this country.

I got down from the train saying good bye to Madras bound Sardarjis who had been my co-passengers for almost 40 hours. My train ticket was made upto my destination and I had to enquire about connecting train that would take me to Samalkot. Luckily a connecting train was leaving within half an hour. It was bound for Vishakhapatnam and I boarded a coach and found a vacant seat to sit on. The coach was not overcrowded and looked cleaner compared to the one I had just left behind. All my co-passengers were Telegu speaking and I could not communicate with most of them except for one or two who understood English. Whatever we may have to say against the English yet they have left us with a uniting common language—English. Those co-passengers who spoke English asked me where from I had come. When I told them that I was from Kashmir their interest in me increased and they asked me many questions about our language and culture.

Soon after leaving the station the train passed over the Godavari river—a huge expanse of water. The railway bridge on the Godavari was the longest ever seen by me and the train moved over it very slowly. The railway track passed through green rice fields for miles and miles on. It was indeed eye catching with greenery broken here and there with patches of huts of the farmers. East Godavari District is aptly called rice bowl of Andhra for the enormous quantity of paddy produced there. The green revolution had not come then and I can guess how much the production of paddy must have increased in Andhra as did the production of wheat in the Punjab after it. The train took four hours to reach Samalkot from Vijayawada. As I got down at the small railway station it was obvious that Indian railways have a uniform pattern of railway stations everywhere except, of course, those of the metropolises and big cities.

My brother Pushkar knew that I was coming but when exactly he did not know. I should have sent him a telegram from Delhi but there was hardly any time left to do so. I knew that my destination was the Industrial Estate and on enquiry the Babu at the station told me in broken English that it was close by and I should take a cycle rickshaw or a bullock cart. When I came out of the station a small statue of Bapu Gandhi with a garland of fresh flowers around his neck greeted me. It made me immensely happy. There was no cycle rickshaw any where near but I could find a bullock cart. Now the real problem was how to communicate to the cart man about my destination and his charges. I looked right and left and could locate a policeman in uniform. When I spoke to him he could not understand a word. However, he did understand the word Industrial Estate and told the cart man who shook his head from right to left. I thought he had refused but the police man indicated me to sit in the cart. The cart man loaded my bed roll and suit case in his vehicle. As I later understood southerners shake their head slightly from right to left to say "yes" which to us northerners means "no". In my mind I thought that the bullock cart would take a long time to reach my destination. I was proved wrong for the cart soon started rolling fast through the streets of Samalkot as the small bull galloped. I had never before seen a bull gallop like a horse. Within fifteen or twenty minutes we were at the entrance of my destination. The guard at the gate guided the cart man as I spoke to him the name of the unit "Mohan Enterprises".

When I got down from the bullock cart and the driver brought my luggage down Pushkar saw me through his office window and came out. After hugging me and paying the cart man his dues he indicated to his peon to bring in my luggage. He made me sit comfortably and asked his peon to get water and tea for me. I was terribly fatigued and wanted to take rest. Sensing my condition Pushkar asked his peon to get a cycle rickshaw and then took me home. His rented accommodation was reasonably good in a well to do locality of the small town. The first thing I did was to wash and change. Thereafter his domestic help served us lunch. He was putting up alone as his wife Pushpa was away at Delhi attending some course as I mentioned earlier. Lunch over my brother advised me to have some sleep and left for his office. I went to sleep the moment I rested my head on the pillow.

I felt relaxed and relieved after a full four hour sleep. By that time Pushkar had returned from his office. Having met after over two years we sat through the whole evening chatting. He told me that he had felt shocked after seeing me fully covered in soot with face blackened by smoke of the stream engine. Diesel engines for trains had arrived but were not being used then by the Indian railways except in some selected sectors. Those days long distance train travel in third class no doubt was not easy but it was affordable. That evening we spoke of our memorable childhood days and how life had changed since then. His cook had cooked fish and rice for dinner. The fish had been gifted by the land lady from her own private pond after hearing of my arrival.

Next morning, the nice and generous land lady invited us for breakfast. The landlord Mr. Narsimhan was a producer of Telegu films. He owned some cinema halls as well. As I enquired about what sort of films were made in Telegu he said they were just like Hindi films—love stories with songs sung around trees. He told me that because of my fair colour he could offer me a role if I learnt to speak Telegu, a difficult proposition no doubt. I thanked him for the offer. In retrospect I think learning Telegu and acting might have changed the course of my life. But that was not to be and I have no regrets about it.

Samalkot is a small town and in addition to an industrial estate, there were two large mills—a sugar mill and a Sago mill—set up by some English men. These mills employed a large number of workers and I hope that these mills are not closed by now. I am sure that the industrial estate must have flourished. The market place was full of activity as it served the neighboring villages. Congress Party was in power and people seemed progressing. Regional parties did not exist then. As it is south Indians are great addicts of tobacco and cinema. Both ladies and gents smoke local made cigars. Cinema is quite popular and whether they eat food or not but watching a film is a must. Pushkar once took me along to watch an old English movie in the only local cinema hall. The cinema hall was an open theatre with asbestos sheet roof and about 200 seats. We were offered the best seats. The hall was fully occupied by old and young men and women and even children. The cinema hall had a single projector so there were several intervals in between change of the reels. It reminded me of films shown by publicity division of Government of India in our villages and towns in fiftees.

A van with a projector, a small screen and a generator would arrive just before it was Dark in an open space in a mohalla or a village. Word would spread and a crowd would gather in no time. For children, there was nothing better than to watch a film in the neighborhood at no cost. Usually it used to be a documentary about the post-independence progress in the country. Some documentaries were good and showed the benefits of education, good hygiene and population control. Sometimes even Hindi films were beamed which attracted larger crowds. It was good entertainment during fifties when Radio was the only medium of entertainment at home. There were only three cinema halls in the Srinagar city then. People by and large and especially women and girls from middle class did not watch films. Watching romantic films was not encouraged by the elders. So youth-school and college students bunked classes to watch Hindi films.

Having stayed at Samalkot my brother had developed friendship with managers of the local mills and industrial estate and with government officials and a local doctor. I was invited by his friends to their club for dinner where they played snooker, table tennis and other indoor games. Most of them belonged to Andhra but there were some from other states also and they had developed a good bonhomie among themselves. At Samalkot I discovered that every well to do household owned rice fields and fish ponds. Rice is staple diet in Andhra and ponds are maintained to harvest fish for their own personal consumption. Rice is consumed with sambar, rasam and vegetables curries. Most people are vegetarians but some consume fish and meat also. Some of Pushkar's friends who had families with them invited us to their homes as well.

Samalkot is very close to the port city of Kakinada on the east coast. It is a very busy city and iron ore is exported to Japan and many other countries from this port where I could see several ships docked. I visited the city several times during my short visit as it is easily approached by bus. A well known medical institute "Kakatiya Medical College" and a large number of other institutions of higher learning are there in the city. I found the food served in hotels good. A meal of rice, vegetables, prawns and an unlimited quantity of butter-milk cost just one and quarter rupee. That was an additional attraction to visit the place frequently.

My return from the brief visit to Samalkot was a pleasant one as my tickets had been booked in advance from Samalkot to Pathankot. Since my classes were to start so I was in a hurry to return. After a day long stay at Delhi I took a night train to Pathankot which reached early in the morning next day. As I mentioned before Jammu did not have a rail link. So there was regular bus service run by the Government Transport and N.D. Radha Krishan Company from Pathankot to Srinagar. The bus stand was close to the railway station. I purchased a ticket in a Government Transport bus and boarded it. It soon after left on its journey to Srinagar. Most of my co-passengers were tourists from Bombay. I still remember vividly that it was 20th October 1962. When we reached Qazigund and the bus stopped for passengers to have their dinner the atmosphere was very tense. The news of China's attack on our borders in Ladakh and north-east the same day had come on the radio. All the passengers in our bus including the driver and the conductor felt tense and the two hour journey from Qazigund to Srinagar was made is total silence. At the tourist bus stand there were no taxis at 11 p.m. The tourists had bookings for their stay in the tourist centre. I was left in a fix but the muslim bus driver came to my rescue. He offered to drop me near my residence on way to his own home. Within a couple of days of my arrival results of first year of M.Sc. were declared and I had cleared with over sixty-five per cent marks. Our classes started immediately thereafter.

The Chinese attack had shaken the country. Mr. Zhou Enlai Prime Minister of China it appears, had grown jealous of popularity of Jawaharlal Nehru in the world politics. India under Nehru had extended hand of friendship to Chinese leaders and coined the phrase "Hindi-Chini-Bhai-Bhai." The formation of a group of non-aligned countries—India, China, Egypt, Indonesia and Yugoslavia—had raised hope in the third world countries in the back drop of cold war that existed between the two main power blocks, viz. the U.S.A. and the U.S.S.R. The atmosphere of cold war was coming in the way of growth and progress of the third world countries. In this situation the attack by the Chinese came as a surprise to an unprepared Indian Army. It is now well-known that the then chief of the Army had expressed his apprehension about Chinese designs and asked for arms, ammunition and training for his troops but his advice was ignored by the Defense Minister Krishna Menon and Prime Minister Nehru.

Actually in 1959 there was an uprising in the Tibet against Chinese oppression in that region. Dalai Lama with his supporters had to run away secretly to India to seek asylum. India could not refuse him asylum as relationship with Tibet goes back to thousands of years. This irked Chinese leadership under Mao Tse Tung and Zhou Enlai and they decided to teach India a lesson. Unable to reach political accommodation on the disputed territory along the 3,225 km. long Himalayan border, the Chinese launched simultaneous offensives in Ladakh and North-East India and crossed the McMahon Line on 20th Oct. 1962 coinciding with the Cuban Missile crisis. Chinese troops advanced over Indian forces capturing Rezang La in Chushul in the West and Tawang in the East. The ill equipped and unprepared Indian forces numbering 10,000 to 12,000 faced well-equipped and well-prepared aggressive force of 80,000 Chinese. Indian soldiers known for their bravery fought valiantly. In the process, we lost 1,383 brave men, 1047 were wounded and 1,696 went missing. On the Chinese side 722 soldiers died and 1,697 were wounded. The U.S.A. offered a hand of friendship and President Kennedy ordered the 7th fleet to enter Bay of Bengal. Chinese thereafter declared unilateral ceasefire on 20th November 1962 but not before grabbing a 23,000 sq. km. of Indian territory which they are still holding and are claiming more.

Documents indicate that the first Home Minister of India Sardar Patel had cautioned Panditji to be careful in dealing with the Chinese leaders who were not trust worthy given their past history. But Panditji was more of a statesman and less of a politician and this set back affected his health. He suffered a mild stroke on 7th January 1964 at Bhubaneswar where he had gone to attend the annual session of the Congress Party. He never really recovered from it and ultimately passed away on 27th May 1964. However, he remained popular with the people of India in spite of the political troubles in his final years.

*****

My third journey by train from Pathankot in company of my cousin Mohanlal, with which I had started my story, had a definite purpose. My sister-in-law Pushpa and brother Pushkar were expecting their first baby and they wished me to be there. Pushpa had completed her short course of study at Delhi and joined her back husband in March 1963. This journey was not much different from the first one that I have described above except that the coaches that we boarded at Pathankot and Delhi were better and cleaner. Moreover, I was not alone and had my cousin with me to give company. Pushkar was expecting our arrival; having grown wiser this time I had sent him a telegram from New Delhi Railway Station. We arrived in Samalkot on 2nd January 1964 and got the good news from my brother that a baby girl had already arrived at a Nursing home at Kakinada on 31st December 1963. Babuji later named her Usha which literally means daybreak. A ray of light, hope and progress had already arrived in Kaul family. My brother just before her birth had received an offer of a better job with perks at Surat in Gujarat and I had been selected by the Public Service Commission at Jammu and placed at number one in the panel of selected candidates. She had indeed brought us luck.

After wash, change and nice hot lunch all three of us rushed to the nursing home at Kakinada where Usha was born. She was a beautiful baby and warmed my heart at her first sight. Being the first baby of our generation she occupies a special niche in the hearts of all of us. Pushpa was discharged from the hospital a couple of days later. Mohanlal left, after stay of a few days, for Bombay where he had to meet the owners of an ink and oil colour manufacturing company for dealership in Jammu and Kashmir. I am glad his mission succeeded. The distributorship that he received brought luck and prosperity to his family. He was a warm and affectionate person but unfortunately he and his wife died of cancer many years later at Jammu.

My brother was asked by his new employers to come for an urgent meeting with them at Surat in Gujarat before joining. So he left Pushpa and baby Usha in my care till he returned after a fort night or so. He employers were so impressed that they asked him to join immediately and return to Samalkot on paid leave in order to bring his family with him. They also offered him comfortable residential accommodation. His employers at Samalkot had already accepted his resignation after he received the offer from his new employers. After having settled down in his new job and occupying the residential quarters Pushkar returned to Samalkot to make preparations for bidding good bye to the place. By now it was already end of January 1963 and reservations for my return journey were made in the first week of February 1963.

My journey from Samalkot to Delhi with a change over at Vijayawada was not incident free. As I got down from train at Vijayawada I went to the enquiry counter to check for my connecting train to New Delhi. There was a break of couple of hours and I thought it proper to take rest in the waiting room. I had hardly settled down when a well-dressed man in his late twenties approached me. After salutations in chaste English he told me that he was an employee of some company at a neighbouring town and had lost his wallet. Since he had no money he needed help to reach his work place. I asked him casually how could I help him. He said it would cost him one and a half rupee to buy a ticket to reach his work place and he would feel grateful if I could help him. I thought for a while, looked at his face and decided to oblige. After some time I went out to buy a book from a stall on the platform. Suddenly my eyes fell on the same man talking to another gentleman on the platform some distance away. Out of curiosity I tried to reach him but he walked away. I approached the gentleman to whom he was just talking and asked him what the fellow was saying to him. He told me the same story of loss of wallet. However, he was lucky as the man on seeing me had walked away. It was obvious the gentleman in question used to approach strangers with the story and earned a living on the railway platform at Vijayawada. I must say it to his credit that he had achieved mastery in his profession to befool unsuspecting travellers!

I had been asked by my adopted mother Shobawati (Mataji) to pay a visit to her nephew Man Mohan Kuchroo who was working as a tutor in the Histopathology Department at All India Institute of Medical Sciences, New Delhi. I was in no hurry to reach Srinagar for my college was still closed for winter break, the idea of visiting my cousin appeared good. So on reaching New Delhi I took an Auto-rickshaw and gave him the address of my destination. Luckily it was a holiday and my cousin staying in the institute's staff quarters was home. He and his wife were happy to receive me and asked the purpose of my unannounced arrival. I explained that I was on my way back from South India. The Institute's staff quarters were then and still are located at Yusuf Sarai. Man Mohan's two bed room flat was on the first floor of the row of residential quarters. Beyond these quarters there was a vast open space which I could see through my window. In far distance I could see the Qutab Minar standing majestically. Delhi in 1964 had not expanded to the extent it has now. Now that open space is covered with concrete jungle even beyond Qutab Minar! One night during my stay it rained and it was quite chilly. When I looked through the window of my room in the morning I found that the rain water collected in pools in the open space had frozen. I did not believe my eyes and went out to physically touch the thin layer of ice. Obviously the night temperature had dipped below zero. My stay with the lovable Kuchroos for a week or so before return to Srinagar was quite comfortable. I again stayed with them in 1976 when Man Mohan had got me an appointment in the Institute's ENT Department for treatment of an ear ailment called 'tinnitus' (constant noise in the ear). It saddens me to think of the affectionate couple. They remained childless and while Man Mohan died in an accident driving his scooter in eightees his wife Raj Mohini had to make it alone for about fifteen years before passing way in 2k.

Chapter 9

G.M. Sadiq Era (1964-71)

On 1st of March 1964 all educational institutions in Kashmir valley opened after winter break and I joined my college at Sopore. The day also marked change in the political scenario in the Jammu and Kashmir state. Ghulam Mohammed Sadiq was sworn in as Prime Minister in place of Shams-ud-din who had resigned. To be fair to Shams-ud-din, he had been earnest in his efforts to streamline the administration. I remember that soon after I had joined my job at Sopore a government order was issued that on a particular day (I cannot recall the date) in December 1963 employees in all government offices and institutions would have to take an oath (a written one received along with the order) under the supervision of the Head of the office to the effect that they would work and act honestly in their dealings and keep public and nation's interests above everything else. His handling of the situation arising from disappearance and later recovery of the holy relic of Prophet Mohammed PBUH had been quite tactful.

With the arrival of G.M. Sadiq a widely respected politician as Prime Minister of the state things started to move rapidly. He ordered release of Sheikh Mohammed Abdullah on 6th April 1964 and conspiracy case against him was withdrawn. Earlier Balraj Puri had held a series of meetings with Sheikh Mohammed Abdullah and a dialogue was arranged between him and Jawaharlal Nehru. In a statement he declared that he had led the state's accession to India and was bound by whatever he said and did till 8 August 1953 but he was not responsible for what happened afterwards. Panditji welcomed the statement and said, "before his (Abdullah's) arrest accession of Kashmir to India had been more or less completed". Nehru was also keen to explore the possibility of a settlement with Pakistan, and it was at his suggestion that Sheikh Saheb went there. Unfortunately Nehru died on 27 May 1964 before he could return from the mission.

The Sadiq Government brought about a number of constitutional amendments in the State Legislative Assembly. Articles 356 and 357 of the constitution of India were made applicable to the state by virtue of which the centre could assume the government of the State and exercise its legislative powers. The nomenclature of the head of the State and head of the government was changed to conform to the uniform pattern of the country. The head of the State hitherto known as Sadr-e-Riyasat as elected by the State Legislative Assembly was now to be nominated by the Central Government as Governor. The head of the Government hitherto known as Prime Minister would be called Chief Minister. The ruling National Conference was converted into Pradesh Congress Committee. These changes were not liked by the people of the valley and they reacted with anger against what they perceived as an assault in their identity. However, the people of Jammu and Ladakh welcomed these changes.

*****

Now that I had a permanent job my parents started getting proposals for my marriage. I had just celebrated my 22nd birthday and was not averse to the idea of having a life partner. When asked by my parents about my opinion I agreed to it with the rider that the bride to be should be good looking and at least a graduate. It is firmly believed in our community that marriages are made in heaven but I did not think so then. Now in hindsight I think there is some truth in it. Within a short time my parents found a match for me and the marriage was fixed for 28 May 1964. It may sound unbelievable to the readers but it is a fact that I saw Promila, my would be bride, on the day of marriage for the first time. This was in keeping with the tradition of our family for parents and elders to choose a match for a marriageable son. In case of my elder brother Pushkar and cousin Nathji too the same tradition had been followed. Many years later the tradition was broken when my younger brothers Pradiman Krishan and Bal Krishan were married. Times had changed by then so had many traditions.

There was hardly gap of a month between the my engagement and marriage. As it is marriages were and still are a long drawn affair among Kashmiris. It involves making preparations for three days of feasting, buying clothes and jewellery etc. All went well till 27 May 1964. On that day, we had organized a feast in the lawns of a neighbour. For the convenience of office-goers the feast started early at 9 a.m. and continued till 2 p.m. When the last batch of guests have had their lunch the sad news of passing away of our beloved Prime Minister Jawaharlal Nehru came. Actually, he had passed away earlier but announcement came late for obvious reasons. With the passing away of Head of the Government, a new person had to take over and Shri Gulzari Lal Nanda, the senior most cabinet Minister was sworn in as the Interim Prime Minister. A pall of gloom fell all-around. In Srinagar life came to a stand still so did everywhere in the country and seven day mourning was announced.

Parimoos my would be in-laws had organized a high tea-party at their own residence but they had to cancel the same. However, they handed packets of eatables arranged for the occasion to the guests who came to attend the party but tea was not served. In order to remove our apprehensions they sent a special messenger to see my parents to confirm that reception of Barat and solemnization of marriage would stand as per programme on the morning of 28 May 1964. That came as a great relief to all because under the prevailing circumstances postponement would mean inconvenience to both the families, their friends and relatives.

My would be in-laws were a family of educationists. My father-in-law Janki Prashad was Headmaster of Government High School Batamallu; one uncle-in-law Prof. Badri Nath taught English literature at the prestigious Amar Singh College and another uncle-in-law Nirajan Nath was an officer in the Civil Department of the Indian Army. Like all other Kashmiri

Pandits including my father they followed the annual almanac issued by the astrologers for religious and social purposes. For all auspicious occasions like marriages dates and timings were fixed by the astrologers. Accordingly my parents and in-laws had agreed to 28th May in consultation with an astrologer as an auspicious date matching with the birth charts of both the bride and the bridegroom. So postponement of the date in view of Nehru's demise would have meant a long wait for another available auspicious date.

The auspicious time for solemnizing marriage on 28th May was 7 a.m. rather an unearthly hour. However, to stick to the auspicious timing it was decided that a small party of ten persons would proceed to the venue of the marriage in two cars to be followed later by other baratis (members of the marriage party) at 9 a.m. It would suite both the parties. Accordingly myself, my father Babuji, Panditji and my two younger brothers proceeded in one car and my maternal uncle Radha Krishan, cousin Nathji and brothers-in-law Jia Lal and Prem Nath with their kids followed in another car. One of my maternal uncles stayed back at our residence to organize and bring rest of the guests in a bus to the reception venue. The distance from our home to the reception venue was hardly three kilometers. The arrangement worked well.

The Hindu concept of marriage is different from that of Muslims. While for Hindus it is a union of bodies and souls for Muslims it is a legal contract entered into by the couple through a "Nikah Nama" and involves a simple ceremony. However, a Hindu marriage involves performance of a number of ceremonies and rituals such as "Dwar Puja", "Kanya Dhan", taking of vowes in presence of fire lit by the Panditji presiding over the whole ceremony. The couple are made to move around the fire to confirm love, loyalty, belongingness, respect for each other and their respective families etc. Among the Kashmiri Pandits a unique feature is the "Pushap Puja" performed at the end. The heads of the couple are covered over by a red shawl held by two young girls and relatives shower flower petals on the couple along with the chanting of prayers in praise of Shiva and Shakti to make their marriage a unbreakable bond.

All through this ceremony the bridegroom holds hands of the bride. It offers the first private moments in their lives to be face to face and exchange silent feelings with their hands and eyes without being noticed. These ceremonies were performed in case of our wedlock under the supervision of our Panditji (priest) Dina Nath who was a highly esteemed Brahmin. One thing that is common between Kashmiri Hindus and Muslims is that the Baratis (Guests) accompanying the groom are well received and entertained with a sumptuous feast by the bride's family. Another unique feature which is common between Hindus and Muslims is "Phirasal" a party given in honour of the couple by bride's family.

Promila's family had organized a grand reception in their own lawns. I got a chance in between the ceremonies to visit the reception venue. It was covered with Shamianas tastefully decorated with buntings and wreaths of flowers. The food served was delicious and guests from both sides were enjoying their meals. The bride and the groom are not allowed to have meals until the marriage ceremony is over. So Promila and myself had to wait.

While our marriage ceremony was going on a lot was happening all over the country. The passing away of Panditji a day before had thrown the whole country into mourning. People of all shades came out on the streets and proceeded in processions towards Lal Chowk (Red square) Srinagar shouting slogans, "Jawaharlal Amar Rahein" and "Hindustan Zindabad". In New Delhi preparations for the cremation of the departed leader had started from the morning. A cremation Pandal was built close to Samadhi of Gandhiji at Rajghat. People from all walks of life had been visiting Nehru's residence the whole previous day and night to pay respects to him. A running commentary of his last journey was broadcast from All India Radio and it was reported that a sea of humanity had gathered on Delhi's roads to pay tearful respects to the man they loved so much. His last rites were performed by his grandsons Rajiv and Sanjay. As our vows were going on we could hear the running commentary going on in an adjoing room where our relatives had gathered to listen to what was going on. Needless to say that Radio was the only audio-medium available those days.

In 1964, television had not arrived in India. Radio and the print media were the only source of news and information. Newspapers published after the demise of Panditji were full of details of his life right from childhood and pages were full of photographs of Panditji's life happenings. There were also photographs depicting scenes of mourning going on at his residence with Indiraji, his grandsons, sisters and close relatives sitting beside his mortal remains. A leader loved by all Indians was no more and it marked the end of an era.

When it was time for me and Promila to take leave emotional scenes were witnessed at her parental house. The parents and relatives especially the ladies started crying tears of joy. Such emotional scenes are a mixture of feelings of joy and sadness at the same time. Joy for settlement of a daughter in life and sadness to send her away after taking all the care of bringing her up with love. The Muslim neighbour ladies lined up clutching each other and started singing and moving back and forth with rhythmic movements. This special type of singing in a chorus along with body movement is called "Roaf". It is common among Kashmiri Muslim ladies to sing like this at moments of joy. Hindus and Muslims in those days participated in each other moments of joy as well as sadness. It is indeed sad that after the mass exodus of Kashmiri Pandits due to turmoil in 1990 we miss such occasions of brotherhood and bonhomie.

Promila was warmly received by the ladies waiting at our residence. Our Muslim lady neighbours had gathered to sing welcome "Roaf" song. A "Rangoli" in our home compound was already there and we were made to stand on it. My mother welcomed Promila in the traditional way by moving a thalli full of sweets, flowers and lighted oil lamps over her head. Both of us were fed sweets before entering the house. A specially decorated seat had been made for Promila by my elder sisters Mohini and Kamta. Soon she was encircled by curious ladies from among the relatives and neighbours. In the meanwhile, I changed and relaxed in the company of my friends aware that we would have to re-visit my in-laws for "dinner". This dinner party is called "sat-raat". Promila was still dressed in her bridal clothes. After she changed to new dress and wore ornaments bought for her by my parents we left for the dinner at Parimoo residence.

*****

Life after Nehru again started to roll back to normal. Gulzarilal Nanda handed over Prime Ministership to Lal Bahadur Shastri after his unanimous election as leader of the Congress Party in the Parliament. He had a reputation of being an upright and honest leader. As time passed, as we shall see later, the country under his leadership, went through a new phase. More than a year after he had been Prime Minister Pakistan attacked India.

*****

With my marriage a new phase started in my life. Meanwhile, I got busy with my job in the college at Sopore. At the time of my joining the college in December 1963 Prof. Maqbool was the Principal. As a student I had known him as a staff member at S.P. college. Prior to his promotion as Principal of the present college he had a good exposure of administration at S.P. College. However, in March 1964 Prof. Maqbool after a tenure of three years was transferred to Govt. College Anantnag and Prof. A.S. Dar who had been on deputation as Director Stationary and Printing was reverted back to his parent Higher Education Department. Prof. Dar had a reputation of an honest and strict administrator. Earlier he had served as the Principal of Govt. College Bhaderwah and left his mark there as an able administrator. As it is his strictness did not endear him to the staff. He took pains to see that class work went on smoothly and with regularity. During his tenure no teacher dared to let students off. His principle was simple, "be strict with teachers and indiscipline among students will disappear automatically". It is no wonder that during his tenure the academic atmosphere improved a lot. He also encouraged sports, debates and other related activities. I admired him as a my role model. Later as a Principal myself I followed his work culture. Given my nature, however, I could not afford to be a stickler of rules like him. Times had changed much since then. For example, I had once to proceed on leave to accompany my ailing sister Mohini to New Delhi for her treatment. He refused leave quoting a rule which required prior sanction by the administrative department for leave other than casual leave. That would take time and it was an emergency. I had to request our staff secretary Prof. Peerzada Ghulam Ahmed to intervene on my behalf. Prof. Dar relented and allowed me to proceed on leave but wrote a rider on my application that the permission was provisional and subject to sanction by the Educational Advisor, who was the Head of Higher Education Department at the time. Sanction did, however, come in due course. Needless to say that many rules have since been changed and College Principals have been given wider powers now.

Campus indiscipline is related with slackness in teaching and administration. As the adage goes, "Idle brain is a devil's workshop." Let there be a free and democratic atmosphere and see to it that students are not allowed to idle away their time. Some teachers do not take classes regularly and let their students roam. This is what creates indiscipline. There should be strictness about entry of outsiders into the campus. Many a time indiscipline is created by entry of mischievous and even unsocial elements into a campus. In this I followed Prof. Dar both in letter and spirit and it helped me to administer with ease. He had also a great regard and appreciation for good and regular teachers. At Sopore I was lucky to have some excellent senior colleagues to interact with and learn from. Prof. Mohd. Latif Beg was the senior most professor. Besides being a good teacher he was a pious Muslim. As a follower of Islamic principles he had instructed officials that his provident fund deductions should not earn interest. Some of the colleagues I was proud to work with were Prof. Muzzafer Ahmed, Prof. Allahdad Khan, Prof. M.L. Shorabi, Prof. G.R. Bacha, Prof. G.Q. Bhat, Prof. P.N. Fotedar. Prof. P.N. Wanchoo, Prof. G.A. Peerzada, Prof. G.M. Bhat, Prof. Pushkar Nath, Prof. K.B. Kachroo, Prof. Abdul Rahim, Prof. M.S. Pandit (he later joined I.A.S.) Prof. S.P. Daftari, Prof. H.K. Khar, Prof. M. Maqbool, Prof. Sannaullah, Prof. A.K. Ogra, Prof. G.K. Moza and Prof. L.N. Saproo. Prof. Saif-ud-din Soz (later a Central Minister) and Prof. Abdul Gani Bhat (later a leader of Hurriat Conference) had also been on the staff of the college prior to my joining and they had been transferred to Govt. College Baramulla. Prof. Chaman Lal Gupta (later a Central Minister) had also been posted to the College after my transfer to S.P. College, Srinagar.

*****

In early April 1964 when Sheikh Abdullah was released from detention there was jubilation everywhere in Kashmir. The Sheikh and his confidant Mirza Afzal Beg revived their party named Plebiscite Front. The bold initiative of Pandit Nehru to send Sheikh Abdullah to Pakistan had come to an end after his sudden demise. However, on 25th May President Ayub Khan had rejected the proposal of Sheikh Saheb for India-Pakistan Kashmir Confederation. During the year 1964 a series of constitutional amendments were brought making Articles 356 and 357 of the constitution of India applicable to the state. The people of the valley were unhappy and protested with unprecedented anger. In response to a call of social boycott (Tarki mawallat) of Muslim Congressmen by Sheikh Abdullah, people declined to attend their marriages, religious functions and even funerals. Meanwhile on 5 February 1965 Seikh Abdullah, his wife and Afzal Beg left for a tour of Europe and West Asia including a pilgrimage to Mecca. He also had a meeting in Algiers with Zhou Enlai Prime Minister of China. The Government of India took a serious view of this and asked him to return immediately. When they landed in Delhi on 8 May 1965 Sheikh Abdullah and Afzal Beg were arrested. Angry protests in the valley followed their arrest.

Following their arrest the students led by Abdul Rashid Shaheen boycotted classes. The Principal along with the staff tried to dissuade the students from boycotting their classes. As a result a large number of students returned to their classes. It was a Friday and there used to be a break for offering prayers. The Principal got an announcement made to the students that after the break a debate was being held and everybody should be present in the college lawns. A good number of students returned after offering Friday Prayers despite exhortations by Shaheen not to. Finding himself ineffective in stopping others he too returned later. When Prof. Dar asked him why he was late, Shaheen did not reply. As the Principal repeated the question he said, "sorry sir". That disarmed the Principal and he allowed him to join the gathering. That day I felt that this young man Shaheen had the caliber to became a leader. Having felt the mood of the students he had decided to join them and when confronted by the Principal he tendered an apology to avoid a confrontation. Flexibility and acting on requirement of the situation are qualities of a good leader. It paid him off later. When he fell short of attendance for appearing in final examination the Principal requested his teachers including myself to give him extra lectures to cover the shortage. A.R. Shaheen later did his postgraduation in Zoology followed by a degree in law. In 1977, Sheikh Abdullah included him as a Deputy Minister in his cabinet. He also represented Baramulla constituency in the Parliament as an M.P. later. Among the many of my students at Sopore Mohammed Abdullah Charoo impressed me as a serious student. After postgraduation in Chemistry he joined the state Higher Education Department as a lecturer and subsequently rose to become Chairman of the J&K Board of School Education.

*****

In 1965, General Ayub Khan President of Pakistan took the misadventure of attacking India perhaps under the impression that India after Nehru was weaker than before. China had attacked India in 1962 and exposed her defense preparedness. On 5 August 1965 between 26,000 to 33,000 Pakistani soldiers under operation "Gibralter" crossed the line of control dressed as Kashmiri locals and headed for various areas within Kashmir to participate in insurgency against Indian rule. Indian forces tipped by local populace crossed the line of control and met with considerable success in capturing mountain positions after a prolonged artillery barrage. By the end of August, however, both sides had relative progress; Pakistan had made progress in areas such as Tithwal, Uri and Poonch and India had captured Haji Pir pass 8 km. into occupied Kashmir.

On September 1, 1965 Pakistan launched, "Operation Grand Slam" in Chhenab sector with the objective to capture the vital town of Akhnoor in Jammu, which would severe communications and cut off supply routes of Indian troops. Despite the failure of operation "Gibralter" Gen. Ayub Khan thought it prudent to attack, with overwhelming ratio of troops and tanks. Pakistan made gains against Indian forces. India responded with its Air Force to blunt Pakistani attack. The next day, 2nd September 1965 Pakistan retaliated and its air force attacked Indian forces and bases both in Kashmir and Punjab. I was witness to two of these air attacks in Kashmir. My colleagues and myself after attending college on that day were returning to Srinagar in a bus. Suddenly at Narbal we heard some blasts. A few minutes later we saw through the bus windows two low flying Sabrejets of Pakistan air force returning after dropping bombs at Srinagar airport. While returning they dropped bombs also on army installations at Pattan and we could hear the sound of these blasts too.

India's decision to open up the theatre of attack into Pakistani Punjab forced the Pakistani army to relocate troops engaged in the operation to defend Punjab. "Operation Grand Slam", therefore, failed and Pakistani army was unable to capture Akhnoor. India crossed the International Border on the Western front on 6 September 1965 making an official beginning of the war. The war lasted for five weeks and caused thousands of causalities besides loss of planes and tanks on both sides. The aim of Pakistan to capture Kashmir by force had failed again. The war ended with a UN mandated ceasefire on 23 Sept. 1965 and the subsequent "Tashkent Declaration" in January 1966. Defeat of Pakistan at the hands of India disappointed Pro-Pakistani sections of Kashmiris. They had seen 1965 war as a possibility of fulfillment of their dream of becoming Pakistani citizens. In Sopore and many parts of Kashmir a pall of gloom fell with the failure of Pakistan's misadventure in Kashmir.

*****

Sopore town had been politically active before the partition of British India in 1947. When Sheikh Mohammed Abdullah set up the all Jammu and Kashmir Muslim Conference in 1932 and then changed it to National Conference in 1939, Sopore was in the fore front. After the accession of Kashmir to India in 1947 a sizeable population of Kashmiris were not happy with his decision. They wanted Kashmir either to accede to Pakistan or become an Independent Nation. However, the Pakistani attack on 22 October 1947 and the atrocities committed by the tribals on the populace left the peaceful Kashmiris aghast and rethink about the option of acceding to Pakistan. After taking over the reins of administration Sheikh Sahab and his team had busied themselves in the Governance of the state. The people had a sigh of relief after the dust raised by the invaders had settled. Those who had left their homes and hearths in the wake of the tribal invasion started to return to their homes. A large number of refugees from Pakistan Occupied Kashmir had also to be settled. The people gave their whole hearted support to Sheikh Sahab's government in settling the refugees and other urgent issues. Two major decisions taken by the new government namely "land to tiller" and freeing the poor from repaying loans taken from money lenders were welcome by the people and made Sheikh Sahab a hero of the masses in Kashmir.

However, as time passed Sheikh Abdullah started showing signs of authoritarian traits and did not tolerate the slightest dissent. He sidelined secular and popular leaders like G.M. Karra in favour of Bakshi Ghulam Mohammed. In July 1953, G.M. Karra formed a Pro-Pakistan opposition party called "Political Conference" in Kashmir. In Jammu and Ladakh people felt alienated as the main focus of Sheikh Government was Kashmir centric. In Jammu Praja Parishad organized anti-government agitation. This angered Sheikh Abdullah. Some sections of Kashmiris were not happy either, with him for having acceded to India. There were also other factors mainly influenced by the U.S., which emboldened the Sheikh to make anti-centre statements in 1952 and 1953. Jammu and Kashmir assembly had elected Karan Singh as Head of the State in November 1952. Discontent in the state and in the rank and file of National Conference resulted in dismissal and arrest of Sheikh Abdullah on 9 August 1953. Bakshi Ghulam Mohammed succeeded him as Prime Minister of the state.

Arrest of Sheikh Abdullah had resulted in a mass agitation in the whole of Kashmir valley. The agitation was put down with a heavy hand by the Bakshi Government and a large number of people had died. The already alienated people of Kashmir were further alienated and Nehru's dream of making Kashmir a willing partner of the Union and a source of strength to its secular basis was shattered. India's moral image also nosedived and the decade long reign of repression and corruption that followed only aggravated the problem.

*****

In the month of January 1966 U.S.S.R's Prime Minister Kosygin arranged a meeting between Ayub Khan and Prime Minister Lal Bahadur Shastri at Tashkent, in the Uzbekistan beginning 4 January for a permanent settlement between India and Pakistan. The Tashkent Conference, under United Nations, American and Soviet pressure compelled the two nations to restore the boundary and the 1949 ceasefire line in Jammu and Kashmir.

The conference was viewed as a great success and a declaration was signed on 10 January 1966. The declaration thus released was hoped to be a frame work for lasting peace and stated that:

1. Indian and Pakistani forces would pull back to their pre-conflict positions, pre-August lines, no later than Feb 25, 1966.
2. The two nations would not interfere in each other's internal affairs.
3. Economic and diplomatic relations would be restored.
4. The two leaders would work towards building good relations between the two countries.

The agreement was criticized in India because it did not contain a no-war pact or any renunciation of guerrilla warfare in Kashmir. In Pakistan also the declaration was not well received and ultimately led to protests against the leadership of Ayub Khan. The day after the declaration Indian Prime Minister Lal Bahadur Shastri suffered a massive heart attack in Tashkent and died there. Lal Bahadur had endeared himself to the people of India for his determined leadership during less than two years as Prime Minister. He had become a National hero following the victory in the Indo-Pak War of 1965. His Slogan "Jai Jawan Jai Kisan" became very popular during the war and is remembered even today.

*****

Promila and myself were expecting arrival of our first baby in second week of February 1966. Her grandmother to whom she was greatly attached died a couple of days before she developed labour pains in the day time on 12 February 1966. It was snowing right from the morning that day. She had been visiting a lady doctor privately who had assured that she would be able to deliver the baby normally at home. Accordingly my sister accompanied me to call the lady doctor home. When she came to visit she said that it was a little complicated and that we should take her to hospital. By now it was late evening. Snow had collected and traffic had come to a stand still. No taxi was available. Finally my cousin Autar Krishan Miskeen used his good social connections and obtained the service of a vehicle of the electric department office situated at Gow-Kadal. Promila accompanied by my mother, aunt, sister and Autar Krishan was taken to hospital where she delivered a baby boy at 3.30 a.m. on 13 February 1966. In the meantime, her parents and uncles too had reached the hospital. The arrival of the baby made the grandmothers and all other relations present happy. Babuji later named the baby boy Anil.

It snowed the whole night and by morning more than 30 cms of snow had accumulated on the roads. Babuji was then posted as Medical officer at Arigam Hospital in Badgam district. The same day he reached Srinagar in the fore-noon and came direct to home. His sudden arrival surprised us for all transport had come to a stand still due to heavy snowfall. He had somehow managed to hire a jeep to reach home. What he said surprised us. He had seen a dream the same night in which a little boy sat in his lap. When he asked him who he was he said, "I am Keshav" (another name of Lord Krishna). My father was a spiritually realized person and understood that his grandson had arrived. His preceptor (Guru) was Swami Nand Lal of Budgam who had initiated him when he was a young man. Babuji had progressed further in his spiritual experiences in the company of Swami Hari Ram during his posting at Drugmulla in Kupwara district. He could foresee things but never revealed them. A day before his death in December 1984 at Jammu he told me that Raju (Anil) had been selected for M.B.B.S. course. The list came out a fortnight later and Anil's name figured among the top five selected candidates. Anil was the first male child of his generation in our dynasty. His birth was as welcome as had been the birth of Usha and Indira (daughters of Pushkar). My brother got a third daughter Anita a month later at Calcutta.

*****

The year 1966 saw the entry of Indira Gandhi in the National Politics as Prime Minister. After the sudden death of Lal Bahadur Shastri in January 1966 at Tashkent, Gulzari Lal Nanda had taken over for a second time as Interim Prime Minister. There were many contenders for the position of the P.M. Unable to agree among themselves, Congressmen on the suggestion of G.M. Sadiq agreed on Indira Gandhi as a compromise candidate. Perhaps they thought that she would be easily manipulated. Gulzari Lal Nanda who was the senior most Minister in Jawaharlal Nehru's and Lal Bahadur Shastri's cabinets believed that he deserved to become Prime Minister this time. He had expressed that he had been acting P.M. twice and deserved to continue. It must be said to his credit that he was a fine Ghandian and was known for his honesty and integrity. However, he was not acceptable to his colleagues. Later they must have regretted their decision to favour Indira Gandhi for the post as she refused to take dictates from any one of them.

Indira Gandhi showed extra-ordinary political skills and tenacity and elbowed the Congress dons—Kamraj, Morarji Desai and others out of power. She held the office of P.M. from 1966 to 1977 and again from 1980 till her assassination in October 1984. She was riding the crest of popularity at the time of her death. India's triumph in the 1971 war against Pakistan and the explosion of a nuclear device in 1974 had helped to enhance her reputation among the middle-class Indians as a tough and shrewd political leader. Indira Gandhi will also be remembered for bringing, "green revolution" in the country by laying emphasis on production by putting inputs to agriculture sector that had already been initiated by Jawaharlal Nehru. The "green revolution" in India subsequently culminated during her rule in the 1970's and transformed the country from a nation heavily reliant on imported grains and prone to famine to being largely able to feed itself and become successful in achieving its goal of food security. Mrs. Gandhi had a personal motive in pursuing agricultural self-sufficiency having found India's dependency on U.S.A. for shipment of grains humiliating.

*****

From my personal angle as well 1966 was an important year for me. My father retired from service the same year and as a natural consequence the yoke of family responsibility fell on my shoulders. My two younger brothers Prediman and Bal Krishan were still in the school. Earlier in 1965, I had applied for research fellowships in the Universities of California and British Columbia. Their response was encouraging but I had to drop the idea of going abroad keeping in view family responsibilities. Conscious that Babuji had developed a heart condition (Angina pectoris), and he would be retiring shortly, it would not be the right for me to go abroad. So I met my teacher Prof. Das to register me as a part time Ph.D. Scholar. He promised to enroll me in the batch of 1969 as he had already enrolled research students till then. My posting at Sopore proved a boon for the fact that the town being close to Wular Lake—the largest fresh water lake in Asia—I got ample opportunity to study fishes of Kashmir in their natural habitat and also made collections for the purpose of laboratory work. Prof. Das kept his word and recommended my name for enrolment as a research scholar under his supervision in the Research council meeting in March 1969.

The year 1967 did not prove to be good for our family. My most affectionate elder sister Mohini Rawal had developed a heart condition and died suddenly in April 1967 at the age of just 32. She was happily married to Jia Lal Rawal but had no child. My parents felt devastated by her sudden passing away. She was not only their first child but a darling. Like her husband Jia Lal, she was a wise person and her counsel was sought by all close relatives. She had transformed her in-laws household and taught at home kids of her elder brother and sister-in-law. My brother-in-law remarried a year later a Punjabi woman Nirmala but kept his relations with our family intact. She bore him a daughter and a son. Nirmala has maintained her relations with us even after passing away of her husband.

*****

The same year, i.e. 1967 there was an agitation by the minority Kashmiri Pandit community against the alleged conversion and marriage of a girl of the community to a Muslim man. It transpired that Parmeshwari working as a salesgirl in a Super Market had developed a relationship with a Muslim colleague. As she did not return home on a certain day her widowed mother panicked and the word spread in Rainawari area of the city where she lived. Police were informed and a search began to trace her. Within a couple of days police found out that she had married a Muslim man with the blessings of his relatives and family. It was alleged by Pandit leaders that she was a minor and should be restored to her mother. The government did not act till an agitation started and later took an ugly turn. Police batten charge on an agitating crowd resulted in death of a youth. This further flared up the situation.

The agitation took communal overtones when some mischievous muslim youth pelted stones on the agitating pandits. Hitherto the Hindu-Muslim brotherhood had prevented any communal incidents from taking place. Unfortunately, however, there were reports of hindus passing through muslim dominated areas like Nawpora, Gawkadal, Nawabazar and Feteh Kadal being attacked and roughed up. I personally know of an incident involving my friend and colleague Kulbushan Kachroo. He was going home on his bicycle when he was stopped by a crowd at Gawkadal and beaten up. His bicycle was thrown from the bridge into the Tchont Kohl below. He somehow managed to escape in an injured condition from the area and went to the nearby Kothibagh Police Station. The Muslim police officer instead of registering his complaint gave him a lecture on the futility of agitation launched by Pandits. In disgust Kulbushan left and managed to receive first-aid from a private medical shop before returning to his home at Rainawari in a Taxi. His marriage was due in a couple of days. In the meanwhile, curfew was imposed in the city to stop further violence. My friend's family had to obtain curfew passes for the marriage party to reach the venue of marriage ceremony.

It goes to the credit of G.M. Sadiq the Chief Minister and D.P. Dhar a Cabinet Minister that they handled the situation with utmost tact and care. The leaders of the agitation were called for talks and given assurances that the matter would be thoroughly got probed and grievances of the community addressed. The leaders of the agitation thereafter called it off. However, it must be added that the agitation did create a feeling of togetherness and unity in the community but their grievances were never addressed. In fact right from the day National Conference came to power K.P.'s were discriminated against in all walks of life. "Under the land to tiller" they lost large chunks of land. In admissions to educational institutions both academic and technical their merit was overlooked. So was with the recruitments, promotions and transfers. The community felt widely discriminated against and the agitation gave them an opportunity to give vent to their pent-up feelings. It was only later that under the instructions from the Supreme Court of India that some relief came in the matter of promotions and allocation of seats in the technical institutions on their own merit. The people of Jammu had also a grievance that their region was being overlooked and did not receive due share in development and services. In April 1967 "Jammu Forum" was formed. Earlier in fiftees Praja Parished during Sheikh Abdullah's rule had been agitating for the grant of regional autonomy. Following his dismissal in August 1953 and taking over of the government by Bakshi Ghulam Mohammed the demand fizzled out. During Sadiq Sahab's regime the demand resurfaced again. Accordingly on 6 Nov. 1967 government appointed "Gajandragadkar Commission" to consider the demands of the forum. After due deliberations for over a year the commission recommended statutory regional development boards, which had far reaching consequences so far as the autonomy of Jammu religion was concerned.

*****

In early March 1968, I was transferred from Govt. College Sopore to the prestigious S.P. College Srinagar my alma mater. It was a dream come true. The vow that I had taken as a student of the college to become a naturalist and teach in preference to the medical profession seemed coming true. Prof. Saif-ud-din was the Principal and Prof. Jagan Nath Wattal headed the Zoology Department at that time. When I had settled down to my new place of posting I picked up the threads of research work that I had started at Sopore. Zoology Department of the College had a good infrastructure for carrying out research work thanks to the efforts of Dr. B.L. Kaw, who headed the department earlier. However, there was need for further development by way of acquiring more equipment, chemicals, books and journals etc. Teaching work being the main concern in the colleges of the state affiliated with the Universities of Kashmir and Jammu much attention was not being given to developing research facilities. When I spoke about developing research facilities in the college to my Head of Department and the Principal they assured of help. It was much later that a research lab in limnology was established at S.P. College Srinagar due to efforts of Dr. D.P. Zustshi and Dr. B.A. Subla. In April 1969 my supervisor Prof. Das provided me facilities in the university by way of literature, equipment and chemicals. My friend M.K. Raina lecturer in the department offered me space in his own room for carrying out my work. So it became easier for me to first attend to teaching in the college and then go to the university which was located at Hazratbal some 10 kms. away. It was becoming difficult for me to manage without my own conveyance. On the suggestion of Promila I purchased a Lambretta scooter for the purpose. It facilitated my work considerably. Now I did not have to rely on public transport and I could work till late hours in the university department. My friend Raina welcomed it because he too could work till late hours in the department on his own research project and return home with me on my newly acquired conveyance.

Initially I hesitated to drive the scooter but my friend and colleague in the college Prof. M.H. Nahvi, who owned a scooter encouraged me. He gave me instructions in the college grounds on his own scooter for a couple of days. Taking courage one morning at about 6 a.m. when there was hardly any traffic on the roads I kick started my scooter and drove it for a few kilometers. The same day I drove it to my college. Later that day after work I returned home driving cautiously. Now I needed a license to drive and applied for the same. When I took the test for it under the watchful eyes of S.P. traffic Aman Ullah Khan I failed and had to apply again. However, the next time I passed the test and got the licence to drive a two wheeler.

*****

On one of the days in the month of September 1969 I had gone to the Fairdeal Motors the distributors of Lambretta scooters for first free service of my newly acquired two wheeler. As luck would have it while waiting in the worksop I saw Bakshi Ghulam Mohammed entering the office of the company which belonged to his son Bashir. Just then it occurred to me to try to meet the Ex-P.M. of the State. I went straight to the office and requested the peon sitting outside to allow me to see Bakshi Sahab. He went in and returned after a while and then let me go in. On entering the spacious office I found Bakshi Sahab sitting alone in a chair. I saluted him and he asked me to take a chair with a smile. When I had settled in the chair he asked me how I had come. I gave him my introduction and told him the reason of my presence in the premises was to get my newly acquired scooter serviced. When he asked me about its performance I told him that I was satisfied. Then taking courage I told him about the incident that had taken place with me about ten years ago when he was the P.M. I knew in my heart that he would not remember a minor incident involving a young man and humiliating him. I told him that the incident had meant a lot to me and it had changed the course of my life. Bakshi Sahab became thoughtful and after a while he looked straight at me and said that he did not remember the incident and if it had hurt me, he was sorry about it. He then continued and said that he had generally tried to do good to the people, including those whom he did not know even remotely. What made him sad now was that those very people whom he had helped the most had gone against him. I told him that the incident had made me strong in my resolution to go ahead in life without anybody's favour. He said that he appreciated it. When I stood up to take leave he too got up, shook my hand and said sorry once again for having hurt my feelings. My bitterness against this once most powerful man simply disappeared from my heart for ever.

*****

The period from the release of Sheikh Abdullah from prison in 1964 upto the emergence of Bangladesh as an Independent country in December 1971 remained full of restlessness and turmoil in the valley. Plebiscite front organized agitations from time to time to keep the pot boiling. It directly affected the life particularly the working in the educational institutions. I recall one such agitation in the summer of 1971 when some mischievous students of S.P. College pelted stones from inside on the police posted outside. The infuriated policemen without seeking permission of the Principal Saif-ud-din entered the campus and indulged in unprecedented cane charge on students as well as staff inside classrooms. One young student of pre-university class, an innocent Pandit boy Satish Nehru was beaten up mercilessly resulting in a head injury. He was removed by the staff to hospital in the jeep driven by Prof. Nazir Ahmed Khan but on arrival the doctors declared him as brought dead. The parents of the boy who was their only son were devastated for no fault of theirs. The Minister of Education Mr. Noor Mohammed came to the college and sympathized with the students and the staff for the unwarranted police action. He also advised students not to indulge in agitations and instead take studies more seriously. The Minister was an educated and well meaning politician but the Plebiscite front had badly vitiated the atmosphere.

*****

On December 3, 1971 Pakistani forces attacked India on the Western front in retaliation to India's involvement in the Bangladesh liberation struggle caused by Pakistani Military Junta's refusal to accept the results of the first democratic elections held in that country in 1970. The Awami National Party had won the majority of seats in the Pakistan Parliament and its leader Sheikh Mujb-ur-Rehman instead of being invited to form government was put behind the bars. In March 1971, Pakistani Army in collusion with religious extremists like

Jamat-e-Islami engaged in systematic genocide and atrocities on Bengali civilians, particularly nationalists, intellectuals, youth and religious minorities. The large-scale atrocities resulted in killing of 1 million people and exodus of 10 million refugees into India and displacement of 30 million people in East Pakistan. As a result the revolutionaries set up a Bangladesh Government in exile in the city of Calcutta (Kolkata) in the Indian state of West Bengal.

India was forced to look after a huge refugee population of displaced East Pakistanis (Bangladeshis). Her diplomatic efforts at the International level proved futile and the Military Junta under General Yahyah Khan did not stop the atrocities on the poor Bengalis. The Pakistan Army's attack forced India to enter war with that country. Overwhelmed by two war fronts, Pakistani defenses soon collapsed on 16 December 1971 and the allied forces of Bangladesh and India defeated Pakistan in the East. The subsequent surrender of Pakistani Army commanded by Gen. Naizi resulted in 93,000 prisoners of war, the largest number since Second World War and emergence of Bangladesh as an Independent country.

During the war our beloved leader true nationalist and Chief Minister G.M. Sadiq died at P.G.I. Chandigarh where he had been admitted for treatment. Consequently on 12 December 1971, Syed Mir Qasim was sworn in as the Chief Minister of the state. It was during Sadiq Sahab's period that greater integration of Jammu and Kashmir with rest of the country took place. He was a cool headed and rational politician and an able administrator. His services to the nation will be remembered for ever

*****

Following defeat in the war the Army Junta of Pakistan handed over power to a civilian government led by Zulfikar Ali Bhutto. He was under great public pressure to get the prisoners of war released from India with the result that a Summit Conference took place between President Bhutto and Prime Minister Indira Gandhi at Simla from June 28 to July 2, 1972. The two countries reached an agreement on July 2, which came to be known as "Simla Agreement". The broad feature of this pact included that the principle purpose of the charter of United Nations would govern the relations between the two countries. The two countries resolved to settle their difference by peaceful means through bilateral negotiations. The agreement also rationalised the ceasefire line in the state as the line of control and committed the two governments to resolve the Kashmir dispute through bilateral talks. The agreement was ratified by the Parliaments of both the nations soon after.

*****

It had now become a routine for me to attend my college for teaching from 8 a.m. to 2 p.m., return home for a quick lunch and then go to the university for research work. My supervisor Prof. Das was a very busy person so it was difficult for me to seek his guidance as often as I would desire. I would seek guidance of Dr. P.L. Duda my teacher and a lecturer in the Zoology department at that time. He helped me in selection of the fish species on which I should work. I would see him even at odd times and he helped without a frown. He later Joined Jammu University and retired as Professor and Head. Another lecturer who had taught me during M.Sc. Dr. Y.R. Malhotra (he later became Vice-Chancellor of Jammu University) also helped me whenever I sought his advice. As mentioned earlier M.K. Raina my friend let me work in his room till late hours which facilitated completion of practical part of my work in the shortest possible time. M.Y. Qudri (he too later became Vice-Chancellor of Kashmir University) was also a lecturer in the department at that time. During the winter vacation months of December, January and February Raina, Qadri and myself were regular visitors to the department and worked hard on our research projects, discussed problems and enjoyed hot food (occasionally including the winter delicacy "harissa") and tea together.

For two years, from March 1969 to March 1971 I worked on my research project and was ready with chapters of my thesis. Now these needed to be shown to my guide Prof. Das for improvements, corrections and final approval. In March 1971 after winter vacations were over Prof. Das returned from Lucknow where his family lived. I met him at his rented residence at Dal Gate and showed him rough proof of my manuscript. He advised me to visit him at his residence in the evenings on alternate days so that he could read, make corrections and suggest improvements. In the month of April 1971, when he had hardly approved four chapters came the shocking news of sudden death of his wife in a road accident. He was devastated and left for his home at Lucknow by the first available flight. After performing the last rites of his wife he returned to Srinagar a completely broken man having left his children in the charge of a spinster sister. It took me some time to gather courage and request him to approve rest of the chapters of my thesis. He was a kind man and loved his students. Gracefully he asked me to continue visiting him at his residence early in the month of June 1971. It took about a month to get final approval from him to start typing the corrected manuscript. Accordingly I engaged services of a typist Tej Krishan, who also happened to be my maternal cousin, to do the typing at my residence. He used to come in the evenings and I would sit with him and dictate the text. Since the text was full of technical terms I had to give him dictation with care and the progress was slow. He had to type five copies at the same time using carbon sheets. Those days computers and photocopiers had not arrived and things were not so easy as now.

Typing took full two months. In the meanwhile, I had also to print photographs of my drawings and microphotos. As luck would have it Promila's maternal uncle was a reputed photographer running a photography shop by name and style "Sat Lal and Co" at Baramulla. On my request he agreed to do this job in the shortest possible time. Typing and photography done the thesis was ready for binding. In this process my friend M.K. Raina (who had been awarded Ph.D. degree by then) helped me in arranging chapters with illustrations, photographs and reference etc. When the binding was done I proceeded to get certificate of originality of the work signed by my supervisor in September 1971. With the permission and blessings of Prof. S.M. Das I submitted four copies of my thesis on 1st October 1971 to the University of Kashmir (erstwhile University of Jammu and Kashmir).

On enquiring from the university I came to know that my thesis had been sent to three examiners for assessment by the middle of October 1971. Normally reports of examiners should come in a couple of months but generally it takes longer. The examiners who are experts in their subjects are generally busy in teaching and research. They are also often away on lecture tours or attending academic conferences. So the universities have to send polite reminders. I was expecting that the reports would come by the end of December 1971 but that did not happen. The first report however, came in the month of February 1972 and two more reports came later. I was told by my friends in the university office that all reports were favourable and a viva was conducted by two external and one internal examiners in May 1972. All the three examiners were satisfied and congratulated me. Now I had to wait for meeting of the University Syndicate where the examiner's reports are placed for final acceptance and clearance for issue of notification. This happened in June 1972 and thereafter an official notification was issued declaring that I had been awarded Ph.D. degree. Around the same time, we were blessed with our second son Kuldeep on 9 June 1972.

*****

Late in the year 1965 my brother Pushkar had resigned his job as the manager of a Plastics Manufacturing Factory at Surat and joined another but much bigger plastics factory at Calcutta. By the year 1968, he had acquired sufficient expertise and knowledge of plastics industry and decided to start his own unit at Calcutta. For this he needed initial capital. He had some savings of his own but needed more finances for the project. He wrote to me if I could arrange some finances for him. Accordingly, I spoke to and convinced Babuji that the project was good and he readily agreed to part with major part of his savings. I also contributed from my own savings and also borrowed some money from a cousin and sent a bank draft to Pushkar. He had also taken a loan from some money lender locally. The project took off well and his business flourished in a few years. Later my two younger brothers left Srinagar for Calcutta for further studies and also joined the family business. The older of the two Prediman Krishan did his B.Sc. Pharmacy from Jadavpur University and the younger one Bal Krishen did B.Com. from Calcutta University. As per our family tradition of marrying sons and daughters when they attain marriageable age Prediman (24) and Bal Krishen (22) were married in September 1973. Alongside the marriage of his sons Babuji also performed the holy thread (Yagneopavit) ceremony of his grandsons Anil (7), Bharat (4) and Kuldeep (2). Prediman was married to Mohini daughter of Shri Prithvi Nath Vass (Kaul) of Rainawari, Bal Krishen was married to Girija daughter of Shri Shambu Nath Jan (Kaul) of Tankipora.

Some time after his marriage Prediman started his own business in Pharmaceuticals at Jammu. Bal Krishen continued to remain with Pushkar at Calcutta to help him run the industrial unit which had grown considerably. They later expanded their plastics manufacturing business on the advice of Jenab Sheikh Abdullah during his visit as Chief Minister to Kolkota. He had visited their factory in 1980 and invited them to start a unit at Jammu. The state industries department provided a plot of land at Gangyal Industrial Estate at Jammu and they established a large unit for manufacture of high density polyethylene (HDPE) water pipes. The unit went into production in 1982 and ran well for many years supplying water pipes to PHE departments of the state. Unluckily eruption of militancy resulted in stoppage of supply orders from government departments of the Valley. With reduction in supply orders the unit started to run into losses.

The problems were compounded by detection in 1997 that Bal Krishen had developed mouth cancer. He was running the Kolkata unit then. Despite all efforts to treat him he could not be saved and died in September 1998. Unwillingly though the Jammu unit had to be closed down to keep the Calcutta unit running. The Kolkata unit too had to be shut down later in the year 2K as Pushkar suffered a stroke. His son Bharat, an actor neither had time nor inclination to continue the family business. Pushkar with whom I was greatly attached died of a severe lung infection at Kolkata on 15 August 2016 but not before birth of his granddaughter Aarya (daughter of Bharat and Bangla actress Jaisri).

Chapter 10

Udhampur Days

After having acquired Ph.D. degree I was planning to start some post-doctoral research project. However, I received my transfer orders to Udhampur in Jammu region in the last week of August 1972. Had I got even a wind of what was going to happen I could have tried to convince my superiors to retain me in the valley if not at Srinagar so that I could continue my research work. The gentleman who replaced me had put in just six months after his first appointment at Udhampur and because of his political links managed pre-mature transfer to his home town Srinagar. I felt badly let down by the administration. Instead of appreciating that I had worked hard to earn a doctorate degree I was being posted to a place where I would get cut off from my field of research.

Naturally my family felt extremely perturbed about it. I was myself upset because it would be difficult to shift to Udhampur along with family. My elder son Anil was reading in a good school and the younger one was less than three months old. I had seven days time at my disposal to join at new place of posting. Gratefully the Department of Zoology at S.P. College organized a farewell party for me during this interval. After the farewell was over Principal Nazir Ahmed Khan took me aside and said that he was not willing to relieve me but he had been under pressure from the administration. He also told me that my students were agitated over the transfer and he had to cool their tempers down and explain to them that despite his efforts he could not stop it as the higher ups were adamant.

Later it came to my knowledge that the Additional Secretary Higher Education had received instructions from the Education Minister to transfer me to teach my father-in-law Janki Prasad Parimoo a lesson. Parimoo had refused to withdraw his writ petition in the Supreme Court of India against the Govt. of Jammu and Kashmir for discrimination in the matter of promotions in the school Education Department. Despite allurements offered to him he had obstinately refused to withdraw the writ petition in the Apex Court. Finally the Govt. of Jammu and Kashmir lost the case in the Supreme Court of India in the matter of promotions in the School Education Department. The Apex court's decision was issued vide Janki Prasad Parimoo V. State of Jammu and Kashmir AIR 1973 Sc 930 (939) 1973 ISCC 420 (1973) 3 SCR 236. 10 January 1973.

I joined my place of posting at Government College Udhampur on 5 September 1972. Principal S.K. Gupta was very supportive and understood my difficulties. He arranged a room for me in the city for my temporary residence till a decent family accommodation was available. Being the senior most in the Department of Zoology the Principal asked me to assume the charge as the head. My other colleagues were Inder Singh Patang, Kanwal Singh Jamwal and Hakumat Singh. They were very supportive and I soon found myself in a comfortable position. My colleagues from other departments especially Botany—Hempal Singh and Elijah Gergan were also very helpful. Other Colleagues like B.L. Zutshi (Pol. Sc.) B.L. Raina (Math), J.L. Raina and M.N. Kaul (Geography) made efforts to find me two room accommodation with kitchen and bath in the city in the shortest possible time. Actually Udhampur was an important town being the District Headquarter and also the Headquarter of the Northern Command of the Indian Army. So there was a great demand for rented accommodation. Our landlord Bihari Lal Nargotra and his family became very close to us in due course of time.

After occupying new accommodation I returned to Srinagar to bring Promila, Anil and Kuldeep with me. At Burn Hall School the Principal, a White Christian Missionary was reluctant to issue school leaving certificate of Anil then a student of class 2 for the simple reason that he was doing well. It was also difficult to leave my parents alone at Srinagar. Back in Udhampur while Promila busied herself in setting home I made efforts to find a good school for Anil. Luckily there was a very reputed Carmel Convent School supported by the Army located at Chinar. It was about 6 kms. away from the city and a Government Transport Bus was engaged by the school authorities for transporting the children, from the city. I met the Principal Sister Heldigarde and she agreed to admit him.

On the first day of his school, I took Anil to the bus stop from where the Carmel School kids boarded their bus. Expecting that he would return home by the same bus along with other kids I waited at the bus stop. When the school bus arrived Anil was not there and I missed a hear beat. I realized instantly that being his first day I should have gone to the school to ensure that he boards the right bus. My first reaction was to ring up the school to find out whether they had retained him after noticing that he had missed the bus. However, as luck would have it a city bus driver who was changing a flat tyre near the school found Anil crying. On asking Anil told him that he had missed his bus to the city. The kind driver gave him lift and dropped at the city bus stop. I was still trying to figure out what to do when I found Anil coming down from a bus. My joy knew no bounds. God had been kind to us but there is a lesson in it. As a parent it was my duty to make it sure on the first day at his school that he boards the right bus to return home. Many such cases of negligence on part of the parents often result in unfortunate incidents.

It was our first experience of living in a sub-tropical climate. Jammu region experiences good monsoon from July to September. It was the month of September when I moved my family to Udhampur and monsoon was phasing out. There were occasional showers and humidity was causing perspiration and general discomfort. So the first requirement was to buy a ceiling fan. At Srinagar we occasionally used a table fan. There were also other things like beds and furniture we needed to buy to live in comfort. I had committed the mistake of selling my three year old Lambretta scooter at Srinagar before my transfer because I wanted to buy a new model of Bajaj scooter. However, my transfer had stalled that. Here I was in need of a conveyance more than any thing else. My college was located on top of a hillock just opposite the hillock on which the Udhampur town is located. The two hillocks are separated by the small rivulet "Devika". As I could not afford to buy a car the only option available was to buy a scooter which was not available off the shelf and I would have to wait.

The "Devika" is considered holy by the people of Jammu in general and those of Udhampur and surrounding areas in particular. The local college magazine is also named after it and I happened to be associated with its publication as convener for many years of my posting at Udhampur. There are a number of springs ("boalis" as locals call them) which feed the Devika. There is a temple complex on the western side of the stream. On its eastern side is the cremation ground. There is a common belief that the Devika is the elder sister of the holy Ganga. So the people of the area immerse the ashes of their dead in it instead of travelling to the far away Haridwar. There is some special quality in water of the stream because ashes and bones of the dead get immediately dissolved in it and the water downstream is as clear as at the source. I believe that the wise elders of yester years had discovered this property of the Devika water and saved their future generations from travelling all the way to distant Haridwar for immersion of ashes of their dead to attain salvation.

Udhampur is the second largest city of Jammu region and fourth largest in the state. It is situated at an elevation of 2500 ft. above the sea level. The climate is sub-tropical and summer temperatures go up to 40°C and rainfall is about 130 cm. mainly in monsoons. The culture is like rest of the Jammu. The main language is Dogri but Pahari and Gojri languages are also spoken. The town is named after Udham Singh eldest son of Gulab Singh the founder of Dogra dynasty which since the middle of the nineteenth century had dominated the area that now constitutes Jammu and Kashmir State. Udhampur is located on the Pathankot-Uri National Highway connecting the Srinagar city to the rest of India. It is an important military cantonment in the India's northern region. The shrine of Vaishno Devi is a major Hindu pilgrimage centre and Kirimchi, group of 4 Shiva temples (11th century) is situated 10 kms. north of the town. Other prominent land marks in the district are Chenani Hydroelectric Project and the Ram Nagar Fort. The region slopes from the Pir Panjal Range of lesser Himalayas on the north to the Shivalik range on the south and is drained by the Chenab and Tawi rivers. Forests of pine, fir and Spruce cover the hills.

Udhampur used to be infested with snakes and scorpions before partition of India. When the partition took place in 1947 and Jammu and Kashmir acceded to India, the town became an important military cantonment. This involved setting up of camps, offices, etc. and movement of men and materials. Some refugees from Pakistan occupied Kashmir were also settled there. Thus the influx of people resulted in construction of roads, buildings and colonies came up in and around the town. As a result the snake and scorpion populations also came down. Like other parts of Jammu Division and plains of India the people of Udhampur use cots for sitting as well as for sleeping in contrast to the inhabitants of Kashmir valley who prefer to sit and sleep on the floor. There is a valid reason for this. The Kashmir valley is free from poisonous snakes. The only poisonous snake found in Kashmir is the Himalayan pit viper (*Ancistrodon himalayana*). In contrast Jammu Division has many poisonous snakes like the Cobra, the Krait and the Russel's viper. All the three are very poisonous. I witnessed at least three snake bite deaths during our stay at Udhampur. A large Cobra measuring 8 ft. was found in a dried up septic tank of our college campus and I got it shot for addition to our Zoology museum.

My landlord and his family were very nice people. They helped us in settling down and made our stay comfortable. Daughters of Mr. Nargotra grew very fond of Promila and our sons Raju (Anil) and Deepu (Kuldeep). In the month of December same year my parents, sister and a niece joined us at Udhampur. During their stay for a fortnight we all visited Mata Vaishno Devi Shrine to pay obeisance. It was our first visit and we discovered the beauty and serenity of the Trikuta mountains where the Cave Shrine is located. Those days the track to the shrine was narrow and rough. However, it has been made wide and very good after the Mata Vaishno Shrine Board came into existence. The first night we stayed at Adh Kanwari and early in the morning next day we reached the shrine. The going was tough but we reached the shrine in time to have a bath, perform Puja and pay obeisance at the sanctum sanctorum inside the mountain cave. The entry point to the cave is a narrow passage leading to the sanctum sanctorum. Kuldeep our younger son was frightened in the dark but soon recovered. There are three pindies or images merged with the rock of the cave representing Kali, Durga and Lakshmi.

After the Darshan we felt happy and satisfied. Those days the entry point was also the exit so the progress was slow. It was only on the instructions of Late Sheikh Mohammed Abdullah that entry and exit tunnels were dug. It has made pilgrimage easy and fast. The number of pilgrims visting the Shrine has crossed ten million per year. It makes Vaishno Devi number two highest visited shrine in the country. Soon we started our trek back to Katra. By the time we reached Katra all of us were tired and wanted to take rest. Luckily we met my colleague Prof. B.L. Zutshi in the market place. His father was the Tourist Officer and he arranged our night stay in the Tourist Guest House. We returned to Udhampur the next morning. After this I visited the Shrine many times again but one visit is particularly important to mention.

In 1975, Anil then nine fell ill and he had to be hospitalized in the Army Hospital courtesy my friend Col. (Dr) R.N. Singh ENT specialist. Initially he had fever and the doctors in the town treated him for typhoid. He had a relapse of the fever and recovered after treatment. After his fever returned third time I really became worried and talked to Col. Singh who advised hospitalization for investigation and treatment. The army doctors found that he had malaria infection and treated him for that. When he was alright I wanted to visit Mata Vaishno Devi for thanksgiving. Anil insisted that he accompany me. I wanted to hire a horse for him but he refused and we made the pilgrimage on foot. Mata Vaishno has been kind to me and my family ever since.

After our marriage Promila had shown no inclination to take up a job and was happy as a homemaker. It suited both of us. In March 1973, however, she got an offer of a job as government teacher being a trained postgraduate. It was tempting to join government service, for soon after she would be over aged and ineligible. We gave due thought and decided that she should accept the offer. Initially she was appointed in a primary school but was later transferred to Girls Higher Secondary School in the town. She liked the job but there was the problem of our younger son Kuldeep. He was less than a year old then. So we had to look for a maid and luckily got one. The daughters of our landlord, who had finished college had taken a liking for Kuldeep to such an extent that he became very fond of them. They also helped us in looking after him.

I had taken my posting at Udhampur as a challenge and wanted to improve the Zoology Department in particular and the college in general in whatsoever way I could. Prof. S.K. Gupta the Principal combined qualities of scholarship and nobility in him. During the short period that I served under him there was a lot to learn. However, an incident cut short his stay and he was transferred. The incident related to misbehaviour of a local boy with a senior girl student who happened to be daughter of an army colonel. Her younger brother also a student of a junior class objected resulting in a scuffle in which he got seriously injured and had to be admitted to the Army Hospital. As a result the Principal suspended the mischievous boy from attending classes and a student agitation ensued.

Meanwhile army authorities had complained to the Government and the District administration had to intervene. While the student agitation was on for revocation of suspension orders of the misbehaving boy, Mr. Bhim Singh, an ex-student leader and advocate at Jammu was requested by the Principal to intervene. A meeting was organized in the college ground where staff, students, the Deputy Commissioner and Police Superintendent beside prominent citizens were present. Mr. Bhim Singh, who had recently returned from a world tour addressed the students and advised them to discontinue their agitation and resume studies. He gave an interesting account of his world tour in his characteristic style and manner. Adressing the students Principal Gupta referred to Mr. Bhim Singh's exhortation to the students and in his forceful and flowery language said "you have just listened to Mr. Bhim Singh about the futility of your agitation and hope you will heed his advice and resume attending classes. He is an intercontinental ballistic missile while you are misguided missiles. I am sure that you will listen to his appeal and call off the agitation." The whole audience burst into laughter, thereafter the issue was resolved amicably and the agitation came to an end.

Principal Gupta was asked to hand over charge to the senior most staff member Prof. Bal Krishan Shastri. In June 1973, Prof. Balraj Sharma took over from Prof. Shastri and he continued till December 1976. During his tenure the college flourished and became a hub of academic, cultural and sports activities in the district. While all this activity was going on in the college a lot of political activity was happening in the state.

*****

In November 1974 while Mir Qasim was the Chief Minister G. Parthasarthy and Mirza Mohammed Afzal Beg signed the "Kashmir Accord" as the representatives of Indira Gandhi and Sheikh Mohammed Abdullah respectively. Accordingly Mir Qasim resigned and Sheikh Sahab was Sworn in as Chief Minister of the state on 25 Feb. 1975 after Congress legislative party offered support to him. Along with him Mirza Afzal Beg, Thakur Devi Das and Sonam Narbu also took oath as Cabinet Ministers at Jammu. Sheikh Abdullah along with his colleagues in the Cabinet and Balraj Puri proceeded by road to Srinagar and stopped for the night at Tara Palace at Udhampur. Ironically though, Sheikh Sahab had spent some years here in this very palace after his arrest in 1953. The college is located just adjacent to Tara Palace and on the initiative of Principal Balraj Sharma teaching staff of the college met with Sheikh Sahab and his cabinet colleagues to felicitate them. It was here that I met and shook hands with the great leader for the first time. I had occasion to meet him a number of times later as well.

Incidentally my father Babuji had been his pet student, when Sheikh Sahab was a teacher in a Government High School at Srinagar. Sheikh Abdullah after taking over as the Chief Minister dissolved the Plebiscite front and the National Conference was revived with him as the president.

*****

In the month of February 1976 the college invited Chief Minister Sheikh Abdullah as the chief guest on the Annual Day function. He very kindly consented and I was given the responsibility of organizing a cultural programme. The cultural department of the district administration was requested to help us in this task. On my suggestion a Kashmiri song "Gulshan Wattan chhu sonuy" in addition to Dogri and Hindi Songs was included. The Kashmiri song proved a hit and the packed college hall reverberated with cheers. Sheikh Sahab accompanied by Bagum Sahiba, Sonam Narbo and his daughter were very happy with the cultural programme and applauded. Later in his address Sheikh Sahab praised the efforts of the students and congratulated them and the college administration. He also stated that he had a dream of a new progressive Jammu and Kashmir state which according to him was possible only through the medium of education especially of the girls.

Earlier in May 1973, we had invited Abdul Gani Lone Education Minister to preside over the college Annual Day. He too was impressed by the talent of our students in the field of song and drama. Prof. Bal Krishan Shastri was officiating Principal at that time after the sudden transfer of Principal Gupta. Later he had proved his administrative acumen during the short stint of officiating as Principal of the Commerce College at Jammu. It is unfortunate that he died in an accident shortly after his retirement.

On Principal Sharma's transfer to M.A.M. College Jammu Principal G.P. Singh took over. He was an old hand having been Principal of Commerce College Jammu for a long period of time. Earlier the Commerce College was a private college run by Jammu Rajput Sabha. Later it was taken over by the state government along with the existing staff whose services were regularized in the government and their seniority fixed.

Accordingly Principal Singh became one of the senior-most Principals in the Higher Education Department. He was a non-state subject hailing from Unna in Uttar Pradesh. As longest serving and dedicated administrator he had run Commerce College very efficiently and made it a prestigious institution of Jammu. It was a very good experience to work with him. Principal Singh later served as Principal of G.G.M. Science College Jammu, Director School Education and Special Secretary to Govt. Education Deptt. from which post he retired. He had allotted the staff quarter vacated by Prof. Hempal Singh on his transfer to me. The other staff quarter was occupied by Prof. S.K. Sood of English. The Principal's residence was a much bigger two storied building with some land around it. As Mrs. G.P. Singh came from a rural background she made full use of the land and even kept a cow. God had blessed the couple with six children (two sons and four daughters) and the produce of the land and milk was utilized by the family. His children and those of Prof. Sood and my children along with the children of officers of the adjacent Police Academy became good friends and the college playground was always live with their sports and other activities in the evenings. Our older son Anil became friends with Asif son of Dy. Commissioner A.H. Banahali, Abhey Kaul son of Dy. S.P. Romesh Kaul, Prabhat son of Prof. Sood and Amiresh and Avdesh sons of Principal G.P. Singh. Like wise our younger son Kuldeep and youngest son of Prof. Sood Babloo became great chums. We socialized with families of our colleagues especially B.L. Raina, M.K. Kaul, J.L. Raina, B.L. Zutshi, Hempal Singh, J.N. Tickoo, S.K. Wanchoo, Sansar Chand, Prem Chand, Harbans Singh, P.C. Gupta, Hakumat Singh, Kanwal Singh, B.K. Sharma, Nihal Singh, D.R. Shastri, Ishwar Lal, Jaipal Singh, M.K. Zutshi, Ms Khema Zutshi, Mohammed Yusuf, O.P. Kailu, Subash Gupta, O.P. Gupta, Vijay Gupta, Elijah Gergan, P.K. Kaul, C.L. Kaul and Ms Jaiki Kaul. Ms Shama Kaul, B.L. Wakhlu, Ms Sajida, Ms Sheela and Ms Kamla to name only a few, colleagues of Promila also had a close association and bonding with us. We became very fond of Wakhlu's daughters Meenakshi and Munnu and B.L. Raina's daughter Sarika.

Udhampur town those days was small but it has expanded now. It is the second largest town in Jammu Division. As is usual in small towns people know each other well. The employees of various government departments generally met in the evenings at the city centre called 'Dhabad'—which consisted of a round central park with a road going around it and shops on the sides. The 'Lambi gali'—long in the real sense opened on the Dhabad on one end and a pond called 'Sailan talab' on the other. There were two other bazars—the Main Bazar and Mukharjee Bazar. While Main Bazar ran parallel to the long lane the Mukharjee Bazar extended up to the administrative complex on the east consisting of District Commissioner's office, Tehsil office, Treasury and the Sessions court, etc. The time we spent at Udhampur from 1972 to March 1980 was without doubt the best part of our lives. It was also the most peaceful period of the whole Jammu and Kashmir State. We were in our youth and our kids were growing. The environment was good and healthy. Luckily the period was also free from any political strife. Except for a brief period of illness of Anil due to malarial fever which needed his hospitalalization our stay at Udhampur was quite good and enjoyable.

The scooter that I had purchased in 1976 came handy when I moved to the college campus. Those days I often used to visit Jammu with wife and children on my two wheeler. I still wonder why and how I took that risk on a busy and hilly National Highway. Was it my bravado or folly? The answer perhaps lies in the fact that in twenties and thirties one is more confident and as one progresses in age the level of confidence goes down. The best option would lie in buying a car but that was beyond my means at that point of time.

Prof. G.P. Singh reposed a lot of faith in me like his predecessor and I was able to help him in submitting proposals for many developmental programmes initiated by the University Grants Commission for the colleges of the country. This included construction of a hostel building, warden's residence and a new block of classrooms. The work on the construction of the hostel and warden's residence had started while I was still posted there. The new classroom block came up later.

Sheikh Abdullah had brought in Prof. Sat Bhushan of the Jammu University as Commissioner of Education. He was a man of ideas and initiated the implementation of several educational reforms of the Central Government. For example, he upgraded the Higher Secondary Schools and proposed to shift the 11th and 12th classes from the colleges to Higher Secondary Schools. For this college teachers were given the task of visiting schools to find out the existing facilities there and recommend if these were adequate enough to implement the scheme. I was associated with one such committee at Udhampur and we found that with a little input by way of laboratory equipment and chemicals and upgradation of library it could be implemented. The existing staff in the higher secondary schools was by and large qualified and adequate. I am glad to say that the shifting of 11th and 12th classes (then called pre-University and 1st T.D.C.) from colleges to the schools boosted the morale of schools teachers then designated as Senior Masters. The Senior Masters who taught these classes were later designated as lecturers. The twin universities of the state also went ahead to introduce the three year degree course at the undergraduate level keeping in with the U.G.C. and the Central Government decisions in this regard following "Kothari Commission" recommendations. As a result of this the boards of study in various subjects had to meet and frame syllabi for the third year of the undergraduate courses. I too was invited to the meetings of the Board of Studies in Zoology at the Jammu University. Prof. Y.R. Malhotra was the Head of Post-graduate Department of Zoology and under his Chairmanship many changes were brought about in the syllabi and courses of study during that period with a stress on job orientation.

My posting at Udhampur gave me an opportunity to study flora and fauna besides the ecology of the Shivaliks and lesser Himalayas. The region represents a transition from the sub-tropical climate of the plains of India to North-Western temperate region of Kashmir. There is a sudden change of fauna and flora as we move further north from Udhampur. For example, cacti like Dandathor and Chitrathor are visible upto Udhampur and surrounding areas, but then disappear altogether when we move further north to Chenani and Patnitop region. The poisonous snakes like Krait, Cobra and Russel's viper and the Monitor lizard are nowhere to be found beyond Chenani. This region is a naturalist's paradise. You get a lot of fauna and flora to study.

As part of our curriculum and field studies I regularly organized trips to Patnitop, Nathatop, Kud, Batote, Sudh Mahadev, Katra and Reasi to give a practical feel and experience of the ecology and environment of the region to our students. I also took them to Kashmir and the neighbouring state of Himachal Pradesh so that they could understand the influence of environment and ecology on the flora and fauna. Generally, these trips were undertaken by Zoology Department in collaboration with Botany Department headed by Prof. Hempal Singh and a brilliant young lecturer Elijah Gergan. I was supported in my efforts by my colleagues Inder Singh, Puranchand Gupta, Hakumat Singh and Kanwal Singh Jamwal. Elijah Gergan a deeply religious person later resigned from service and became a full time Christian Missionary and head of Moravian Mission School at Leh.

These trips and outings resulted in collection of specimens for Botany and Zoology Museums of the college. I have always believed that museums play an important role in educating people and it has been my endeavour to enrich museums in the institutions where I served. I consider it my good luck that I had a chance to visit some of the best museums in the country such as Calcutta Museum, Bombay Natural History Museum, Salar Jang Museum Hyderabad and some in the U.K. (London, Cardiff, York, Liverpool and Edinburgh) and European countries (Belgium, France and Switzerland).

In December 1976 Babuji and Amiji (my parents) had gone to Calcutta to spend the winter there with my brother Pushkar and his family. During his stay there Babuji developed some serious health problem and Pushkar advised me to come over. He was shown to a number of Doctors and on the basis of X-ray (CT scan and ultrasound were not known then) one surgeon suspected malignancy of Gall Bladder and advised surgery. We put our heads together and decided to go for the surgery. The surgery revealed no signs of malignancy anywhere. He had gall stones and a rare condition namely tuberculosis of intestines which gave the symptoms of loss of appetite and loss of weight mistaken by the surgeon as those of malignancy. After his discharge from hospital treatment for TB was started at Calcutta and within six months he was hale and hearty.

*****

In the meanwhile political situation in the state was changing. In March 1977, Sheikh Mohammed Abdullah resigned as Chief Minister after Congress Party withdrew support in the assembly. Governor's rule was imposed and assembly was dissolved on the advice of the Council of Ministers. June 1977 elections were hailed as the first free and most fair elections conducted by the Election Commission of India on the instructions of the Prime Minister Shri Morarji Desai. Results were declared on 4 July 1977 and the National Conference got 47 out of 76 seats. Sheikh Mohammed Abdullah once again took over the reigns of the state as Chief Minister till his death on 8 September 1982.

Babuji's illness in 1976-77 had made me think that my aging parents needed my presence at Srinagar and I should approach my department to transfer me back from Udhampur. Accordingly I met the Education Commissioner Prof. Sat Bhushan in Feb. 1978 with the request that I be transferred to Srinagar, having already put in six years at Udhampur. I also requested him that my transfer orders be issued before the start of the new academic session so that my kids do not lose an academic session. In Kashmir Division academic session started in March and ended in November, on the contrary in Jammu Division academic session started in April followed by summer vacations from August, and ended in March the next year.

Higher Education comes under the State cadre and college teachers can be transferred from one Division to another Division. However, transfer of employees from one Division to the other faces opposition especially from Kashmir to Jammu. Generally employees consider transfer from Kashmir to Jammu as a punishment because it becomes difficult for them to go back when they so desire. So when I approached Prof. Sat Bhushan, being a straight forward person, he said that it might be difficult for him to transfer me at that time. However, in September 1978,

I received my transfer orders to Srinagar which did not suit me because my kids would lose an academic session if I shifted them to Srinagar then. When I approached the Commissioner and reminded him of my request not to transfer me in the mid session for the sake of my kids he was annoyed. I felt that an employee is not entitled even to seek a suitable time for transfer, and before I could get myself relieved from Udhampur for joining at Srinagar another order was received posting me to G.G.M. Science College Jammu for a period up to ending Feb. 1979. Accordingly I joined at G.G.M. Science College Jammu.

I had just joined at Jammu when a student agitation broke out in the whole Jammu Division against some incident involving police excesses on protesters at Poonch. The agitation continued for several days and took an ugly turn on a particular day when students pelted stones on police personnel on the canal road allegedly from inside the college ground. The infuriated men in uniform rushed into the campus, as some of their colleagues were injured by the stone pelting and beat up anyone and everyone whom they could see. They also entered staff room and the Principal's room and damaged furniture. They did not listen to the Principal Bhardwaj's pleas and beat up staff members including myself. I saved my head with a chair and they attacked my legs with their batons. One of my colleagues from the Chemistry Department Prof. Munshi Ram received head injuries due to lathi blows and he had to be taken to P.G.I. Chandigarh for specialized treatment. That day I saw with my own eyes what police brutality means.

The teaching community felt badly hurt by the uncalled for violence of the police men and called on the Chief Minister Sheikh Abdullah the same evening. The staff led by Principal M.R. Bhardwaj and President College Teacher's Association Prof. Mohinder Sharma were made to be seated in the hall by the Chief Minister's staff. Soon after Sheikh Saheb came to meet us and listened to us patiently. He said that he had been informed about the entry of the CRPF men into the Campus without orders and beating up staff and students alike. He further said that he had felt as if he had himself received the blows. He said that he had started his career as a teacher and had the greatest regard for the builders of the nation and assured us that the guilty police officers and men would be punished for their uncalled for behaviour. This pacified us and we left.

Although my transfer to Jammu had been made for a limited period of three months yet due to some academic exigency I had to continue there till March 1980 when my transfer order to Women's College Nawakadal Srinagar was issued. So I stayed on at G.G.M. Science College Jammu for about fifteen months. However, I enjoyed my posting there because the academic atmosphere was quite good under the Principal M.R. Bhardwaj who was a good administrator and tolerated no nonsense. It was during this period that on the persistent complaints of discrimination by the people of Jammu that the State Government appointed Sikri Commission in May 1979 to inquire into their grievances.

Chapter 11

Return to the Valley

I was transferred to Government College for Women, Nawakadal in March 1980 against a senior and reputed teacher Prof. M.K. Munshi. The Principal Mrs. Krishna Misri was not happy to relieve a teacher of high repute against a person about whom she had no idea. In government service orders are to be obeyed so I was allowed to join. Although Prof. Munshi enjoyed a very good reputation as a teacher, yet he had not moved out of Srinagar for a long time and the government was under pressure from those who were posted outside Srinagar. Principal Misri tried to retain him but she could not succeed in her efforts. As time passed Mrs. Misri came to know me better and entrusted the University Grants Commission Schemes for implementation to me. I was able to formulate some very important schemes like COSIP (College Science Improvement Programme) and COHIP (College Humanities Improvement Programme) which were accepted by the U.G.C. for implementation along with sanction of grants. In the meanwhile, Principal Mrs. Krishna Misri whom I had come to admire as an able administrator, was transferred to Women's College M.A. Road Srinagar, a premier female educational institution, earlier nurtured by eminent educationist Ms. Mahmooda Ahmed Ali Shah. She was relieved by Miss Bilquis Fatima. It was soon after her joining that grants for the COSIP and COHIP were released by U.G.C. It pleased her greatly and she congratulated me for it. I had also proposed to U.G.C. for grant of eight fellowships for teachers to undertake research leading to Ph.D. degree under Faculty Improvement Programme. This was also granted.

I immensely enjoyed my work at Women's College Nawakadal from March 1980 to June 1986 and found that lady colleagues are excellent co-workers. Principal Bilquis Fatima was a committed educationist and administrator and took pains to improve the educational standard of the institution which primarily served educational needs of the female students from not so well off sections of the society. Most of them were first generation learners.

*****

In view of his failing health Sheikh Mohammed Abdullah nominated his son Farooq Abdullah as his successor. This was resented by his son-in-law Ghulam Mohammed Shah the senior-most National Conference Minister in his cabinet. When Sheikh Sahab died on 8 September 1982 a grieving Dr. Farooq Abdullah was sworn in as Chief Minister with the blessings of Mrs. Indira Gandhi. Sheikh's death plunged the whole valley into grief and mourning. People loved him as a leader and in his death they saw end of an era.

His funeral procession started from the polo ground and the whole route was thronged by people on both sides right upto Nasim Bagh near the famous Hazratbal Shrine where his mortal remains were laid to rest on the shore of Dal Lake. The Prime Minister Mrs. Gandhi came all the way from Delhi to attend his funeral. Dr. Farooq Abdullah took over the leadership of the National Conference but this succession led to a bitter conflict with his brother-in-law G.M. Shah emerging as a rival candidate. The June 1983 assembly elections again returned National Conference under Dr. Farooq Abdullah to power but the internal quarrels had not dissipated. Defection of the G.M. Shah group from National Conference led to fall of Dr. Farooq Abdullah's government on 2 July 1984 and G.M. Shah (NC-K) assumed power with the support of Congress (I) from outside. This ushered in a period of unprecedented communal violence and misrule in the state (Balraj Puri 1993).

For the first time in its history, the state witnessed serious communal violence during Feb.-March 1986 which paved way for the promulgation of Governor's rule on 7 March 1986 followed by president's rule on 7 Sept. 1986. Although Farooq

Abdullah had become C.M. with the blessings of Mrs. Indira Gandhi in succeeding his father, yet he proved too immature in his understanding of politics. He dropped experienced and senior-most Cabinet Ministers of his father like D.D. Thakur and P.L. Handoo who could have advised him on various issues. Instead he joined hands with the opposition national parties and hosted their conclave at Srinagar on 5 and 6 October 1983. Mrs. Gandhi was not amused. To make matters even worse on 14 January 1984 six Congress workers were killed in police firing on a protest demonstration. On 11 Feb. 1984 Maqbool Bhat founder of Kashmir Liberation Front was hanged for terrorist activities and buried in Tihar Jail. A lot of resentment was registered by the people of Kashmir. On 26 April 1984 Jagmohan was sworn in as Governor of Jammu and Kashmir in place of B.K. Nehru. He dismissed Farooq Abdullah Ministry on 22nd July 1984 and G.M. Shah his brother-in-law was sworn in as chief minister.

*****

As I have stated earlier Ms. Bilquis Fatima had taken over as the Principal of Women College Nawakadal. She entrusted many ongoing programmes to me. The college introduced a programme wherein additional part time teachers were appointed from the grants received from U.G.C. in order to help weak students. The college being located in the downtown the girl students mostly come from educationally backward classes. Most of them being first generation learners their level of scholarship was comparatively low and the programme helped them gain ability and self-confidence. Some other programmes introduced by the principal such as games, debates, singing and dancing helped students to overcome their shyness and inhibitions.

One of the important activities of the Higher Educational Institutions in the State are annual educational tours for 15 to 20 days. These are organized by colleges with support from the Higher Education Department during the months of December and January every year. Nawakadal Women's College organized a 20 day tour in December 1982 and January 1983 under my charge. A party consisting of fifty girl students, five teachers including myself and an assistant were seen off in two buses by the principal and parents of the students on 20 December 1982 from the college campus. Arrangements for our stay for a night at Jammu had been made in the Women's College Gandhi Nagar. The journey from Srinagar to Jammu was smooth and we were received in the college by the Principal Ms. Savitri Rampal. The arrangements for our stay were good. The next day we boarded Bombay bound Superfast train from Jammu. Incidentally students and teachers from Women's College M.A. Road Srinagar under the charge of Prof. (Mrs.) Kaul and Prof. (Mrs.) Sugra Hafiz were also travelling by the same train in an adjacent coach.

The train pulled out of Jammu Station at about 5 p.m. and soon gathered speed. It had to stop at only a few stations and the journey would be completed in just 28 hours. Indian Railways had recently introduced Superfast trains and it was one of them. Our journey involved just one night and one day as compared to the one I had performed as a student in 1962-63 from Pathankot Station in over forty hours involving two nights and a day. Our first night travel was quite smooth but during the next day while I was sitting and chatting with my students Mr. Hriday Nath Miskeen the assistant accompanying M.A. Road tour party came rushing from his coach. He requested me to accompany him to their coach as an unusual situation had developed there. I joined him along with my assistant Ashfaq Ahmed and we hurriedly reached the adjoining coach. What met my eyes was something I had not expected. Some girls of M.A. Road College were dancing along with a group of four young men on the floor of the coach to the tune of a Hindi Film song. Students and other passengers in the coach were watching in amusement and clapping. The perturbed lady staff of the college were sitting and watching helplessly. They had obviously sent Mr. Miskeen to me with the hope that I would intervene. I immediately understood seriousness of the situation and something needed to be done. With all the strength in my lungs I commanded, "stop". To my utter surprise and that of all others present in the coach the dance came to a sudden halt and the participants looked at me in disbelief and dispersed. My command had obviously worked! The four boys and all the girls, except one tall girl wearing high heel sandals and shoulder length hair, took their seats. This girl kept standing and said to me, "sir we are on a tour and it is our right to enjoy". Looking straight in her eyes, I said, "yes you are on a tour and it is your right to enjoy but you cannot disturb other passengers in a public place. The train coach is a public place". She felt convinced, said "sorry sir" and took her seat.

Lest the dance start once again I decided to cool down and sit with the students and staff of M.A. Road College for some time. I explained to the students that they were expected to behave properly in a public place and dancing with men not known to them was not proper. The young men were listening quietly and continued to sit in their seats. After some time I left for my own coach. An hour or so later all the four young men came to see me in my coach and apologized profusely for their behaviour. They told me that after completing engineering course they had been selected by O.N.G.C. as trainees and were on their way to join duty at Baroda, which was a couple of hours away. They had got with them a packet of sweets and offered me some. I declined but as they insisted and said by this gesture of mine they would feel satisfied that I had forgiven them. I obliged them with a smile. The tall and intelligent muslim girl, I am given to understand, is a successful Advocate in the Supreme Court of India today. I feel equally sure that those boys must have done pretty well in their careers and hope that they are occupying high positions in their respective organizations now. In retrospect I feel that those boys and girls had not committed any crime and were simply following the dictates of their youth.

The train reached Bombay on time. The Dy. Resident Commissioner Mr. Bhat along with his staff was waiting for our arrival at the railway station. He had arranged transport and accommodation for the students and staff of both the colleges in a high rise building in Central Bombay. Needless to say that we already had our dinner in the train. A ride in a lift to the top floor of a high rise building in Bombay (Now Mumbai) was a new experience to most of my students. After making ourselves comfortable all of us went to sleep.

The next few days of our stay in Bombay were very busy. From day one of our stay after breakfast we would move out. We visited the Malabar Hills, Choupati, Gateway of India, Hotel Taj, Race Course, Planetarium, Taraporawalla Aquarium, Bombay Zoo, Prince of Wales Museum and Juhu Beach. The visit that my students enjoyed the most was that of the Elephanta caves. As luck would have it Begum Sheikh Abdullah was also visiting the caves along with her elder daughter Mrs. Khalida Shah on the same day. I requested her to meet and talk to our students which she gracefully agreed to do. It was very nice and satisfying for all of us to spend some time with her.

Our next destination was New Delhi. Principal Bilquis Fatima was waiting for us at the Kashmir House, where she had made arrangements for our stay. We stayed in Delhi for a couple of days and nights and visited important places in the capital such us Rashtrapati Bhawan, Parliament House, Red Fort, Qutab Minar, Delhi Zoo and Chandni Chowk before returning to Jammu. At Jammu we were again welcomed on our return by the Principal of Women College Gandhi Nagar. After a night stay in Jammu we returned to our homes and hearths at Srinagar on 9 January 1983. My students had returned home a happy lot, having seen how diverse and wonderful their country is. As I have said earlier educational tours should form an essential part of study as these help the students to know their country better.

During my posting in Women College Nawakadal we held a number of functions and invited dignitaries to participate. Prof. Chaman Lal Sapru a literary figure invited Prof. Harivansh Rai Bachchan to address our students in one of the functions. The famous dancer Sonal Mansingh was invited to perform in the college hall under the SPICMACAY programme. The youth Congress leader Kumari Shailja also paid a visit to the college to interact with the students. She later became a Central Minister. Several Vice-Chancellors also participated in different programmes organized by the college. In May 1983, the college invited Dr. Farooq Abdullah to witness a cultural programme presented by the students on the Annual Day function. On his arrival in the college accompanied by his wife Ms. Molly he walked straight in the lawns of the college, located on the left bank of river Jhelum, and waved to the boatmen and women in his characteristic style to their utter surprise and joy.

After Mrs. Indira Gandhi was assassinated on 31 October 1984 the college organized a condolence meeting in which many prominent persons including academicians and politicians participated to pay tributes to her. I also spoke about her contribution to the advancement of science and environment in the country. My speech was later published by the *Kashmir Times* in its issue of 18 December 1984.

The day Mrs. Gandhi was assassinated I had to drop my parents at Srinagar Airport on their way to Jammu. Babuji was suffering from a lung condition and doctors had advised him to move down to warmer climate of the plains. Since my younger brother Pradiman Krishan was living at Jammu there was no problem to move him there. It was at the Srinagar Airport that we learnt about Mrs. Gandhi's assassination. The news brought a pall of gloom all over the country. This was for the last time that I had to drop Babuji at the Airport since he passed away at Jammu after less than two months later.

On 15 December 1984, I received a message late at night that Babuji was seriously unwell having contracted pneumonia. The next day I took the first flight to Jammu. Despite his sickness he enquired from me about welfare of my wife and sons and also spoke to me in feeble voice about certain important things. It never occurred to me that he was saying all those things knowing that his end was near. He lived only for a few hours after that. The whole night my mother, brothers Pushkar and Prediman and myself stayed awake by his bed side. He was conscious all the time and in meditation as usual. When my mother asked him in the morning whether he remembered Shiva, he nodded and uttered the words "Su-Hum" (I am he and he is I). At around 10 a.m. our mother noticed that he had not passed urine since the last night. Pushkar rang up the physician Dr. Kudiar who was treating him. He came at about 11 a.m. and examined him and prescribed some injections. Ten minutes after the physician had left he had a heart attack and passed away peacefully. All of us except Bal Krishan and sister Kamta were by his bed side when the end came.

Our mother Suma (Sumawati) faced the loss of her husband with composure. She consoled and advised us to stop crying, switch on the cassette recorder and play the *Bhagwad Gita*. We obeyed her and an atmosphere of peace prevailed. Babuji had been a sober, soft spoken and deeply religious person. He was gentle, kind and compassionate person and always spoke of treating fellow humans and animals with love. His end had been peaceful and we followed whatever our mother wished us to do. Our youngest brother Bal Krishan who was at Calcutta at that time was informed. He desired that we should wait for his arrival for the last rites. Since flights those days were not as frequent as today, he had to take a late night flight from Calcutta and the connecting morning flight from Delhi to reach Jammu. It was also the wish of our mother that Bal Krishan should be present during the last rites. So we had to postpone the cremation till the next day.

Generally Hindus prefer to immerse the ashes of their dear ones in the holy Ganga at Haridwar. However, it has been a tradition of Kashmiri Pandits to immerse the ashes of their dead at "Prayag" the confluence of the river Jhelum and Sindh stream at Shadipur near Sumbal town in north of Srinagar. At the confluence there is an island on which stands an old stunted chinar tree which has not grown beyond a point during the last two hundred years thus earning the nick name "Prayagech booni" (the stunted Chinar of Prayag). A child who does not show normal growth and remains stunted is referred to as "Prayagech booni". It was the wish of our mother that Babuji's ashes should be immersed at Shadipur to keep the family tradition. So my sister Kamta, Promila and myself flew to Srinagar on a cold December day in 1984. It was snowing at the Srinagar Airport and we took a taxi for Shadipur stopping enroute at my in-laws house at Nursingarh Srinagar to pick up a Panditji for performing the religious rites.

To reach the spot we had to cross the river Jhelum in a boat. There is a temple by the side of the confluence of the two rivers. After performing Puja (veneration) by the side of the river I had to take a boat to the middle of the confluence for immersing the ashes. Before and after the immersion I had to have a dip in the ice cold water of the river. It was quite an experience to have a dip in cold water with snow flakes falling on my body. I had observed in my childhood some Brahmins at Ganpatyar ghat having a morning dip during winter in the *Vitasta* even while it snowed and the temperature went below zero degree celsius. I had wondered then how they managed it but understood now that with determination nothing was difficult to do. Needless to say that we had to observe fast for the day. After the immersion was over we went as decided earlier to the house of our cousin Nathji at Rainawari for dinner and night stay. The next day, we moved to our Nai Sarak home and stayed there for a couple of days for our neighbours, relatives and well wishers to meet us and offer their condolences. Thereafter we returned to Jammu to take part in other rituals and ceremonies for the peace of the soul of our revered father.

On return to Srinagar at the end of February 1985 we tried to settle down without Babuji. It was difficult as we missed him. Suma had shown great courage in the face of loss of her husband after a long association of over fifty-two years. Inside, however, she was not reconciled to the loss. However, after a couple of months later she started showing signs of being unwell. I showed her to physicians and they treated her but there was no improvement. Among the top physicians at Srinagar Dr. Nasir Ahmed Shah and Dr. Ali Jan had a good reputation. There were also some surgeon of repute like Dr. Ghulam Nabi, Dr. Girdhari Lal and Dr. Brij Mohan Bhan. Kashmiris have a penchant for giving nicknames. Even Doctors and Professors are not spared. So one Surgeon was called "Puj" (butcher) not because his patients died on the table but for the rough manner of his dealing with them. In fact his patients recovered faster than those of other surgeons. Similarly one Professor whose nose ran most of the time the prefix "Zukam" (bad cold) was added to his name.

I was advised by my friends to consult Dr. Ali Jan. It proved a good piece of advice. He asked me about her history followed by an examination and opined that she was suffering from depression due to loss of her husband. He assured me that she would recover after proper treatment. He also advised her not to brood over her loss and prescribed some medicines. Thankfully she recovered within a couple of months and led a normal life thereafter.

Our son Anil had been selected in January 1985 for undergoing medical training at Govt. Medical College Srinagar. His name figured among the top five selected candidates and hard work had paid him off. Selections to medical and engineering courses were made by the state government on the basis of a test conducted every year followed by an interview. It was generally alleged that interview marks were manipulated to select favourites. There may have been some truth in it. To tilt the balance in favour of certain candidates who were lower down in the merit list allotment of more marks in the interview could help them. Earlier only the merit at 10+2 level had been the basis of selections for technical institutions but due to pick and choose policy adapted by the government some affected people had knocked at the doors of courts of law. Therefore the C.M. Sheikh Mohammed Abdullah had ordered that selections be made on the basis of a test conducted by a Selection Authority. Anil was a beneficiary of that policy and got selected on his own merit.

In fact after passing 10+2 with distinction I had got him admitted to part 1st of B.Sc. course at S.P. College Srinagar. He took keen interest in debates and sports activities while at S.P. College. He stood first in the Inter College debate organized by the Kashmir University. He also represented Kashmir University at the Inter-University debate at Aligarh Muslim University and got second prize there. He also represented Kashmir University in some other Inter-University competitions. Quite early in his school his teachers had observed his aptitude for writing and participation in debates and quiz programmes. They encouraged him and even as a student of medicine his interest in sports and debates continued and he brought laurels to his college. Our younger son Kuldeep too showed keen interest in debates and competitions and brought laurels to Model Academy Jammu and later BITS Pilani.

*****

I had been back in Srinagar after a gap of eight years. During these years there had been a visible change in Kashmir. The number of Mosques had increased (it is believed with the Saudi money) and one could see slogans written on walls exhorting Muslims to say their prayers (namaz) regularly. On the face of it there is nothing wrong in asking people to say their prayers but there was more to it than met the eye. As a matter of fact Muslims of Kashmir are a religious lot and say their prayers especially on Fridays. In fact, there are standing government instructions to allow employees offer Friday prayers in mosques of their choice. However, during Sheikh Abdullah's term as Chief Minister after 1974 the Jamat-e-Islami had become very active and spread a wave of Wahabi/Salafi islam. There was an inflow of maulvis from outside Kashmir, mostly Uttar Pradesh and Bihar. One could see them moving around here and there and in the Bazars. Some had even got married to Kashmiri girls. Perhaps Sheikh Abdullah was aware of their presence and the threat that they posed to the Sufi culture of Kashmir. He had tried to stop the spreading tentacles of Jamat-e-Islami but could not do much in containing them. His death helped the Jamat and they played a role in radicalizing Muslims of Kashmir, who have a history of Sufism. As a matter of fact Kashmiri Muslims have always been under the influence of Sufi peers and fakirs. The valley is full of shrines of Sufis which are visited by both muslims and hindus to pay obeisance and pray for the welfare of their near and dear ones. Although Wahabi/Salafi Islam frowns upon such practices, yet Kashmiri muslims continued to visit Shrines of Sufi peers and dervishes and offering prayers there as it suited their temperament. However, inroads were made by some Wahabis and separate mosques of Ahal-e-hadit came into being for offering prayers. These people criticize the Muslim men and women who visit shrines of Sufi peers and fakirs. The microscopic Ahmadi Muslims too have separate mosques to offer prayers.

Thus the seeds of radicalization had been sown in Kashmir in seventees and early eightees with dangerous consequences for the state as well as the country as a whole. I could perceive the change in the staffroom of my college where lady lecturers instead of talking about current affairs or academic matters discussed and exchanged, Islamic literature in circulation, amongst them. That the radicalization of the Muslims of Kashmir would finally lead to exile of Kashmiri Pandits very soon never entered my mind then. It did, however, strengthen my feeling that I should not invest my savings in constructing a new house at Srinagar despite an urgent need to do so. My parental house at Nai Sarak did not fulfill our needs. Whenever my brothers and their families from Calcutta and Jammu came visiting in summer we felt overcrowded. I felt the need of a bigger house. Our family owned an acre of land near Srinagar sufficient to build a palatial house or four separate cottages. In fact, my brother Pushkar was in favour of building four independent cottages on the plot of land but I persuaded him to keep the plan on hold. Instead I went ahead with the construction of a house on a plot of land owned by us at Jammu. As situation later turned out my decision proved to be a correct one.

*****

The period of rule of G.M. Shah was that of chaos and confusion. There were regular hartals and demonstrations throughout 1985. On 15 August 1985, there were wide spread demonstrations in Kashmir and police had to resort to firing. I was witness to a slogan shouting abusive crowd which came from Gawkadal side and entered Ganpatyar temple and vandalized it. The infuriated Kashmiri Pandit youth of the area came out of their homes and confronted the communally charged Muslims and fought them with their bare hands and the latter then took to their heels. In the month of February 1986 crowds of Muslims entered temples and shrines in Anantnag district in South Kashmir, roughed up priests, broke images and idols and set temples and houses of Pandits on fire. It was alleged that a particular political party was behind these attacks on Hindus.

As the word of attacks on temples reached Jammu, it infuriated the Hindus there. As a result some Kashmiri Muslim labourers were roughed up by a crowd at residency road in Jammu. The situation was now taking a communal shape and the State Government led by G.M. Shah was dissolved on 7 March 1986 and the state came under Governor's rule. During the period of winter from last week of December 1985 to ending

February 1986 we were putting up at our newly constructed house at Sarwal Jammu.

G.M. Shah also known as "Gulla Shah" was the Chief Minister for less than two years. To his credit it must be said that he was a no-nonsense man and a strict and well meaning administrator. He had, however, a week streak in his character. He was short tempered. I was witness to an incident in his private office which showed that he was indeed a short tempered person. My brother Pushkar had been invited by the State Government to start an industrial unit at Jammu. He had installed sophisticated machinery for manufacture of high density polyethylene (HDPE) pipes used for potable water in place of the traditional galvanized iron (G.I.) pipes. The government public health (PHE) department officials were not showing any interest in buying HDPE pipes in place of G.I. pipes. Some of them were even giving preference to buying HDPE pipes from manufactures from outside the state in contravention of the government policy of encouraging local units. So Pushkar wanted to draw the C.M.'s attention to this fact. He arrived from Jammu to see him and I accompanied him. We were advised by his staff to take our seats and wait for our turn in the big room at the head of which sat the C.M. in a chair. Before it was our turn to talk to him a lady from Sopore requested him for a job for her educated daughter. He politely told her that he did not make appointments and her daughter should apply to the concerned department for it. If suitably qualified she would be appointed. The illiterate lady did not quite understand what he had said and repeated her request for his help. When she persisted he lost his temper and asked his staff to throw her out of the room. The hapless Woman thereafter started to cry adding to his anger. We felt terribly sorry for the lady. Mr. Shah, however, soon cooled down and asked us the purpose of our visit. Pushkar explained to him in some detail. Being sharp he immediately understood the problem and asked his assistant to take the representation and put it up to him for action in his office. He was a man of action and ordered an enquiry in the matter which ultimately helped my brother to sell his pipes to government departments.

Chapter 12

Back in Jammu

Now that Babuji for whose sake I had moved to Srinagar was no more and we had a newly constructed house at Jammu, I felt that it might be a good idea to get myself transferred back to Jammu. When the secretariat moved to Srinagar in the month of May 1986 I applied for my transfer through my Principal Prof. Sugra Hafiz who had joined after retirement of Ms. Bilquis Fatima. She was reluctant to forward my application and I had to persuade her to do so. As luck would have it Prof. R.K. Bhan from Zoology Department of Science College had also moved an application for his transfer to Srinagar. The government had no problem in transferring both of us without dislocating anybody in the process and an order was issued in June 1986 wherein Prof. Bhan and myself had to exchange our positions. Later after I joined at Jammu I learnt that Prof. Bhan for some reason had changed his mind and was considering to withdraw his application.

My posting at Women's College Nawakadal was quite pleasant and eventful in many ways. I made friends with many male professors who in the absence of a separate staffroom used to assemble in the staffroom of Physics Department headed by Prof. G.M. Kuchhai. He was a thorough gentlemen besides being religious and God fearing. Prof. C.L. Sapru was a literary person and I learnt many things from him. Prof. Vinay Handoo I knew from Udhampur. Being an intellectual and a knowledgeable person he would initiate discussions on varied topics of interest not necessarily related to academics. Profs. Ashok Raina,

M.K. Thusoo and S.N. Kaw (Physics), Prof. Sharma (Music), Mr. Sardari Lal (Tabla master) and Mr. Yaqoob Bazaz (Librarian) were all pleasant people and I enjoyed their company. My departmental colleagues Profs. Shanta Mam, Raj Dulari Agha, Hamida Siddiqi, Dr. Neena Bambroo, and Ms. Hasina were very supportive and cooperating. From sister department of Botany Prof. Sheela Kaul, Dr. B.A. Wafai, Dr. Ashrafa Jeelani and Dr. Kawoosa were very cooperating in many ways concerning Inter-disciplinary matters.

Prof. K.L. Gupta Principal of Science College knew me from the days when he was posted as Dy. Education Commissioner in the Civil Secreteriate. He was happy and welcomed my transfer. Once settled down in Jammu I felt that Promila too needed to join me. When I contacted officials of the School Education Department in the civil secretariat for her transfer I was told that since it involved transfer from one Division to another consent of the Director School Education Jammu was required. Luckily for us Prof. G.P. Singh with whom I had worked at Udhampur was the Director at that time. When I approached him he took no time to give me a letter of "No Objection". Thus Promila's transfer to Jammu transpired in a short time and she joined me at Jammu in September 1986. In the meanwhile, I got our younger son Kuldeep admitted in Model Academy—a prestigious school at Jammu. Our elder son Anil was studying medicine at G.M.C. Srinagar and continued to stay with my biological mother Suma and adopted mother Shuba at Srinagar home. They joined us in January 1987 when Anil's College closed for winter vacations.

*****

An understanding had developed between National Conference and Congress following the dismissal of G.M. Shah Government in March 1986. This paved the way for return of Dr. Farooq Abdullah to power and he was administered the oath of office on 7 November 1986 at Jammu. The understanding later had a far reaching consequences for the state and the country. The National Conference and Congress fought elections together for the State Assembly in March 1987. A conglomerate of 14 Muslim parties of Kashmir had earlier in January 1987 formed a "Muslim United Front" to fight elections. It was alleged that many leaders of MUF were arrested before and during elections and there were also allegations of rigging. This ultimately proved disastrous for the state and the country since seeds of militancy had been sown. Many young men crossed over to POK and were trained by ISI and Pakistan Army for carrying out militant activities in Jammu and Kashmir. Kashmiri Pandits became the first target of the Militants resulting in their mass exodus from the valley.

*****

In Science College I got busy soon after my joining. Principal K.L. Gupta was an honest and dedicated educationist. He had endeared himself to the teachers and students. He knew about my work at Womens College Nawakadal. One day he called Dr. S.K. Chada who was looking after U.G.C. programmes in the college and asked him to associate me with him. This association proved very useful for both of us and for the college. Together we were able to formulate many programmes including faculty improvement programme for the college. This programme benefitted many willing teachers who were able to improve their qualifications and acquired M.Phil. and Ph.D. degrees without undergoing any financial loss. They were paid their full salaries while they were away for improving their qualifications at the universities of their choice. Moreover, after acquiring higher qualifications they were entitled to additional increments. This scheme proved a boon and many college teachers benefitted from it. Earlier many of us holding M.Phil. and Ph.D. degrees had in fact to fight hard for many years for additional increments. It was only after Prof. M.R. Puri an eminent educationist was deputed from University of Jammu to work as Director of Higher Education that he persuaded the government to grant one and two advance increment for M.Phil. and Ph.D. degree holders respectively.

Way back in 1975-76 a movement for organizing college teachers of the state was initiated in Jammu by a group under leadership of Prof. Mahinder Sharma. After initial hiccups it was decided to have separate wings of college teachers association for Jammu and Kashmir divisions with a common programme, aims and objectives. In Jammu for the first time elections for the association were held, I believe, in 1975. The first and foremost demand put forth by both wings of the association was to do away with separate grades for lecturers and professors. It was proposed to have a running scale. The discrimination made in selection from among lecturers to professors scale as was done earlier had been later challenged in the court of law. The left out senior lecturers had then approached the State High Court which upheld the right of senior lecturers for promotion and quashed the selection order. A running scale had, therefore, become the chief demand of the college teachers and the government had agreed. The demand was implemented in the state grade revision for employees in 1982. The state had it's own pay scales for college teachers. There were only two cadres viz. lecturers and professors instead of three viz. lecturers, readers and professors as in U.G.C. scales.

The next demand of the college teachers was to implement the University Grants Commission Pay scales to them as was done in the case of university teachers in 1973. Some college teachers had their reservations about it because there was no provision of a running scale and in these pay scales promotions were made again on the basis of selections. So this demand remained unfulfilled till 1988. It had been propagated by some people that implementation of U.G.C. pay scales would throw positions of college teachers open to citizens of India which was against the provisions of Article 370 of the Indian Constitution. The Chief Minister Sheikh Abdullah had been convinced about it and he had categorically refused to implement U.G.C. pay scales for college teachers. He favoured separate State pay scales for college teachers instead.

*****

March 1990 witnessed beginning of a mass exodus of Kashmiri Pandits from the valley in the wake of armed insurgency. Actually insurgency had started in 1989 itself when low-scale bomb explosions took place in Srinagar city. This was followed by first political murder when a National Conference worker Yusuf Halwai was shot dead by militants on 21 August 1989. This was followed by murder of BJP leader

Tika Lal Taploo on 14 September 1989. On 4 November, former Sessions Judge Neelkanth Ganjoo, who had sentenced JKLF founder Maqbool Bhat to death, was also shot dead. In between some more persons belonging to intelligence agencies, telecommunications and social activists were also shot dead. This created fear of terror among Pandits, Nationalist Muslims and Sikhs who started Migrating to Jammu in small numbers from November 1989 itself. On 8 December 1989, Rubaiya Sayeed daughter of Union Home Minister, Mufti Mohammad Sayeed was kidnapped by JKLF militants. She was released on 13 December 1989 in exchange for five JKLF imprisoned leaders who were given a free passage to POK.

On 19 January 1990, Jag Mohan was appointed governor and Farooq Abdullah resigned as Chief Minister. A reign of terror was unleashed thereafter by the militants. Kashmiri Pandits were threatened by militants to leave the valley or face consequences. Posters were openly pasted on their doors and announcement were made from mosques exhorting K.P.'s to leave the valley. The night of 19 January 1990 will ever remain etched in the memory of Pandits who were openly threatened through recorded announcements on public address syetems made simultaneously from mosques throughout the valley to flee the valley or face death. On 13 February 1990, Lassa Koul Director of Srinagar Doordarshan, a dear friend of mine, was shot dead. This was the beginning of mass exodus of Pandits, nationalist Muslims and Sikhs from the valley.

*****

Thus, the policy continued till in 1988. The college teachers agitated and the government under C.M. Dr. Farooq Abdullah agreed to implement U.G.C. pay scale from 1988 instead of 1986 (date from which the new U.G.C. pay scale had come into effect under 1986 Pay Commission of Govt. of India recommendations). Mr. Vijay Bakaya the then Education Commissioner played a very positive role in convicing C.M. for grant U.G.C. scales in favour of college teachers. The President of C.T.A. Jammu, Prof. Surjit Singh Sevak in consultation with his colleagues agreed to it and the agitation was called off. Later that year Prof. Sevak was made a member of the State Service Recruitment Board (SSRB).

In the year 1990, I became actively involved in the college teachers association of Jammu division and was elected Treasurer. Prof. N.N. Sharma and Prof. Narinder Singh were elected as President and General Secretary respectively. At the very first meeting of the new executive it was decided to persuade the government to grant implementation of the U.G.C. pay scales with effect from January 1986. The state then under Governor's rule was run by Advisors and Commissioners. Ms. Sushma Chaudhari was education commissioner and we convinced her that if the pay scales were implemented from January 1986 it would not help college teachers alone but would benefit the state exchequer as well. Actually the U.G.C. rules categorically stated that those states which would implement the pay scales in toto from 1986 would get 100% reimbursement of the difference of pay of college teachers. We had worked out that by not implementing the U.G.C. pay scales from January 1986 the state exchequer would lose a few crores. We had worked out that by not implementing the pay scales from 1986, the state would have to pay the difference due to raise of pay from its own coffers. However, if the scales were implemented from 1986 the pay arrears of teachers would be paid by the U.G.C. from that date, i.e. 1 January 1986 and the state would also be benefitted by a few crores of rupees. She encouraged us to meet the Advisors Mr. Jamil Ahmed and Mr. Ved Marwah. Accordingly Prof. N.N. Sharma, Prof. Narender Singh and myself met and convinced them with facts and figures that implementation of U.G.C. pay scales with effect from 1986 would benefit both the college teachers and the state. Our efforts brought fruit and orders to implement of U.G.C. pay scales to college teacher from 1 January 1986 were issued to the joy of all.

*****

The years 1987 and 1988 proved to be full of turmoil. The decision of the government to curtail annual durbar move of departments from the summer capital Srinagar to winter capital Jammu resulted in an agitation by Bar Council of Jammu on 7 November 1987. Finally, the agitation was called off on

14 November 1987 after the government rescinded the Durbar Move order. Similarly, there were protests at Srinagar in June 1988 against a hike in the power tariffs. When demonstrations turned violent on 10 June 1988 police resorted to firing resulting in death of three people. This was followed by bandh and protest calls till 13 June 1988. The discontent continued to simmer and there were massive Anti-India demonstration in the whole of Kashmir on 15 August 1988 and the government was forced to impose curfew.

Following the death of General Zia-ul-Haq President of Pakistan in a plane crash demonstrations were organized in Kashmir on 17 August 1988. As demonstration continued and became violent police had to resort to firing and four people died on 18 August. This did not quell the discontent and on 26 August three more people died in police firing. The curfew that had been imposed on 15 August was finally lifted on 27 August 1988 after 13 days. Curfew had caused a lot of inconvenience to the public and they had grown wary of it. The lifting of the curfew came as a great relief to the people. Ironically when Bhutoo was hanged in Pakistan by Zia-ul-Haq people of Kashmir had demonstrated against it also. Now they were agitating against the unnatural death of the same dictator who had hanged his benefactor. Bhutoo had chosen Zia as chief of the Pakistan Army over and above the head of many of his seniors. Such was the politics of Kashmir.

Underlying all this apparent discontent in the valley as became obvious later in 1989 and 1990 was the role of ISI in bringing discontent among the people of the valley against India. Earlier they had started the silent islamisation by encouraging Jamat-e-Islami to spread its tentacles and preaching hatred against India by the maulvis brought in from outside the state. All the time, as became clear later the reports sent by the intelligence agencies and the state governor were swept under the carpet by Rajiv Gandhi who it is alleged was misled by Dr. Abdullah's assurances that all was well. The joining of hands by the Congress and N.C. had brought bad luck and disaster to the state and the country.

On 24 March 1990, Mir Mustafa independent MLA was kidnapped by Hizbul Mujahideen and killed on 28 March 1990. On 6 April, Kashmir University Vice Chancellor Mushir-ul-Haq and his private secretary Abdul Ghani and HMT General Manager H.L. Khera were kidnapped and killed. Killing spree which had started in August 1989 continued unabated. On 21 May 1990, Mirwaiz Maulvi Mohd. Farooq was shot dead at his residence. The killing of Maulvi Farooq resulted in resentment among the people against the militants. At this point of time the government should have acted in a wise manner to create a wave of contempt for the militant violence. But unfortunate events followed. In the mourning procession of Maulvi Farooq, there were militants who fired at the security forces in the down town. In a panic reaction the security forces fired on the mourners resulting in death of 50 persons. Earlier also 35 people had been killed on 20 January as a result of firing by the securing forces on a crowd protesting against night-long house to house searches in Srinagar. The Government of India in a panic reaction replaced Jag Mohan by Girish Chander Sexena on 26 May 1990 as Governor of Jammu Kashmir (Balraj Puri, 1993).

*****

In 1992 elections of C.T.A. were held and Prof. Sevak who had been repatriated from SSRB back to college service and posted at Science College stood for election as president against Prof. N.N. Sharma and defeated him. I also lost in the election to the General Council. Prof. Sevak had won because he had endeared himself to the college teachers community during his earlier stint and got U.G.C. pay scales implemented. I must also add that meanwhile Principal K.L. Gupta retired in February 1992. He had handed over charge to Prof. P.L. Bakshi, the senior most staff member who too was due to retire by the end of March 1992. However, Prof. Bakshi took the initiative to get the bills of arrears of pay (due to implementation of 1986 pay scales) prepared for drawal from the treasury before the end of the financial year. But for his initiative the funds would have lapsed.

*****

As a result of mass exodus of Kashmiri Pandits to Jammu a great administrative problem had resulted. A section of the population of Kashmir became displaced. At this juncture the people of Jammu at the behest of Hindu social organizations and BJP accommodated a large number of K.P.'s in their homes. They also helped them by way of rations, clothes and other items to cope with the situation. The government also accommodated the displaced people in schools and other government buildings and M.A.M. stadium. The Hindu social organizations opened the doors of dharmshalas and temples to accommodate some people. It was a period of great distress for the community. School and college going students had to be accommodated in the educational institutions. On the initiative of many leaders of displaced teachers like Prof. B.L. Zutshi, Dr. Ashok Munshi, Prof. J.L. Bhat, Prof. Arvind Gigoo and many others the government decided that for the displaced students separate evening classes be held in the existing government schools and colleges. For this purpose services of school and college teachers who had also migrated were utilized. Thus at Science College, M.A.M. College and Govt. College Udhampur evening classes were started with the help of lecturers/professors who had migrated. Likewise evening classes in schools at Domana, Mishriwalla, Bakshi Nagar, Batal Balian and Shastri Nagar were also started for the benefit of students.

Prof. Jia Lal Kotwal was transferred as Principal of Science College in March 1992 from Government College Udhampur where he had put in about two years. He was an able and strict administrator. The first and the foremost thing that he did was to stop the youth of different sports clubs of the city from playing in the college grounds probably in order to maintain discipline. However, this was resented by sports lovers of Jammu. These grounds had been used by the young men of the city besides the college students for more than half a century for the simple reason that there were not may play grounds available. The centrally located parade ground had become useless for sports purposes because it was often used for holding political and religious rallies and even for commercial exhibitions.

I must, however, say it to the credit of Prof. Kotwal that he opposed the proposed conversion of the college playground on the river Tawi side into a stadium. It was the period of Governor's rule and he personally met Gen. (Retd.) Krishana Rao and got the proposal shelved. It was indeed in the interest of the premier institution of the city to retain its playgrounds for future generations of students. This good step of Prof. Kotwal in fact helped me later in the year 1999-2000. As Principal of Commerce College I initiated the process of construction of a hostel in a part of Science College ground with the active cooperation of Principal Surinder Saproo and help of Chief Minister Dr. Farooq Abdullah and Education Minister Mohd. Shafi.

In the State of Jammu and Kashmir college teachers have from the inception in early twentieth century enjoyed a special place in the society. Higher education was highly valued and the college teachers were respected for their dedication to the cause of education. Some very eminent teachers had laid the foundations of higher education in the state. Till 1947 the few colleges of the state were affiliated to the then Punjab University Lahore. Some very eminent Principals and Professors including English men had nurtured these institutions and the result was that the students who had passed out rose to high positions in the state and country. Thus the colleges of the state had a rich environment in which academics and sports thrived. There was a culture of decency, grace and politeness combined with strict discipline. This continued for quite some time even after the partition and establishment of Jammu and Kashmir University in 1949. This culture had attracted many alumni to enter the coveted service of teaching in colleges. With the passage of time, however, the service started losing its sheen. The profession could not remain unaffected in the face of changing materialistic environment. Many college teachers who had earlier avoided the lure of money started private coaching to earn an additional income in order to provide more material comforts to their families.

*****

In August 1992, I was transferred to Govt. College Bhaderwah. However, due to militancy and a threat perception I did not join and proceeded on leave. The period of my leave lasted for about three months and I utilized it well. My work and writings in the fields of wildlife and ecology of Himalayas had earlier earned me an award from Food and Agriculture Organization on the World Food Day on 16 October 1991. I had been invited to New Delhi by FAO to receive the award. It had naturally encouraged me. I thought it proper to invite articles from various experts of Himalayan ecology and environment to compile a compendium of articles in a book form. The effort proved worth its while for the response that I received was overwhelming. I received over thirty articles and research papers from research workers and authorities on the Himalayas. I selected and edited some 25 articles and compiled them in the form of a book tilted *Ecodegradation of Himalayas Causes and Remedies*, with a foreword by Mr. Kamal Nath, the then Minister of Environment and Forests Government of India. The volume saw light of the day subsequently in 1994.

I had made a representation to the Governor against my transfer to Govt. College Bhaderwah and was subsequently posted in Govt. College for Women Parade Ground Jammu in October 1992. Thus my long leave period came to an end. My stay in this college for about four years proved quite fruitful for the institution and to me personally. As Head of the Zoology Department I renovated the museum, purchased new laboratory equipment and chemicals and books for the library in view of the recent changes in the syllabi and courses of study at the undergraduate level. I also organized seminars and extension lectures with the help of the Principal Reeta Jatinder and active cooperation of my colleagues. Prof. Reeta Jatinder Principal of the college was a literary luminary and a radio artiste. She had great literary taste and encouraged me. I felt quite comfortable under her guidance. She had earlier been President of College Teachers Association and understood the problems of colleges and college teachers. Since I too was associated with the CTA, it was but natural that we mostly agreed with each other's point of view.

*****

On 28 October 1992, our elder son Anil tied knot with Anjila Shah daughter of Dr. Nasir and Dr. Girija Dhar in a simple civil marriage solemnized at the New Delhi residence of Supreme Court Judge Justice A.S. Anand. It was a simple function attended by close relations of both the families and some common friends like Mr. Makhan Lal Fotedar Union Health Minister, Mr. Sri Kanth Raina and Mr. Vijay Dhar. That evening Dr. Nasir arranged a reception at the sprawling grounds of Army officer's club which was attended by friends and relatives from both sides. We also threw a reception party at Hotel Maurya Sheration the next day for friends, relatives and well wishers from both the sides.

*****

After transfer of Mrs. Jatinder as Secretary of the J&K Cultural Academy Prof. Sukanya Dogra Head of the Chemistry Department took the charge as principal. A lady full of grace and charm she continued the good work of administering the college. She organized additional teaching classes for weaker students. She also started coaching classes for students belonging to socially weaker sections to help them compete in the competitive examinations for admission to medical and engineering colleges. Having a science background she encouraged endeavours of science faculties besides the arts and social sciences faculties. My experience of running University Grants Commission projects was utilized to the full by Prof. Dogra.

*****

In August 1996, I was promoted as principal after a long wait due to reasons I have mentioned earlier. There was a complete paralysis of administration in the education sector during the Governor's rule which started in January 1990 and ended only after the elections in 1996. A culture of adhocism had taken over. In 1992 selections to Principal's posts were about to take place but a disagreement between Commissioner of Education and Chairman of Public Service Commission on a minor issue stopped the whole process. A comparatively junior teacher who had not been invited to appear in the interviews for principal's selection had gone to the court and got a stay.

The bureaucracy due to lack of interest did not get the stay vacated. This is how bureaucratic delays and red tapism can slowdown progress.

Adhocism often leads to inefficiency as there is no accountability. Ad hoc teachers do not deliver so well as they are aware that their services can be terminated. There is a classical case involving a certain Degree College. Services of a lecturer appointed on ad hoc basis were not terminated on time and he continued to be in his post due to connivance of a clerk and laxity of the principal. When the error was detected by the higher office the lecturer had crossed the mark of six months. Then he refused to be terminated and went to court. The government on court directions had finally to make services of a wholly undeserving person permanent. Similarly at another Govt. College when the principal was transferred he handed over charge to an ad hoc lecturer (all lecturers in the college at that time were ad hoc appointees). This gentleman took it to his head and thought that he was a permanent principal even though he was not even a permanent lecturer. In the meanwhile, government transferred a senior lecturer as in charge principal of the college. The ad hoc lecturer holding charge refused to hand over to a permanent senior lecturer. The situation should not have been allowed to arise in the first place. When the Principal of the college was transferred he should have been instructed to stay and hand over charge to an in charge being posted simultaneously. It appears that he was in a great hurry to join at his home town where he had been transferred.

Such was the scenario existing in the Higher Education Department in August 1996 when I was promoted as principal. I had to replace an in charge principal at Govt. College Kathua. Luckily Prof. I.S. Patang holding the charge had been my junior at the university. In addition to his own charge as Head of Zoology Department he was holding additional charge of the principal after retirement of Prof. B.L. Bhardwaj in the month of May 1996. I was greeted with warmth by the staff of the college and a new chapter began in my career. It was an opportunity to implement my ideas for improvement of higher education. Government College Kathua was established in 1961 with an enrolment of 28 students. At the time of my joining the roll was 3000. The campus was spread over an ecofriendly area of about 40 acres. It was a coeducational institution. The college besides the administrative block, lecture theatres, laboratories had also an auditorium to carry out extra curricular activities. The college had a rich library having collection of over 50,000 volumes. Moreover, latest journals, magazines, periodicals, etc. were also subscribed. The college had separate boys and girls hostels and a few staff quarters. I added two more hostels and a Home Science Block during my posting to the college affiliated to the University of Jammu.

As expected it took me some time to get accustomed to the institution and the staff even though I had earlier visited the college in connection with conduct of university examinations and also as an executive member of College Teachers Association. However, short visits even when frequent do not give one the real feel of an institution. A day after joining I requested the staff secretary Prof. Vijay Sharma to arrange a staff meeting so that I could address and interact with them. At the very start I told my colleague to consider me the first among equals. I told them that we had to rub our shoulders together and bring the college to a level where it could be noticed. I also told them that they should not fight shy of sharing their problems with me; they would always find me there to help them. At the same time, it was expected that they would perform their duties honestly with a sense of devotion and commitment because as teachers there was a great responsibility lying on their shoulders. The message was well taken as the eventual university results indicated. With the passage of time I could feel the warmth of the staff and students.

The first and the foremost problem that I encountered was the shortage of staff. There were 3000 students on rolls and as many as sixteen faculties but only 75 teachers. The college was short of at least 15 teachers. So my first and foremost job was to persuade higher education department to provide additional teaching staff. Luckily I enjoyed a good working relation with Dr. Muzzafar Khan, Director of Colleges and he supported me. As luck would have it the government agreed and provided the additional staff I had asked for. It helped improve the working of the various departments and I received a shot in my arm. My next problem was shortage of hostel accommodation for girls and boys, more so for the former. I took up the matter with the administrative department in the month of October and soon received a query whether a pre-fabricated block would serve the purpose. I immediately sent my consent in view of the great pressure I was facing for accommodating girl students. Therefore in a matter of just three months an additional block of pre-fabricated hostel rooms with modern facilities like wash rooms, common room, kitchen and dining hall came up. This accommodation came handy when we organized a week long National Social Service camp in the college in February 1997 in which students from as many as fourteen universities participated.

The N.S.S. National Integration Camp organized at the Kathua College campus from 22-28 February 1997 under the auspices of University of Jammu and Ministry of Human Resources Development, Govt. of India turned out to be a big event. Such a National level camp was organized for the first time in a college campus in the state. The college was fit to organize the camp in all respects but there was the problem of accommodating the guests. We were looking for it in the town when the godsend opportunity of building a pre-fabricated hostel for girls came. I got the accommodation ready ahead of the camp and it came handy. All the guests could be properly accommodated. The district administration also cooperated by providing water, electricity, health and hygiene facilities well before the camp was held. One big problem was the face lifting of the auditorium and the buildings. For this I had to contact my friend Kamlesh Gupta the Chief Engineer R&B. He was kind enough to provide funds for this purpose to the concerned executive engineer of Kathua, a very honest and upright officer. He got the job done very nicely well in time and the campus received a good presentable look. The auditorium also got a good facelift. The camp was inaugurated by the Governor Gen. (Retd.) Krishna Rao on 22 February 1997 and it proved a big event. In his inaugural speech the Governor dwelt at length on the need of unity among the people to safeguard the nation against the nefarious intentions of our neighbours. He praised and congratulated the college management for holding such a big event. Earlier we had got a tree planted by him in the campus and he had enquired from me about the number of universities and institutions participating in the camp.

The inauguration was also attended by the Vice Chancellor Jammu University Prof. R.R. Sharma, Deputy Commissioner, Senior Superintendent of Police, Sessions Judge, officers of the University, Principals of Jammu Colleges, officers of various departments and prominent citizens of Kathua. The big event being the first of its kind at Kathua it was largely attended. On my request the Governor also released first volume of my edited series *Advances in Fish and Wildlife Ecology and Biology* on the occasion. During the lunch that we had organized for the Governor and other guests at the Fish Seed Farm Kathua he enquired from me about the reasons behind the mass Fish Kill in the "Mansar Lake" which had happened recently and was widely reported in the media. It had been reported in the media that the lake had been poisoned which had resulted in the death of a large number of fish. I had to explain to him in detail that the kill was not a result of poisoning but was a natural phenomenon which also occurred elsewhere in world due to change in weather conditions and temperature variations in winter.

The camp continued for eight days during which a number of activities were carried out. The participants actively took part in all these activities. Visits to Mata Vaishno Devi and to Mansar Lake were also organized. I personally accompanied the participants and explained to them about the origin of lakes and myths about them and most importantly the ecology and importance of lakes and other water bodies as sources of potable water, fish and good recreation. It was followed by a good question answer session.

The camp was attended by a number of dignitaries including the Minister of Education Mr. Abdul Qayyum, the Minister of Law and Parliamentary Affairs Mr. P.L. Handoo the Minister of Information Mr. B.A. Nengroo, Prof. R.R. Sharma Vice

Chancellor, Mr. Vijay Bakaya Additional Chief Secretary and Commissioner of Agriculture and Mr. Patnaik Principal Chief Conservator of Forests besides prominent citizens and officers like Director Environment and Remote Sensing, Joint Director Field Publicity, District Field Publicity Officer Kathua Mr. Sanjeet Khajuria, Director AIR Kathua Mr. M.K. Raina Officers of the University and Principals of Jammu Colleges. The grand success of the NSS camp, which was widely reported in the State and National Press and electronic media was undoubtedly the result of cooperation that I received from Prof. Ram Murti Sharma Camp Commander and Prof. R.K. Gupta besides Prof. Inder Singh, Prof. Vijay Sharma, Prof. Ram Saroop and other teaching and non-teaching staff.

*****

The month of February 1997 had been particularly lucky for me and my family. It began with the arrival of our first grandson Ahan at Delhi on 1 February. His parents Tina and Anil had completed postgraduation in gynaecology and surgery respectively at All India Institute of Medical Sciences and were working as Registrars there at that time. My wife, myself and Tina's parents were present at the Mother and Child Nursing Home when Ahan arrived and brought joy to all of us. I had to rush back to Kathua to look after the arrangements for holding the NSS camp mentioned above. Luckily for me it also passed bringing credit to the college, the staff and of course to myself as well.

*****

When I had joined the Kathua College the academic session had just started. A new course on "Fish & Fisheries" was introduced from that year. It was a U.G.C. supported programme. Grants for purchase of equipment and books had been placed at our disposal but the real problem was of teaching staff. The course was to be started by the Zoology Department which was already understaffed. Since I was myself a fisheries specialist I told Prof. Inder Singh, the Head of Zoology to let me teach the course till staff is provided by the department. So I started teaching the course myself. It was for the first time that a principal was taking a class in the college. The word spread in the town and I started receiving phone calls appreciating the gesture from thankful parents and community leaders. I told them that I loved teaching and in view of the shortage of staff it was also my duty. The course was started in view of the fact that a national level fish breeding and seed farm existed at Kathua. It was under the State Fisheries Department and we could take our students to train them at the farm. Kathua District has two parts, one part called Kandi that is perennially short of water due to its hilly terrain and another part which is full of streams and ponds. There are numerous ponds in the hilly terrain also, which are used for storage of rain water. These ponds and newly dug ones can be used for fish culture which can provide employment to the unemployed. The plain part is also very good for fish culture. Two qualified lecturers were later provided to the college during the second year to take care of teaching the fisheries course. In the meanwhile, I had developed a rapport with the fish farm management and the Director Dr. Nisar Ahmed Jan to provide facilities to our students which they thankfully did till the college developed its own ponds and other infrastructure later after funds were made available by the Department of Higher Education.

During an academic inspection of the local D.A.V. Higher Secondary School for girls the principal told me that the school was teaching Home Science subject and in the absence of this subject in the college the girls had to give it up. She suggested that we should start the course in the college. I told her that her suggestion was good and I would try to implement it. It appeared to me that these girls were deprived of benefit of a good course due to its absence in the college and I immediately took up the matter with the Higher Education Department. Simultaneously, I also spoke about it to the Education Minister and the Vice Chancellor of Jammu University during their visit to the college for N.S.S. camp in February 1997. Both were pleased by my suggestion and within a period of three months my proposal for starting a Home Science Department was conceded. As a result three posts of lecturers for teaching Home Science were sanctioned and funds were provided to build a Home Science Block. The chief architect of the government Mr. Gupta visited the college soon after and I showed him the location where the building should be built. I was glad that in August 1997 construction of the Home Science Block had started. It was completed after my transfer to Jammu but I had the satisfaction that a useful subject was introduced and a new block for it built on my initiative.

After taking over I had found that the college had amassed large amounts of money as local funds under various heads, two of which attracted my immediate attention. Under one fund called "mutual benefit fund" I found that a substantial amount of money was lying idle in the bank. The fund is basically to provide help to the needy students. While there deservedly are scholarships and free ships available to students belonging to SC/ST categories there are none for meritorious students belonging to other social categories. Since the college had students coming from a very large area, being the only college in the district, I felt there must certainly be some poor and deserving students from among Muslims, Brahmins and Rajputs, etc.

Accordingly I framed a committee of three senior professors and asked them to get a notice issued calling for applications from deserving students from other than SC/ST categories for financial assistance. A large number of students both boys and girls applied. They were asked to submit income certificates and thereafter called for an interview. Those who were found deserving were paid cash amounts out of the available funds. It therefore became a precedent for future to help the deserving needy students out of the fund.

Another local fund which had accumulated over the years was "college magazine fund". The college magazine *Ravi* had not been published for the last ten long years for unknown reasons. A magazine is an extremely important periodical issued annually to inform the students and the community about the activities of the college for an academic year. It also provides an opportunity to students to write essays, articles, poem, etc. and help them develop their journalistic and creative writing skills. Many writers, poets and journalists develop the art of creative expression in the institutions where they study. As such I felt that we should start the publication of the magazine from the 1996-

97 session. I called a staff meeting and put forth my proposal. Everybody welcomed the idea and many suggestions were put forth. So a magazine committee was constituted and student editors were selected by a written test. Quotations from printers were invited and scrutinized for placing orders. In a period of less than six months *Ravi* was published. In August 1997, when the college re-opened after the summer break, the magazine was distributed to delight of all especially the students. For even the senior most of them it was a new experience because nothing of the sort had passed through their hands since they had joined the college. An ex-student who had seen the magazine wrote me a letter of appreciation for bringing out a college magazine which he had not seen during the three years when he was a student.

In September 1997 a very serious situation arose in the college. I had gone on leave to New Delhi for treatment and surgery of my younger brother Bal Krishan at All India Institute of Medical Sciences. He had been diagnosed as suffering from mouth cancer. I had handed over charge to Prof. Inder Singh the senior most professor before proceeding on leave. After the surgery of my brother was over I returned and came to learn about the unfortunate death of a 1st year girl student in the hospital at Jammu. The girl student had joined the college in August 1997 and returned to her home at Billawar after falling sick. She had been admitted to Billawar District Hospital and later discharged after preliminary treatment. Despite her ill health she had insisted to attend the college. Her older brother was a student of 3rd year in the college and had tried to dissuade her but failed. After attending her classes just for one day she fell ill again at night in the hostel. She had rectal bleeding. When the matter was brought to the notice of the girls hostel warden Ms. Reeta Bhagat, she immediately got her shifted to the District Hospital Kathua. Her bleeding, however, did not stop despite blood transfusion arranged by the college management. Late in the evening the same day doctors at the District Hospital advised that she be shifted to Medical College Hospital at Jammu.

As the District Hospital ambulance was out of order, Prof. Inder Singh arranged a private vehicle and sent the girl student along with her brother, another student and medical assistant of the college to Jammu a distance of 90 km. late at night. The girl student was admitted in the Medical College Hospital at Jammu but died soon after. Her body was shifted to her village Sukrala Mata in Billawar Tehsil. A pall of gloom fell on the college as the message of her death reached us. I had joined back the same day and called my staff members and asked them to hold a condolence meeting in the college grounds. A condolence resolution was passed and two minutes silence observed. The students were advised to go to their homes in silence as a mark of respect for the departed soul.

When the college reopened the next day a word reached my ears that a section of the students were agitated over the death of the student allegedly due to negligence of the girls hostel superintendent Ms. Reeta Bhagat. I immediately called Prof. Inder Singh and Ms. Bhagat to know the facts first hand. They confirmed what I had already heard and I felt satisfied that they had done whatever they could under the circumstances. Thereafter, I called the President of the student's union and his executive members and asked them pointedly if an agitation was being planned. What they said surprised me. They told me that the students were angry as to why the girls hostel superintendent and Prof. Inder Singh did not accompany the girl to Jammu. I told them how could they be accommodated in a small Maruti van as the patient was accompanied by a medical assistant, her brother and his friend beside the driver. Even if they had accompanied in a cramped and overloaded vehicle how could they have saved her. In fact an error of judgment had been committed by the doctors at the District Hospital by not referring the patient early in the day to medical college Hospital Jammu. A bigger vehicle or private ambulance could then have been arranged from Pathankot town in the Punjab. The union President and his colleagues were satisfied and assured me that no agitation would take place. Their assurance not withstanding I contacted the District Magistrate and Senior Superintendent of police and told them about the possibility of a student's agitation on the issue which they were already in know of. They assured me of the precautionary measures required at their end. I also formed a committee of three professors headed by Prof. Vijay Sharma, H.O.D. Mathematics and a member from the District Administration nominated by the Deputy Commissioner to probe into the incident and report within seven days. Simultaneously I sent a detailed report of the incident to Mr. Ajit Kumar Commissioner/Secretary to Government, Education Department, to keep him informed.

I also decided that a group of teachers including myself and some students visit the residence of the girl student at Sukrala Mata village in Billawar Tehsil. The next day our college bus full of students, teachers and myself went to the village some 40 km. away from Kathua to express our sympathies and offer condolences to the family. We were told by the family members that the girl student was already very weak and sick and that she had remained admitted at the Billawar Hospital for quite some time. Obviously her disease had not been properly diagnosed. Had she been admitted in the Medical College Hospital, Jammu she might not have died. Her insistence to attend college, even though just for one day, proved fatal as her problem had taken a serious turn. They told us that they were satisfied that the college administration had done its best to help her under the circumstances and thanked it for the same.

In order to remove any misunderstanding and apprehensions of the public I organized a meeting of eminent citizens of Kathua in the college in which senior teachers Prof. Inder Singh, Prof. Vijay Sharma, Prof. R.M. Sharma, Prof. Bhagat, Prof. Malhotra also participated. We explained to them the whole episode, including the steps taken by the college to get the girl student treated first at District Hospital Kathua and later on the advice of doctors there shifted her to Medical College Hospital, Jammu. We also told them about our visit to the residence of the student to sympathize with her parents and what they had told us about her sickness prior to joining the college even though just for a day. The eminent citizens understood our position and assured that they would prevail upon their wards and other students not to agitate and to attend classes regularly.

Privately also I met the leaders of various political parties and Sh. Lal Singh the local M.L.A. to help the college administration in maintaining peace and harmony for smooth conduct of class work and normal functioning. To their credit I must say that they helped the college administration and within a few days the college was back to normal academic and other activities.

Students are a volatile community. More often than not they are misguided on petty issues by political parties resulting in campus unrest and loss of precious academic days. If they are not properly handled and guided they agitate and then sometimes things go out of control and unsocial elements take over and disturb peace in the campuses.

My efforts did not go in vain and within a week the college was working as usual. A situation which could have flared up and created difficulties for the college management and district administration fizzled out. One important factor of great help was the good working relationship that I had developed with the staff and a close relationship with students by interacting with them. But there were lessons to be learnt. If the educational administrators and teachers work closely together and are helpful to their students and take care of their genuine demands the chances of strikes and agitations can be reduced and avoided. There is also a need of keeping eyes and ears open and prevent the unsocial and mischievous elements from entering the campuses and influencing the students. I will dwell upon this elsewhere.

The enquiry committee came out with a report within the stipulated time and confirmed that the college administration and the hostel superintendent had acted quickly and tried to save precious life of the girl student. However, by the time the student had returned from her home at Sukrala Mata to attend the college severe damage had already occurred to her health. Had her health condition been diagnosed properly at the Billawar Hospital earlier, she could have been taken directly to Medical College Hospital Jammu for treatment. By the time she was admitted to the District Hospital at Kathua her condition had deteriorated.

The college was short of furniture especially desks. I had already started the process of getting the broken furniture repaired within the campus. Orders were also placed for purchase of 100 desks from the government factory for which calling of quotations was not needed. On my joining I had found that the main staffroom and other departmental staffrooms were in a bad shape. I spoke about it to the staff secretary and departmental heads and told them that finances to carry out refurbishing of the staffrooms would not be a problem if they agreed. They expressed their willingness and accordingly the broken and repairable sofas and chairs were identified and a list made. A tender was floated and a on the basis of the lowest quotation received the job was entrusted to a local firm. We also bought new curtains from the Jammu Super Market for which no tendering was required. The staffroom was painted and the washroom repaired. As the repaired sofas arrived the very look of the staffroom changed. The departmental staffrooms too gave a changed look with new curtains and furniture. It is important to have a pleasing environment at one's workplace. This is as important for teachers as for all other professionals.

Since the college was a co-educational institution we had a sizeable number of girl students. To make them comfortable there already existed a large common room. It too needed refurbishment and I ensured that the girls felt comfortable. My predecessor had purchased about fifteen glass boards. However, these were not fitted in the classrooms for some reason. I told my office to obtain services of a professional who could fit these in the classrooms. Once fitted both teachers and the students felt happy, former for the simple reason that it was easier to write on them and the latter for clear visibility.

Before the annual examinations started in the month of March 1997 I called a meeting of the staff both teaching as well non-teaching and told them that these must be held in the most fair and transparent manner. I also spoke to the Senior Superintendent of police to provide services of some police men to ensure that no outside persons were able to enter the campus and create disturbance. As the examinations concluded in the month of April 1997 the university authorities who had paid surprise checks praised conduct of these examinations. Subsequently when the results were declared we had much to celebrate about. The top two positions in the Science Faculty of the University of Jammu went to our college.

The new Academic session started with enthusiasm in August 1997. Admissions to 1st year had actually been made earlier by the admission committee during the vacations soon after the declaration of results of +2 examinations by the School Board. The admissions were made as per the norms set by the University of Jammu. For admission to science stream the minimum percentage was set at 45%. Although much lower as compared to many universities in the country yet the demand for admissions for science stream was high. There were pressures from students, their parents and even from politicians but we could not oblige them for obvious reasons. However, many people did not take refusal kindly.

The college roll went up to over 3500 that year. Academic, co-curricular and extra-curricular activities picked up soon and all went on smoothly. The construction activities had also started and I concentrated my energies on further improvements of the campus. I approached the local M.L.A. Choudhary Lal Singh and requested him to pay out of his development funds for the repair of the breached boundary wall of the college. Some people were using the broken boundary wall to trespass and make a short cut to reach the main road from their homes and vice versa. Some people even let loose their cattle in the college ground for grazing at night. The cattle would damage the garden and flowering plants. Mr. Lal Singh was an ex-student of the college and immediately agreed. The boundary wall was repaired and trespassing and cattle grazing came to an end. I must add here that during my tenure at Kathua Chaudhary Lal Singh whole heartedly co-operated with the college administration.

Beside academics I also encouraged cultural troupes to visit the college and perform there. Among these I recollect the impressive performance of a troupe from Manipur in the college ground. It was about the loss of the nest built by a pair of birds and the consequent pain suffered by the mother of the little chicks killed by a predator. It left an impression on the audience.

In sports too especially cricket and athletics our boys and girls did quite well and shone at the inter-college tournaments.

Holding of seminars, workshops and debates on current topics and themes like environment, food security and role of education in development had become an important part of the college activity during my tenure at Kathua. Since these programmes were widely reported in the media Govt. College Kathua came into limelight and was talked about everywhere. During one of the visits by Mr. P.L. Handoo, Minister for Law and Parliamentary Affairs to Kathua, the Deputy Commissioner told him in my presence that the college had become a prestigious and elitist institution. Honestly speaking the remark made me feel flattered.

While the session was going on in full force, orders of my transfer to Govt. SPMR College of Commerce Jammu came in the month of December 1997. Prof. Aman Rathor Principal was transferred to the School Board as Secretary and I was asked to take over charge of the prestigious Commerce College. Dr. A.K. Malla was promoted to take charge from me. I received the orders with mixed feelings. My concern was that the work of development that I had initiated at Kathua college should continue. I knew Dr. Malla as a classmate at the college and the university and I was aware of his capabilities. That was a big consolation. On the other hand, I was happy for going back to Jammu. I would certainly miss my colleagues and students. My colleagues like Profs. Inder Singh, Vijay Sharma, Ram Murti, Shastri, Malhotra, Reeta Bhagat, R.K. Gupta and Ram Saroop had been a great support during my tenure for which I would always remember them.

*****

I took over charge at commerce college Jammu on 16 December 1997. As the things stood Commerce College had been an all male institution but now with the introduction of BBA course, a few female students too had joined. I was not a stranger to the staff being known to them as an active member of College Teachers Association. They received me with considerable warmth. As is the practice the first thing I did was to address the staff to elicit their cooperation.

Educational institutions close for winter break in Jammu Division for ten days with effect from 22 December every year. In pre-independence era these were called Christmas holidays. During this period students are sent on a tour to some part of the country as I have mentioned earlier. The transport and stay expenses are brome by the state and the students have to spend for their food only. It is a voluntary exercise and only a limited number of students opt for it. In commerce college a large chunk of students come from the local business community. When I joined arrangements for the tour were almost complete. The tour in charge Prof. Kohli, however, was feeling uncomfortable due to some problem that he was confronted with. He was feeling hesitant to share it with me. I had to assure him that he could freely speak to me if there was a problem and it would be my endeavour to find a solution. He then came forth with a problem which rather surprised me. According to him some four or five tough boys from the area, who were not on the rolls of the college had been managing to accompany the tour parties for some years. They would go to the railway station, mingle with our boys and pass off as a part of the tour party consisting of nearly a hundred students. The railway officials normally do not take a head count of tour parties and they would travel without tickets with our boys. I immediately understood that some of our own students must be friendly and conniving with them. These boys I was told were regular visitors to the college canteen as well and no one dared to object to their presence.

It was definitely a serious problem and I realized that to run the college peacefully I would have to act fast and asked Prof. Kohli to give me the names of these boy with their addresses. When he had given me the list I phoned the S.H.O. of the area and requested him to drop in the college as I had to speak to him about an urgent matter. When he came to see me, I told him about the problem and showed him list of the mischievous elements. After seeing the list he said that he would need an official letter to take action and left. A letter was got typed immediately and delivered to him in his office within an hour. On receiving my letter he rang up to say that appropriate action would follow. The police officer acted quickly and the tour party left peacefully minus the miscreants. I never saw any trace of those boys in the college thereafter. The problem had been solved once for all, thanks to fast action taken by the police officer.

When the college reopened in January 1998 many problems cropped up. Two issues which were very serious concerned the syllabus of the BBA class started a few months ago and recognition of the course by the Jammu University. The syllabus that was being taught had been prepared by the Board of Studies tentatively but not approved by the academic council. Actually the course needed recognition by the concerned body of the university. This had not been done by my predecessor so it fell on me to get it done. For preparation of the syllabus, the Management Department of Jammu University suggested that the college should get syllabi of the course from some universities where the course was being taught. Since this would take time, I thought it proper to form a committee of three teachers headed by Prof. Bharti (HOD) to visit some neighbouring universities in Punjab, Haryana, Himachal and Delhi and interact with the concerned faculty and return with syllabi taught there within as short time as possible. The committee members left in the right earnest and surprised me with their alacrity. They returned with the syllabi for all the three years of the course after visiting five universities within just five days. They then sat for another week or so in the college overtime and prepared a thorough syllabus for the three year course. A special meeting of the Board of Studies in Management was convened by the university authorities with Prof. Ashok Aima HOD as Chairman and our teachers as members in the Jammu University. The syllabi were approved by the concerned authority in the shortest possible time. Of course, there was a problem, the University Syndicate which approves the courses meets once in a year and the meeting had already been held for 1997-98. However, to my relief, I was told that the rules gave special powers to the Vice-Chancellor to give provisional approval under special circumstances till formally approval by the syndicate. Prof. R.R. Sharma Vice-Chancellor was very considerate when I told him about the problem. He understood it and since his provisional permission was needed only for running the 1st year course, he readily agreed to do so. We immediately set the ball rolling and with the cooperation of Mr. Ram Saroop Director Colleges Development the approval was received well in time and that settled our worries.

Soon after I had taken over charge of the Commerce College, one Mr. Bhat Assistant Director of Indira Gandhi National Open University met me. He told me that the Government of Jammu and Kashmir had agreed to make space available for a study centre at Jammu. He also said that he was given to understand that the Commerce College had some space which could be made available. There was no such information available to me at that time so I asked him to see me again after some days. After he left I made enquiries from my office and came to know that my predecessor had spoken about Mr. Ajit Kumar, Commissioner Education having enquired if the request of IGNOU could be entertained by the Commerce College. A thorough personal check up of accommodation available in the college campus indicated that there were a few rooms in one of the wings which were not being used for quite some time. They required repairs for use and if made available to IGNOU there would not be any interference in our normal working as these were approachable from another gate of the college. After satisfying myself I enquired from Dr. Muzzafer, Director Higher Education, if any commitment had been made to IGNOU authorities about it. He invited me to his office and then both of us met Mr. Ajit Kumar for a discussion. Mr. Ajit Kumar seemed to be keen to start study centers of IGNOU in the state beginning with Jammu. No one could disagree with the benefits that such study centers would provide to those students who for some reason cannot join a regular college. But I told them that the college will require the accommodation itself to meet future increases in enrolment to run the present courses and any new courses we might start. So we could lend accommodation for a limited period of three to five years after which time IGNOU should acquire their own accommodation. Subsequently, Mr. Bhatt was also called for discussions and told about our conditions. He agreed to the conditions laid down by us. Soon agreement papers were signed followed by handing over the accommodation to IGNOU. I am happy to state in retrospect that it was a good decision to accommodate IGNOU for the obvious reason of promoting higher education.

The Minister of Education, Mr. Abdul Qayyum had himself started career as a college lecturer but had left after joining politics. He had a stint earlier also as a Dy. Minister of Education and took keen interest in the education sector. He was particularly concerned about fair conduct of examinations. So he visited the examination centers in March 1998 himself accompanied by the Vice Chancellor. Such visits have a salutary effect on the system of examinations and help stop malpractices. He was impressed with the conduct of examination at the Commerce College and conveyed it to me through his personal staff.

*****

In 1998 a student agitation erupted following the release of selection lists of Medical and Engineering colleges. The number of selected candidates in Medical colleges from Jammu was far less than those from Kashmir. The students from Jammu alleged that there was a clear cut discrimination. Although selections were made on the basis of an entrance test, it was alleged that the government was making unfair selections. The agitation took a serious turn when all the city colleges decided to participate under the banner of "Jammu University Students Front". The students of three main colleges namely Science College, Commerce College and MAM College gathered near the "Shahidi Memorial" outside the gates of Science College and blocked traffic on the Canal Road. On the first day, there was a standoff between the students and police. Contrary to the advice of my colleagues I went out and talked to the students and asked them not to block the road. I told them if they had any grievances they could agitate peacefully inside the campus of the college and write them on a paper and I would pass it on to the government. A large number of students were convinced and they returned to the college grounds. I asked them to sit down in the lawn and write a memorandum, give it to me and then go to their homes if they do not want to attend the classes. The students shouted slogans against the government for the unfair treatment of Jammu region and thereafter dispersed. After some time the mob on the road turned violent and police resorted to a lathi charge in which many students were injured. Some policemen also received injuries including a Superintendent of Police who fractured his leg. One of the students received serious head injury and he had to be hospitalized.

*****

At the Commerce College a certificate course in computers was introduced. It was open to our own students and also to outsiders for a small fee. We had hired the services of a very competent person to run the course. He was himself running a computer training centre in the city. In the year 1999, government appointed a permanent computer science lecturer in the college and I had to discontinue the services of the gentleman, reluctantly though. We also introduced a course in accountancy.

Student agitations are nothing new. Being young and emotional students can be easily exploited by those who have their axe to grind including the political parties. Sometimes these agitations turn violent and police resort to use of force resulting in serious injuries and fatalities. There is a permanent reminder of this fact outside the main gate of the Science College in the form of a "martyr memorial". In the year 1965-66, the students of Agriculture College R.S. Pura had launched an agitation against the government decision to declare agriculture assistants cadre as non-gazetted officers. Earlier the agriculture graduates were appointed as agricultural assistant in the gazetted cadre. The agitation was joined by the students of all the city colleges. It continued for several days and when it took a violent turn outside the Science College and the Old Jammu University campus (the Present Commerce College) on the canal road police resorted to firing in which some students died. Police bullets even entered the classrooms of the University Campus and many postgraduate students were also reportedly injured.

*****

We organized seminars and workshops on a wide range of themes and invited prominent persons from the society, media and academics to speak to our students. Among them I remember Mr. Teja Singh and Lalla Dwarka Nath (former Chairmen of Public Service Commission), Mr. Ved Bhasin (Chairman Kashmir Times group of Publications), Mr. Jatender Bakshi (former Chief Engineer), Dr. Syed Nasir Ahmed Shah (former Principal of G.M.C. Srinagar), Prof. Abrol (HOD Commerce J.U.), Prof. Vijay Prakash (Principal Science College), Prof. Kartar Nath (Principal M.A.M. College), Mr. Kuldeep Khoda (I.G.P., later Director General Police), Mr. M.M. Khajuria (former D.G. Police), Prof. Zahoor-ud-din (Registrar J.U.), Prof. Devinder Singh (Director College Development), Mr. Bodh Raj Bali (State Cabinet Minister), Mr. Dilaver Mir (former Cabinet Minister), Prof. A.N. Sadhu (HOD Economics J.U.), Mr. S.S. Kapoor (Education Commissioner and Later Chief Secretary), Prof. Mohd. Abdullah Charu (Chairman School Board), Dr. Muzzafar (Director Colleges), Prof. R.D. Sharma (Professor Commerce Dept. J.U. later Vice-Chancellor) and Prof. Ashok Aima (HOD Business Management later V.C. Central University Jammu). The college regularly published a magazine titled *Karan* and a newsletter for which Prof. K.L. Bhalla (HOD English) took great pains. A brochure giving information about the college and admission policy was also published every year. Cultural activities and sports activities formed an important part of programmes of the college.

The college did not have a hostel of its own. Since it was the only college providing courses in commerce in the Jammu Division we had a large number of students who came from far flung areas. For them we had arrangement with M.A.M. College and G.G.M. Science College for providing accommodation to a limited number of our students. Some students were forced to find their own accommodation which was an additional financial burden to their parents. With this in mind I approached the Chief Minister Dr. Farooq Abdullah to help me. He asked me if the college had some land available for the purpose. I told him that there was a small piece of land available in the college. He directed the Managing Director of J&K Projects Construction Corporation (JKPCC) to visit the site. The latter sent his team who found the piece of land too small. Then

I suggested that G.G.M. Science College be asked to make land available for the purpose. The ball was set rolling and I persuaded the principal of the Science College Dr. Surinder Saproo to help me in the process. I must express my gratitude to him as he cooperated and showed some vacant land out of which one site was selected for the purpose. The government acted quickly and the Minister of Education Mr. Mohd. Shafi took personal interest in the project. In the meanwhile, I retired and my successor Prof. Reeta Munshi then took keen interest in the project till it was completed. With the construction of a hostel of its own the Commerce College became self-sufficient to accommodate students coming from far flung areas.

*****

I would like to add here with regard to the student agitation mentioned earlier that the City College Principals were involved by the administration in a discussion regarding the agitation and it was agreed that student leaders be assured of a probe into their grievances. The agitation was thereafter called off by the student leaders. In the meanwhile much classroom work was lost. As it always happens a probe is ordered and finally nothing comes out of it. Even after this agitation the problem of fewer students from Jammu region getting selected in the competition for admission to the Medical Colleges continued. It later came to light that a number of cases of selections of wards of influential people were made possible by malpractices at the time of conduct of the test such as impersonation and leakage of papers to students who paid huge sums of money for it. Many such instances of malpractices in competitive examinations, at the national level too, for admission to high profile institutions and courses have come to light. These instances shake the very confidence of the aspirants and put a question mark on the reliability of conduct of these competitive examinations.

*****

With the introduction of BBA course we were feeling shortage of classrooms and laboratories. Not that lack of space was a problem for the purpose. In fact, there was a whole block of rooms available for the purpose, above the auditorium hall. At one time the Department of Biological Sciences of the University of Jammu functioned there. The block was in a dilapidated condition. It needed renovation. The college had idle funds available under the head of 'library security'. When students are admitted, the college charges from them a small amount as security which is refundable. Generally when students pass out they do not ask for the refund. Over the years the amount had swollen to a couple of lakh of rupees. This amount was sufficient to meet the cost of renovation. I contacted the administrative department for permission to utilize this amount for the purpose. The department agreed subject to the condition that a notification be issued in the newspapers for refund up to a stipulated period of time after which the amount would be forfeited. Accordingly a notification was issued in the local newspapers giving a period of one month. Only a few ex-students responded and they were refunded their security amount. When the stipulated period elapsed we asked the Govt. P.W.D. to give us a detailed estimate of the work. This they did in about a month's time. Thereafter the work was allotted to them in April 2000. The job was completed by the P.W.D. within three months. The block was ready before new session started in August 2000. We got the block inaugurated by Prof. Chaman Lal Gupta then Minister of State for Defense on 30th October 2000.

During the Kargil war one of our former students named Major Ajay Jasrotia had died fighting the enemy. We felt quite proud of a former student having sacrificed his life for the country. I therefore thought that the college library be named after him. A staff meeting was called where I put forth my suggestion. The staff members, some of whom had taught him, welcomed the idea. So all arrangements were made, a photograph was got from his parents enlarged and framed. It was put inside the library with a plaque bearing his name below it. A proper inauguration by Prof. Chaman Lal Gupta Minister of State for Defense G.O.I. was done in presence of parents, and grandparents, staff and students to honour the martyr on 30th October 2000.

*****

During 1998-99 academic session I changed the admission policy. It resulted in far reaching consequences in the academic standard of the institution. The college used to admit mostly plus two students from commerce and arts streams. There were just 50 seats left for those from science stream. So only 50 meritorious students from science stream were admitted while other applicants were disappointed. When I looked at the admissions made during the previous years, it became obvious that the cut off points for those from commercial stream students was far below as compared to those from science stream. This automatically affected the results. I approached the Higher Education Department and Jammu University to allow me to increase the intake capacity from 500 to 600 in the first year. They readily agreed because I did not press for additional staff. This opened the way for making a change in admission policy. I ordered that henceforth admission will be made purely on merit basis from commerce, arts and science streams. A common list was issued (instead of two lists as was done earlier) initially for 500 seats. After these seats were filled up; another list was issued to complete the full quota of 600 seats. This policy allowed entry of meritorious students from science stream as well as other aspirants from commerce and arts streams. As a result no applicant from whatever stream was denied admission. The quality of teaching and learning improved and the results also showed an upward trend. This policy ultimately helped the college to improve the standard and quality of commerce education. It also had an impact on the overall improvement of image of the college as became clear during the subsequent years. Commerce college which earlier had an image of rowdy teenagers on its rolls was transformed into a college of gentlemen. Admission of girl students in BBA also helped in improvement in the behavior of the students.

*****

During the year 1998, I remained mentally disturbed due to the serious illness of my younger brother Bal Krishan that I have mentioned earlier. I had a number of times to rush to Delhi and Mumbai for treatment of his Oral cancer. Despite our efforts in which, my sons and brothers helped he could not be saved and died at AIIMS New Delhi in September 1998.

Consequently the marriage of our younger son Kuldeep with Meeru, daughter of Mrs. Gyan and Mr. K.L. Dhingra, his colleague at Tata Consultancy Services which was finalised earlier had to be delayed due to untimely departure of Bal Krishan. Thank heavens the marriage could be solmnised at New Delhi six months later in March 1999 in presence of and with blessings of all elders from both the sides. They were blessed with a son, our second grandson Upmanyu on Christmas day in the year 2002.

*****

Our first batch of BBA (Bachelor of Business Administration) passed out in the year 2000. Most of them did extremely well in their final year examination held in March 2000. While some got immediate employment others applied for MBA in various institutions of the country. One of our girl students was admitted in IIM Calcutta and another one was selected by *Times of India* for administrative training course. On the whole, it gave me immense satisfaction that our students were doing well and Commerce College had emerged as a prestigious institution of Jammu. When I finally retired from service on 31 October 2000 I had the satisfaction of leaving an institution with a good reputation and a new image.

*****

During the summer of 2k I was deputed along with other staff members to supervise the conduct of Joint Medical and Engineering Entrance test being held at some centers at Srinagar. Actually as a consequence of the selections during the previous year and student agitation the government had decided that for conduct of these examinations, teams from Jammu would supervise the test at Srinagar and those from Srinagar would supervise the test at Jammu to eliminate doubts of any wrong doing. This gave me an opportunity to pay a visit to S.P. College Srinagar my alma mater. I was appalled to see the degradation of this premier institution that had occurred during the years of militancy. Militancy had not only dismantled the academic atmosphere in the educational institutions but even destroyed some buildings and infrastructure present there. Some girls schools and colleges were set on fire to discourage female education. Restrictions were put on the movement and dress of females especially students. S.P. College was in a bad shape. Gone were the lush green grounds and lawns which previously bore flower beds and now wore a deserted look. The Botanical garden from where we used to get materials for practical studies had turned into a jungle. I felt dismayed.

*****

After a break of many years I visited the college again in summer of 2013 and was pleased to see that things had started to change for better. Although the playgrounds seemed to have been dugout (perhaps for some repair work), yet the lawns bore flower beds as before. The buildings which appeared in disrepair during earlier visit gave a better look. The Botanical garden looked better but had not regained its pristine look. Some new buildings had been built and some more were in the process of construction. I did not get time to interact with students and the staff to ascertain the academic status. The Principal, however, told me that things had changed for better. Several years of militancy had disrupted normal academic and other activities of the institution. I was told that other institutions in the valley had suffered similarly during the painful years of militancy.

Chapter 13

The Seventh Exodus

In the chequered history of Kashmir persecution of the aboriginal natives, namely Kashmir Pandits, took birth the day Shah Mir set his foot on the soil there. According to Jonaraja, "Shah Mir from Swat arrived in Kashmir in the year 1313 AD along with his family, during the reign of Suhadeva (1301-20), who employed him and utilized his services. In subsequent years, through his tact and cunning Shah Mir rose to prominence and became one of the celebrities of his time. Later, after the death of the King Udhyenedeva (brother of Suhedeva) in 1338 AD Shah Mir managed to assume the Kingship himself and thus established the Shah Mir dynasty in 1339". From the fourteenth to the end of the twentieth century, the Kashmiri Pandits had to migrate from the valley to places outside seven times. The phenomenon that had started in fourteenth-fifteenth century continued with gaps, and the last (seventh) forced mass exodus took place in 1990; paradoxically what is also termed as migration took place under the very nose of the Central Government that professed to be secular.

The Muslim rule in Kashmir lasted from 1339 to 1819 AD. The local sultanate rule that lasted for a period of 247 years was the most troublesome for the Pandit community. Sikander, the iconoclast, ruled Kashmir for twenty-four years (1389-1413) and decimated the community to such an extent that only eleven families of the Pandits survived. It was the period during which the Pandits in the Valley were put alive into gunny bags and thrown into the Dal Lake at a place which to this day is called

"Bata Mazar", meaning graveyard of the Pandits. All their religious places were desecrated and lofty temples at Martand (Sun temple), Bijbehara, Awantipur, Pattan, Parihaspur, Lodhu and many other places were reduced to rubble. It was also during these 247 years plus the Afghan rule of 66 years (1753-1819 AD) that many Pandit families including Kauls, Nehrus, Kunzrus, Zutshis, Kathjus, Hangloos, Hastoos and others bade good bye to the valley and fled to other Indian cities for their settlement.

Events, however, took a favourable turn for the community during the rule of Sultan Zain-ul-Abidin (1420-70) popularly called "Badshah" and Kashmiri Pandits heaved a sigh of relief. The change of heart was brought about in the Sultan by the well-known physician Shri Bhat who cured him of a serious life-threatening disease. To reward his services, the Sultan relented and accepted his request to exempt the poor and suffering community from the unjust and oppressive taxes. He further obliged him and even persuaded the displaced Pandits to return to the valley. During the rule of Badshah, Kashmir progressed in all spheres of life and this period was indeed a golden era in the otherwise bleak and oppressive Muslim period.

The Muslim rule in Kashmir came to an end in 1819 AD, when Kashmir came under the Sikh rule. It marked the end of a long period of persecutions suffered by the Kashmiri Pandits during the Muslim rule. The Sikh rule lasted for a short period and was followed by Dogra rule (1846-1947). During this period of about hundred years the Kashmiri Pandits did not have to migrate and indeed was the most peaceful period for all the inhabitants of the state. As Pandits had a tradition of literacy and education they were employed on small and middle level jobs in the administration and also as teachers and physicians. Though a few of them got some administrative positions the important decision-making ones were held by the Dogra and Punjabi officers. Those Pandits who owned land took to agriculture and survived. Some even engaged themselves as small traders to earn a living.

The Dogra rulers are often accused of exploitation of the Muslims in general and peasantry and artisans of the valley in particular with some justification. They are alleged to have been subjected to heavy taxation which impoverished them. The Pandits were not the rulers but as employees, their services were utilized to collect taxes and they were seen by the Muslims as a part of the oppression. The truth, however, is that pandits by nature are kind and considerate people. A kind of forced labour called "begaar" was imposed on artisans as well as peasants. No doubt this institution existed even before but during the Dogra rule it reached its climax. Mercifully the institution of "begaar" or "forced labour" was officially abolished in 1920 during the rule of Maharaja Pratap Singh. Credit must also be given to the Dogra rulers especially Pratap Singh and Hari Singh in modernizing Jammu and Kashmir. They brought to the state industry, modern education and opened numerous schools for the purpose. Technical institutions, libraries and museums were established. Particular attention was given to arts, crafts and growth of literary activities. They encouraged poets and literary people and a lot of literature was published during their rule. They also encouraged collection of rare books and manuscripts. The two major libraries, one at Srinagar and another at Jammu, are a proof of the same. A network of roads and construction of bridges made communication easier. The Dogra rulers enacted laws to safeguard forests and wildlife. They also promoted trade and commerce. According to R.K. Sher, "one of the most important jobs done by them was to get land settlement done by Sir Walter Lawrence. The end of Dogra rule in 1947 in the wake of tribal raid and the establishment of a popular government under Sheikh Mohammed Abdullah, marked the beginning of another era of persecution for the Kashmir Pandits". Mr. Sher further writes, "there was no end to this persecution, of course not in the crude ways as was the case during the rule of the Sultans. Mirza Afzal Beg's advice to National Conference cadres was that they should not kill Pandits but find out ways and means by which their source of sustenance is withdrawn and in this process they would steadily and slowly leave the valley. This process was started in right earnest from 1950 and land reforms were implemented in quick succession for obvious reasons. The Hindus particularly the Pandits of Kashmir, were deprived of their landed properties, the sole means of their sustenance, and they were rendered paupers. Under the garb of land reforms entire landed properties were expropriated to the state without compensation and thereafter distributed among the Muslim peasants".

Not getting satiated with this step service rules were contrived under the pretext of giving due representation to the unrepresented or under represented communities so as to debar Kashmiri Pandits from joining the state service even on merit. The State service became the preserve of Muslims and just to look secular, a few Pandits having clout with the National Conference, were also taken into government service. The pressure on the means of sustenance of the K.P.'s was so acute that 80% of the youth born after the partition, left the state in search of livelihood. The remaining 20% were absorbed on pure merit in the Central Government offices and the banks operating from outside having branches in the State. In the State service supersession of senior, diligent and competent Pandit officials became rampant in the administrative machinery (R.K. Sher 1995).

During the Dogra rule from 1846 to 1947 the population of Kashmiri Pandits remained stable at 14 to 15%. After the land reforms in 1950 about 20% of the Pandit population left Kashmir. In 1981 the population of the Pandits in the valley had reached just 5%. Even this small fraction of Hindu population was an eye sore for the Islamists who had grown vocal over the years and Pakistan inspired insurgency provided the right opportunity to ethnically cleanse the valley. In 1990 almost all the Pandits living in Kashmir valley were forced to leave. In fact, Pandits had started leaving the valley in search of employment after their agitation in 1967. The majority community came under the magic spell of Islamists from across the border which forced the Pandits to flee their homes and hearths. Nobody stopped them from leaving. Local newspaper *Aftab* published a press release on Jan. 4, 1990 issued by Hizb-ul-Mujahideen asking the Pandits to leave Kashmir. *Alsafa* newspaper repeated the warning. These warnings were followed by Kalashnikov-wielding masked jihadits carrying on Military type marches openly.

Other methods to frighten the minority community were also utilized. Explosive and inflammatory speeches from public address systems of mosques became frequent. Audio cassettes carrying similar propaganda were played to instill fear into terrified K.Ps. Threatening letters and notices were pasted on their doors wherein they were asked to leave immediately otherwise their children would be harmed. The letters openly declared that Kashmir was only for the Muslims and there was no place for the kafirs in the land of Allah. These warnings signaled implementation of Jihadist's intentions quite blatantly. Quite a few brutal killing of Hindus were carried out in the first fortnight of January 1990 to bring home to the miniscule minority the intention of the insurgents. The Muslim majority kept quiet. Not a word was spoken even by those who were sympathetic to the Pandits for fear of their own lives. They quietly advised their Pandits friends to leave.

The night of 19 January 1990 proved to be the last nail in the coffin. During that night chosen intentionally by Islamic radicals to force the Pandits to run for their lives witnessed macabre happenings the like of which had never been witnessed before even in the darkest hours of Kashmir's history. Farooq Abdullah had resigned and Jag Mohan had taken charge as Governor just the previous night at Jammu. Though curfew was imposed, it had little effect. The mosque pulpits continued to exhort people to defy curfew and join jihad and terrorize the Pandits.

In the words of Col. T.K. Tickoo, "as the night fell, the microscopic community became panic stricken when the valley began reverberating with the War-cries of Islamists, who had stage managed the whole event with great care; choosing its timing and the slogans, interspersed with martial songs, incited the Muslims to come out on the streets and break the chains of "slavery".

These exhortations urged the faithful to give a final push to the kafirs in order to reign in the true Islamic order (Nizem-e-Mustafa). These slogans were mixed with precise and unambiguous threats to the Pandits. They were presented three choices—Ralive, Tsalive ya Galive (convert to Islam, leave the place or perish). Tens of thousands of Kashmiri Muslims poured into the streets shouting, death to India and death to kafirs."

These slogans, broadcast from the loudspeakers of every mosque, numbering 1100, exhorted the hysterical mobs to embark on jihad. Those who had organized such a show of force in the middle of the cold winter night had only one objective; to put fear of death into the hearts of the already frightened Pandits. In this moment of collective hysteria, gone was the façade of secular, tolerant, cultured, peaceful and educated outlook of Kashmiri Muslims which the Indian intelligentsia and the liberal media had made them to exhibit for their own reasons. Most of the Kashmiri Muslims behaved as if they did not know who the Pandits were. This frenzied mass hysteria went on till Kashmiri Pandits despondency turned into depression as the night wore itself out.

For the first time after independence of India from the British K.Ps found themselves abandoned to their fate, stranded in their own homes, encircled by rampaging mobs. Through the frenzied shouts blood curdling sloganeering the assembled mobs, the Pandits saw the true face of intolerant radical Islam. It represented the complete antithesis of the overrated ethos of Kashmiryat that was supposed to define Kashmiri ethos. It was the longest, coldest and the most frightful night experienced by Kashmiri Pandits in their lives.

The Central Government was caught napping and the army and paramilitary forces, in the absence of any orders did not act. The state police and administration also did nothing. The frightened Kashmiri Pandits found themselves left to the mercy of God and found best protection in huddling indoors and frozen with fear. They spent the night without a wink of sleep. They could clearly see writing on the wall. They had to leave the valley to avoid the fate of Tika Lal Taploo and many others. Another mass exodus of Pandits was inevitable. By day break it became clear that Kashmiri militants had decided that K.Ps had to leave the valley. Their vicious jihadi sermons and blood curdling shouts and threatening slogans like "Zalimo, O Kafiro, Kashmir Hamara Chhod Do" (you tyrant infidels leave our Kashmir); "Kashmir Main Agar Rahna Hai Allah-Ho-Akbar

Kahna Hai" (if you want to live in Kashmir you have to say God is Great); "Islam Hamara Maqsad Hai, Quran Hamara Rasta Hai" (Islam is our objective, Quran is our constitution); "Kashmir Banawon Pakistan, Batav Variae Batneiw Saan" (We will turn Kashmir into Pakistan with K.P. Women, but without K.P. men) (Col. T.K. Tikoo 2014).

To save their honour and life there was no alternative left for the Pandits but to leave the valley. The radical Islamists had planned it so meticulously in utmost secrecy that no Kashmiri Pandit got even the slightest wind of it. They were taken unawares with the result that property worth billions of rupees was left behind just to save their honour and life. Prior to taking this decision to force Pandits to leave, more than a hundred of them had already been slain. They left the valley for an uncertain future, penniless and with bare minimum clothes. To add salt to the injury the canard was spread that Pandits had left the valley on the instructions of the Governor Jag Mohan. One may ask: does anyone leave his home and hearth for an uncertain future at the behest of some one? What about the nationalist Muslims who too were forced to leave the valley?

It must be said to the credit of Mr. Jag Mohan that he exhibited great administrative acumen. He organized relief to such a large number of displaced people at Jammu, Udhampur and Kathua with great efficiency. The displaced people had become refugees in their own state and country. They were accommodated in government buildings, schools, sports stadia and tents. The Governor posted an honest and able officer Mr. Vijay Bakaya as Divisional Commissioner to overlook the relief and rehabilitation arrangements. The dimension of the problem was such that all the displaced people could not be accommodated. The good and generous people of Jammu came to their rescue and opened their doors to accommodate them. Even industrial sheds, garages, cowsheds and stores were cleared to accommodate them. It was a huge task to accommodate all and was indeed done with great efficiency.

Those Kashmiri Pandits who preferred to stay in the valley were not spared either. Wall posters in fairly large letters proclaiming Kashmir as an "Islamic Republic" had became a common sight in the entire valley. So were the prominent advertisements in local dailies proclaiming that the struggle was to establish supremacy of Islam, in all walks of life and any one putting hurdles would be annihilated. Press release of Hizb-ul-Mujahideen published in the morning edition of the Urdu daily *Aftab* of 1 April 1990 proclaimed, "Kashmiri Pandits responsible for duress against Muslims should leave the valley within two days". *Alsafa* of 14 April 1990 carried the news—"with Kalashnikov in one hand Quran in the other the mujahids openly roam the streets singing the "Tarana-e-Kashmir". Under such circumstances majority of those Pandits who had stayed back also left deserting their homes. Those Pandits and Sikhs who stayed back were punished for their stubbornness. In January 1998, 23 people—men, women and children in Wandhama village were taken out of their homes at night and killed in cold blood. In the name of Jihad even a two year old child was not spared. In July 1992, 121 Biharis and in March 2000, 26 innocent and God fearing Sikhs after offering prayers at a gurudwara at Chithisinghpora village were brutally gunned down. Same year in the month of August 32 Hindus including 29 Amarnath pilgrims were gunned down at Pahalgam. Again 24 Hindus were killed at Nandimarg village in March 2002.

The terrorists did not restrict their killing sprees to the valley alone they killed 17 Hindus on 13-14 August in 1993 at Kishtwar. Two mass killings in May 1996 and January 1998 resulted in 16 and 17 deaths at Simbar and Prankot villages in Doda district. The killing continued through the years 1998, 1999, 2001, 2002, 2003, 2004, 2005, and 2006 in Doda, Rajouri, Poonch, Udhampur and Jammu Districts. The purpose was to instill fear among Hindus and ethnically cleanse Doda, Kishtwar, Reasi, Rajouri and Poonch districts as well.

In the aftermath of the exodus of Pandits from the valley 18,000 houses were torched, about 150 places of worship and temples were desecrated, damaged and demolished. Numerous temples were burnt down, damaged and destroyed between 7 to 9 December 1992 after demolition of Babri Masjid at Ayodya by Hindu zealots on 6 December 1992. Even ancient ruins of temples protected as monuments by Archaeological Survey of India were not spared. Many Hindu educational institutions were also burnt down. In summer of 1995, 7 tourists from Gujarat were abducted from Dal Lake and killed in cold blood.

The Pakistan inspired, aided and abetted insurgency has ruined Kashmir and Kashmiris, including Sikhs, Hindus and Muslims. The mindless violence has cost not only precious lives but broken the special social fabric for which Kashmir was well known. The Hindus indeed lost their roots but the Muslims too lost their cherished Sufi culture to radicalized Islam. In the process the loss has been of the ethos and way of life peculiar to the Kashmiris.

One may ask who has gained from the mindless violence during the last twenty-six years. Certainly not the Kashmiris. While the Hindus lost their homes, hearths and livelihoods the Muslims suffered loss of life and experienced untold sufferings and lost peace of mind. There was an exponential increase in mental illness cases in the valley. Some people involved in insurgency might have gained financially but majority of the Muslims have been at the receiving end from the militants as well as from the armed forces doing their duty.

The situation is ably summarized by M.J. Akbar, "Pakistan does not want Kashmir now. It will want Kashmir within its boundaries in future, but not now. Its designs are much more dangerous than that. It first wants to bleed India well and particularly through Kashmir, and Punjab for it should be apparent to us that today's Kashmir is far more useful to Islamabad as a festering sore within India rather than a potent sore within Pakistan. The idea of an independent Kashmir, incidentally, is the biggest fraud, perpetrated on the subcontinent; no one with standing army—nor to mention a flying Air force is going to allow it" (Byline Sep. 29, 1991).

Recently the former President of Pakistan General Musharaf, facing treason charges in his country, said in an interview to a T.V. channel that Kargil war was forced upon India in retaliation for creation of Bangladesh. General Zia-ul-Haq who started insurgency in Kashmir did so with the same mindset. These Army men failed to realize that it was General Yahya

Khan and his foreign Minister Zulfikar Ali Bhutoo who did not allow Mujib-ur-Rehman, a Bengali leader to became Prime Minister of Pakistan despite having won majority of seats in the Parliament. Instead they arrested and put him in Jail in West Pakistan. They thus themselves sowed the seeds of creation of Bangladesh. Pakistani Generals have time and again said that they have not forgotten the humiliation of their defeat in 1971 and will go on inflicting a thousand wounds to bleed India. The proxy war in Kashmir initiated by them is a result of this mindset that has forced Kashmiri Pandits to become refugees in their own land.

Chapter 14

Wrath of *Vitasta*

September 2014 will remain etched in our memory for a long time to come for the deluge it brought to the State of Jammu and Kashmir. The State witnessed disastrous floods across majority of its districts caused by torrential rainfall. It also affected Pakistan Occupied Kashmir. Nearly 277 people in the Jammu and Kashmir state and 280 people in POK died due to the floods. It all started on 2 September when heavy rainfall started during the last stage of monsoon in India. This triggered flooding and landslides in Jammu and Kashmir and POK. On 5 September, the *Vitasta* (Jhelum) river at Ram Munshi Bagh was reported to be flowing at 22.40 feet (6.83 m) which was 4.40 feet (1.34 m) above the danger mark at Srinagar and 33.6 ft (10 m) at Sangam. The discharge rate in the river was recorded as 70000 m^3/s against discharge 2500 m^3/s. The Chenab river and its tributaries were also flooded causing heavy causalities and loss of property in Jammu region. As per the official sources several thousand villages across the state had been inundated and submerged completely or partially but Srinagar city was the worst affected. According to Greater Kashmir of October 8, 2014, "for five straight days before September 7—when the devastating flood ravaged the city—the meteorological department had sent alerts to the Jammu and Kashmir Government about the abnormally high rainfall hitting the Pir Panjal belt in south and central Kashmir. At one point the department even 'went beyond its duty' to warn the government that continuous rains could trigger flashfloods and landslides and disrupt road and air transport. Despite the MET warnings and alerts sent to the top administrative officials including the Divisional Commissioner Kashmir and Flood Control Department nothing was done. The specific warning sent by the MET on September 3 to the government four days before Srinagar sank, first time over a century—that ought to have sent alarm bells ringing".

Mr. Pawan Kotwal Commissioner/Secretary Flood Control Department, explained at a press conference on 30 September 2015 that on 6 September evening, a day before flood hit Srinagar, the government was expecting weather to improve after sky got clear of clouds and the level of water in *Vitasta* which was running 22 feet at Srinagar would at the most rise by another foot and would be manageable. Usually the government pressed alarm buttons when water rises to 18 feet in *Vitasta* at Ram Munshi Bagh (Srinagar) but even at 22 feet, the government was 'hoping' for situation to improve! With many parts of Anantnag and Pulwama districts submerged under five to eight feet of water for two days, it was any body's guess that flood water would ultimately move down to Srinagar.

Traditionally in a flood-like situation in the past, the government would order opening of two important locks the Kandizal embrankment and Dal Lake gate at Srinagar to ease pressure on *Vitasta*. Why this was not done? When the discharge in Jhelum had started to build towards the highest ever figure of 1.2 lakh cusecs against 1.4 lakh cusecs recorded in 1902, it should have alarmed the government. The carrying capacity of the river is 45,000 to 50,000 cusecs. But for some unknown reason nothing was done till the furious river breached embracement and flooded parts of the city mostly on its left side. Vast areas of the city were flooded with 10 to 15 feet of water. Whole buildings or parts of them crumbled and thousands of people were trapped in the upper floors and attics of their homes. Hundred were swept away or died in a watery grave inside their houses. *Vitasta* was in a great fury and took her revenge.

The flood took everybody by surprise and exposed the government's unpreparedness. Despite MET warnings as was obvious from the fact that some ministers and bureaucrats got trapped in the deluge and were battling for their survival. A senior minister was evacuated from an office near Ram Bagh after some days, while family of a junior minister was rescued a day after Srinagar was flooded. Even police was caught napping. A top police official was seen rushing to Sadder Police Station in slippers (Greater Kashmir 9 Oct. 2014). In order to reduce pressure Dal Lake gate lock was subsequently opened. As a result the flood waters entered and inundated all the buildings inside and outside the lake. An aeriel view of the city showed most parts of Srinagar and surrounding areas converted into a huge lake.

As admitted by the Chief Minister Omar Abdullah on 11 September there was no government for 36 hours and he resumed functioning thereafter with six officers in a room. It was indeed a deluge for everyone. Even the army cantonment area on the right bank of the river at Badamibagh was inundated along with the civilian population living in these areas. As stated by the Chief Engineer irrigation and flood control department in an affidavit before the State High Court the flood water would have created more devastation had it not breached embankment at Kandizal (in Pulwama) in the morning of September 4, which was followed by three more breaches within the area on September 5 and 6, subsequently at Dongripura and Kakapura on September 6, 2014.

The gravity of the situation was such that the Prime Minister Shri Narendra Modi after an aerial survey called it a "national calamity". In Srinagar, most of the city was submerged under the flood water. The river Jhelum spilled over submerging Pantha chowk, Batawara, Sonawar, Raj Bagh, Jawahar Nagar, Gogji Bagh, Wazir Bagh, Tulsi Bagh, Ram Bagh, and neighbourhoods like Chhanapora, parts of Rawalpra, Natipora, and Bemina.

According to Raj Nath Singh the Home Minister of India, several thousand villages across the State had been hit and 390 villages completely submerged. In actual figures 2600 villages were reported to be affected in Jammu and Kashmir, out of which 390 villages were completely subermerged, 1225 villages were partially affected and 1000 villages were affected in Jammu

Division. The first and second storeys of the houses and hotels in Raj Bagh that were packed with tourists were submerged. Hundreds of boats had been brought from Delhi and other parts of the country for rescue operations. Along with locally available army and civilian boats these were used to evacuate the trapped people.

According to official figures available, the air force used 82 aircraft and helicopters in the rescue work. Ten battalions of Border Security Force, 329 columns of Indian Army and 300 boats were used in the rescue operations. According to then Home Secretary, Anil Goswami, 10 VSAT systems were air lifted to restore critical telecom towers and satellite link from Bardula had been provided for crucial communication. The Indian army showing their ingenuity used some old fashioned Indian Juggar and converted their trucks to Mobile charging platforms for people to charge their mobile phones in the absence of electricity.

To provide food, water and medicines to the people, two IL76, one C-130J and one AN32 aircraft carried a total of 50 tons of supplies. 300 boats were dispatched to south Kashmir for evacuation of people from submerged areas. Armed forces including B.S.F. and National Disaster Response Force (NDRF) rescued over 200,000 people from different regions of Jammu and Kashmir. Bharat Sanchar Nigam Limited (BSNL) launched an operation on a war-footing with Indian Army and Indian Air Force (IAF) to restore mobile services through satellite network and telecom network.

According to Lt. General Subrata Saha of the Indian Army the rescue operations of the army would not have been possible without the assistance and efforts of the local youth. Every second or third boat of the Army went to the local volunteers. "The Army salutes the efforts put by the youth of the valley", he said, "if not for these local youth, who have guided us to reach the places I cannot say how we could have been able to accomplish the mission".

The Prime Minister of India, Narendra Modi offered an assistance of ` 745 crore ($120 million) to the state, this was in addition of ` 1100 crore ($180 million) already earmarked for the disaster. Chief Minister of Maharashtra announced aid of ` 10 crore ($1.6 million); C.M.'s of Madhya Pradesh, Tamil Nadu, Gujarat and Andhra Pradesh announced assistance of ` 5 crore ($810,000) each. The government of Telengana sent 50 water purifiers worth ` 2.5 crore ($410,000) for safe drinking water. Chief Minister of Jammu and Kashmir announced the relief assistance of ` 200 crore to the flood victims. An amount ` 3.5 lakh for the kin of those killed and an initial financial assistance of ` 75,000 for lost homes was also announced. Free ration of 50 kg of rice per family for a period of six months was also announced.

Air force dropped packets of food, biscuits, medicines and bottles of mineral water to the people stranded in first and second floors of their homes. It was indeed a herculean task to reach out to the people who were in great distress. Local NGO's, social and political organizations reached out to the people with succour. Yasin Malik made contact with the Pujaris and the Hindu yatris numbering around 200 stranded in the Dashnami Akhara at Maisuma and supplied them with rice, pulses, flour, sugar, water, tea leaves and other necessities for which they openly expressed gratitude to him.

In the Jammu Division, landslides triggered by heavy rainfall had damaged roads, dozens of bridges, buildings and crops. The rivers Chenab and Tawi were in great spate and vehicular traffic had been stopped on the Jammu-Pathankot highway. Katra bound trains were halted. The Jammu-Pathankot road was opened when the water level receded on 8 September. Srinagar-Leh highway was re-opened on 9 September. The State Government requested the Central Government to supply 25000 tents and 40000 blankets for the affected people on both sides of the Pirpanjal range.

At the time of writing the valley of Kashmir and particularly Srinagar and the surrounding areas have returned back to normal. The damaged structures including about 50 bridges however, remain to be repaired and restored. The preliminary assessment of damage and loss to property was a whopping ` 5000 to ` 6000 crore.

Following the calamity it was but natural for people in the civil society as well as in the government to ponder over the causes which led to it. The government came out with the theory that the flash floods around Kounsernag and Vaishew were the main cause of abrupt rise in water level in the Jhelum in the intervening might of September 6/7 which drowned the city. However, skeptics in the civil society doubted this as the main cause of the flood of this magnitude. They instead blamed the administration for their laxness and unpreparedness to meet the challenge. A senior minister of the coalition government blamed his successor for stopping the dredging of river Jhelum for one and a half years after he had left the department.

To my mind the nonstop incessant and unseasonal rain caused by Western disturbances for almost six days in the first week of September were mainly responsible for the disaster. In some places the rain fall was 400 per cent more than the monthly average. The magnitude of the floods would not have been so damaging had the people of Jammu and Kashmir in general and those in power ever since 1947 not fiddled with nature. Before 1947, Jammu and Kashmir had a well managed forest wealth, but after independence the forests, which till then had been protected from the ravages of deforestation became victims of vandalism-indiscriminate felling of trees. Lakhs of hectares of forests became degraded; while some degraded forests were cultureable, others were a "dead loss". It was indeed unfortunate, because deforestation brought in its wake floods due to soil erosion on mountain slopes (Kaul 1991).

It was barely a year ago that Uttrakhand was devastated by floods. There, also the rainfall was unexpected and extremely high. It killed more than 5000 people mostly pilgrims. We cannot ignore the fact that high levels of man made carbon emissions are causing change in global weather patterns and its natural consequence, i.e. climate change. The carbon emissions are heating up the atmosphere faster than normal. It is alarming to note that scientists who study monsoon patterns predict that heavy rain events will increase over the subcontinent in the coming years. The inter-governmental panel on climate change reports confirm that climate change will lead to increase in frequency, intensity, spatial extent, duration, and timing of extreme events. There is also evidence that Himalayan region will be worst hit with extreme rain events. Given that Himalayas are the world's youngest and most fragile mountain region, it spells big trouble. This is further compounded by the mismanagement of natural resources such as forests, lakes and water channels.

Most of the natural drainage channels have been destroyed due to utter mismanagement. It started with the Nalamar Project. The Nalamar channel was filled and converted into a road without thinking much about the consequences. The first causality of this project was degradation of the Dal Lake. Subsequently, all the back channels and wet lands in the city were filled up and converted into colonies. The traditional system of flood management was to channalise the water from the mountains into lakes and water channels. The interconnected Dal, Nageen and Anchar lakes were not only beauty spots but also its sponges.

As reported by Muddasir Ali (Greater Kashmir Oct. 9, 2014) an unprecedented growth of illegal residential colonies and government institutions in the flood basins had added to the already existing bad situation. The entire flood basin from Kandizal to Lasjan and the entire stretch of Nowgam-bypass have been converted into illegal residential houses. These had served in the past as water absorption basins. Similarly once flood basins Somerbugh, Soiteng, Padshahi Bagh, Kursoo and part of Pampore have also been turned into residential colonies. There has been mushrooming of illegal concreted structures in Jhelum embankments and basins, shrinking their water retaining capacity. In his report to the Jammu & Kashmir High Court, Deputy Commissioner Anantnag has pointed out that out of the total width of Jhelum, only one-fifth has been left out without encroachments.

The moot point is whether all these encroachments, illegal constructions were possible without the knowledge and connivance of government officials and politicians in power. Corruption, favoritism and vote politics has brought us to this situation. Srinagar Municipal Corporation must explain how such huge complexes like Srinagar Development Corporation, State Motor Garages, Hajj Authority and Jhelum Valley Medical College, etc. were allowed to come up in flood prone Bemina.

The horror inflicted by the flood of September 2014 could have been largely avoided had the administration been alert and taken the forecasts of heavy rain seriously. On the contrary, it chose to take it easy till the Jhelum unleashed its fury and drowned the Srinagar city and surrounding areas. It appeared that the holocaust unleashed by floods would turn the valley of Kashmir into Satisar once again for the sins committed by her inhabitants including the rulers. The inhabitants of the valley had chosen to say goodbye to common sense in favour of greed. All sorts of greedy characters appeared on the scene soon after the independence. The natural resources like forests were virtually looted and paupers turned millionaires overnight. Land mafia grabbed government land in connivance with unscrupulous government officials. Unauthorized colonies came up everywhere including on the banks of the Jhelum. As if it was not enough the river *Vitasta* considered holy for centuries by the inhabitants of the valley was desecrated and polluted.

At the end of the day it becomes imperative for us to listen to the warning of nature and take forecasts of the weatherman seriously. It is a well-recognized fact that climate change is a result of global warming. To avoid further holocausts, caused by floods we need to ponder seriously and take immediate measures so that a repeat of 2014 does not take place. To begin with the degraded forests must be restored on a massive scale and aforestation programmes must be taken in hand vigorously. Dredging of the river Jhelum, flood channel and Hokar sar must be taken in hand on a priority basis. Another flood channel must be dug starting from Kandizal area to relieve pressure on the Jhelum whenever floods occur. The lakes and wetlands must be restored to their original health using modern scientific techniques and methods. Pollution must be checked and there should be a proper management of solid wastes. Dumping of solid wastes into the Jhelum and other water bodies must stop. A sewerage system must be built on priority in all cities and towns and no municipal waste should be allowed into rivers, streams and lakes.

Our fore fathers had not assigned a sacred status to the rivers, lakes and water bodies for nothing. They had understood their importance in their daily lives. It should be understood that environment, of which rivers, lakes and wetlands are part, is not a waste bin into which we can dump anything at will. There is a limit even to the capacity of a waste bin. When it overflows with dirt and muck, the whole surrounding turns foul. Nature has bestowed our state with everything that is desirable and good for our economy and well-being. Let us restore the pristine glory of the *Vitasta*, other rivers, lakes, wet lands and forests so that the state of Jammu and Kashmir flourishes with wealth and beauty for all times to come. We owe it to our future generations to hand them down a beautiful and prosperous Jammu and Kashmir.

Chapter 15

Puri to Pontefract and Paris

I retired from service on 31 October 2k after rendering over 36 years of eventful government service. In December the same year Promila and myself left for Kolkata to attend the wedding of my niece Meenu with Satya. Attending the wedding was emotionally important for us because my brother Bal Krishan (Meenu's father) had died over two years ago. The wedding was well attended and passed off smoothly. Meenu had chosen a very nice young man Satya from a reputed and respectable Bengali family and that was a matter of great satisfaction to all of us.

When the marriage ceremonies were over we left Kolkata to visit Odisha. I had earlier visited Puri on a pilgrimage along with brothers Pushkar and Prediman and parents in January 1969. We had then visited Konark and Bhabuneswar also. Odisha had fascinated me and I wanted Promila to share my experience. We made Bhabuneshwar our headquarter and from there made daily forays to places of interest. Besides Jagan Nath Puri we visited Konark Sun Temple, Lingaraja Temple, Udayagiri and Khandagiri, Nandankanan Zoological park, Dhauligiri hills, Ashoka Rock Edict, and also Chilika Lake and Bird Sanctury.

The Konark Sun Temple is without doubt a piece of amazing architecture. The tall white marble statues of Vishwamitra and Maneka making love and other statues in stone are fascinating master pieces that have withstood the vagaries of time. One cannot but appreciate the hands that have depicted Kama Sutra perfectly and in detail in stone. The beautiful and buxom lady holding a mirror to see her image is awesome. Watching the biodiversity in the Chilika Lake and the Bird Sanctuary was an experience of a life time.

At Lingraja Temple, the caretakers maintain registers for the benefit of visitors. It reminded me of a similar tradition at Mattan (Martand) Temple in Kashmir. A visitor is asked the name of the place wherefrom he comes and a register is opened to see if someone from his family, clan, village, town or city have ever visited the temple before. My wife was amazed to see her name besides my name, that of son Anil, and those of my parents, brothers and sisters and also of grand and great grandparents recorded by my father Babuji during our visit in 1969. It is a good practice and pleases the people who come for a visit and see names of their family, relatives or even neighbours recorded in these registers. I used the opportunity to update the family record, including names of my sons Anil and Kuldeep, daughters-in-law Tina and Meeru and grandson Ahan. Upmenyu was not born then.

*****

Our older son Anil after serving as Registrar in General surgery at All India Institute of Medical Science for several years went to England in the year 2k for pursuing F.R.C.S. Intially an eminent Scientist W.J. Owen had offered him a position of Honorary Registrar—Surgery at the famous Guy's St. Thomas Hospital London for a period of six months. Thereafter he had an offer as a Senior SHO-General and Vascular Surgery at Pontefract General Infirmary, West Yorkshire in November 2k. His wife Tina was working as a gynecologist at Safdar Jung Hospital New Delhi at that time. She gave up that position and along with three year old son Ahan joined Anil at Pontefract.

After our return to Jammu from a visit of Kolkata and Odisha in January 2001 Anil and Tina invited us to pay them a visit during summer. We readily agreed but we needed to get our expired passports renewed. It took a couple of months. In the meanwhile, Anil sent us the requisite documents for submission along with our applications for grant of visa to the British High Commission in New Delhi and we applied for British visas. We were interviewed and instantly granted visas for six months.

That set the ball rolling for our first visit to the United Kingdom. Anil had also advised us to apply for a Schengen visa that would allow us borderless travel within 28 Nation Bloc of European countries. Since Britain was not a member of the bloc we had to apply for Schengen visa to the French Embassy in New Delhi. It was also granted within a couple of days.

Thus in the first week of July 2001 we took an Emirates Airlines flight to Manchester with a short stop over at Dubai airport. As our plane started to descend, the picturesque scenery of England caught our attention. The first impression that we had in our minds was that of a beautiful country with rivers, streams, lakes and mountains full of tree cover and greenery. The rows of nice looking houses with colourful tiled roofs added to the charm and beauty of the landscape.

As the plane descended further to land we noticed the well planned wide roads, parks, gardens besides the lovely and clean buildings arranged in rows. It was a complete contrast to many unplanned congested and disorderly colonies of the Indian cities and towns mostly shorn of greenery. We instantly fell in love with England. It reminded me how I wished as a primary school boy to visit the country of smart Mr. and Mrs. Edmund the British Christian Missionary teachers who along with their gentle German Shepherd dog used to visit our Haba Kadal school at Srinagar. In their lovely British accent Hindustani they spoke to us about importance of discipline, order, cleanliness and hygiene in our lives. The word picture of a clean, green and orderly city created by them in my mind instantly materialized before my eyes.

Tina and Ahan were waiting for us at Manchester Airport while Anil was busy performing some surgery at Pontefract Infirmary. They had come in a Taxi and received us warmly. Soon we were on our way to Pontefract, in West Yorkshire. I sat in the front seat beside the driver. In Britain they still continue with Right hand drive and keep to the left. After leaving Manchester the taxi took to the four lane motorway and was fast approaching one of the most beautiful and scenic areas of the United Kingdom namely the Pennines. Often described as the "Backbone of England" the Pennine hills form a more or less continuous range stretching northwards from the Peak District in Derbyshire, around the northern and eastern edges of Lancashire and greater Manchester, through the Yorkshire Dales past the Cumbrain Fells to the Cheviot Hills on the Anglo Scottish border.

It was less than 45 miles drive from Manchester Airport to Pontefract. We were soon in our home—one of the many two storeyed row houses built over a hundred years ago and yet in good shape. Anil had been allotted the two bed house located just opposite the hospital across the Friarwood lane. We were welcomed by smiling Sunflowers planted in the front Lawn by none other than our dearest four year old Ahan. He was genuinely feeling proud about it. The house had a sitting room, a leisure-cum-dining room and a kitchen in the ground floor and two good bed rooms and a large washroom. Anil came home soon after our arrival. After having lunch together we were advised to go to sleep to overcome jetlag.

When we got up from deep slumber it was well past seven in the evening. The sun was still shining bright in the sky in northern hemisphere. Days are much longer in summer and sun sets almost at 10 p.m. and rises at about 5 a.m. the next day. So nights are much smaller. The reverse happens during winter when days are smaller and nights are long. The summers are quite pleasant and you do not need fans. In fact, most people do not possess fans in their homes. You might come across pedestal fans here and there which can be counted on finger tips. That day we spent the evening chatting and reviving old memories.

Pontefract is one of the five famous towns in the Wakefield district, West Yorkshire with a population of about 29,000 people. It's name originates from the Latin Pontefractus which, means 'Broken bridge'. The town is famous for "Pontefract Castle" which was built around 1070 by Elbert d lacy and as a consequence the town suffered terribly throughout the English Civil War years. Oliver Cromwell described Pontefract castle as, "one of the strongest inland garrisons in the Kingdom". Now-a-days, Pontefract castle is absolutely ruined, and it is incredibly difficult to visualize how vast once it was.

Nonetheless, this mighty stone castle was a real force to be reckoned with and had such a feared reputation that it was even mentioned in the works of Shakespeare. Writing in the late 1500's Shakespeare used Pontefract castle (at his time Pomfret castle as a setting in two of his historical plays, Richard II and Richard III. In Richard II, the King is dragged to Pomfret castle where he ruminates on his life when imprisoned in the dungeons—and is killed as the play ends. In Richard III, Rivers is dragged to the castle, and describes it thus.

III. iii. 9
O Pomfret, Pomfret! O thou bloody prison!
Fatal and ominous to noble peers!
Within the closure of thy walls
Richard the second here was hack'd to death.

Other unfortunate events occurred in the castle. It was the place where Henry VIII's fifth wife, Catherine Howard, began her affair with Thomas Culpeper. Both were eventually beheaded for their ill-advised liason.

The castle was demolished after the townspeople's petition to the Parliament, begging for the same. It had been a long-time source of trouble for them, before and after the English Civil War. So the townspeople were too happy to see it's demolition.

Pontefract has now received grants from various sources for improvement, repair and renovation of the castle to make it fit for the tourists to visit. It is undoubtedly the most important historical castle in the whole of Yorkshire, and is well worth a visit. Other important towns close to Pontefract are Wakefield, Doncaster and Leeds.

Pontefract has been a market town since the middle ages and its location on deep sandy soil made it one of the few places throughout Britain where liquorice plants could be cultivated. While liquorice growing stopped some time ago, other long-standing traditions such as its public race course continue to provide entertainment for visitors and inhabitants alike.

After overcoming jetlag we settled down and found ourselves in very good company. Ahan had made friends with two little girls Loren (6) and Kaity (5) daughters of our immediate neighbours Mrs. and Mr. Bonner. After their parents left for work in the morning the pretty dolls would join Ahan and the home came alive with activity. The girls found themselves at home and would open well stocked refrigerator for juice, biscuits and cookies, etc. The kids became very friendly with us and occasionally would order us to accompany them to the park just across the road, adjacent to the hospital for cycling. It was a good pastime for us. While Tina busied herself in the household chores (she had not taken a job till then) we gave company to the kids in the busy park.

The English and all other Europeans love flowers and greenery. So you find their homes always displaying flowers in their window sills and in lawns. Flower beds are there everywhere, along the roads and in the roundabouts. There is greenery everywhere in the form of grass and plantations. You will not come across any one throwing used bottles, tins, empty cigarette packets, empty match boxes or any used items on streets. There are waste bins everywhere and people throw used things like packets, wrappers, etc. in them. Owners walk their dogs and remove their poop from footpaths in small polythene bags (that they carry in their pockets) and dump in the nearest bins kept by councils for the purpose everywhere in towns, cities as well as in villages. It helps keep surroundings clean, free of litter and prevents spread of infectious diseases.

As we got adjusted and accustomed to the place it became a regular habit to go for morning walks. Pontefract is more or less hilly like most of the Northen England and there was a small hill called "Rookery" with lots of trees and birds lying close of a mile away from our home. It became our favourite spot for going on morning walks there everyday. At the top of the hill, there was a huge agriculture farm belonging to a rich farmer who lived nearby. It was harvest time and we watched how wheat was harvested mechanically from cutting, to thrashing, winnowing and then packing of the grains. The straw too was rolled and then bundled and packed in polythene sheets mechanically. Sometimes, we discussed the farm practices with the farmer who would readily answer our queries. It transpired from these discussions that crop rotation was followed with sugar beat, mustard, peas and wheat sown alternately. The produce was good. We were surprised to know that farmers received substantial amounts of money from the government as subsidies to keep them in the job of farming.

Britain is a welfare state in the real sense. From Anil we learnt that the National Health Service (NHS) provides treatment free of cost including consultation, tests and medicines. Elderly are given passes for free travel in buses and trains within their own district. They also receive pension (if they do not have any other source of income). The homeless are provided accommodation as per their requirements by the local councils (equivalent of our municipalities). Education in government schools is free upto GCSE or O-levels (equivalent of our matric). The homes of poor and elderly are insulated at government expense against cold. They also receive benefits in the form of cash for heating their homes in winter. Utmost care is taken of the pregnant women and new born babies. For child welfare there are schemes that ensure that children are looked after well by parents and grandparents. Counselors visit homes and spend time with families and their children to see for themselves that kids are well fed, well dressed and live in clean hygienic conditions. Generally people love their children immensely and take good care of them. Despite all the safeguards some parents do ill treat their children; this happens only in broken homes where parents are divorced, poor or drug addicts.

With the opening of schools after summer break Anil and Tina started looking for a good nursery school for Ahan in the vicinity of their home. Luckily they found a good private school which was about half a mile away from home. Tina would drop Ahan in the morning and get him back in the afternoon using their car. When for some reason she could not go I would accompany him. Before his admission he had been going to learn swimming at a nearby swimming pool. Occasionally, I would accompany him. It was a wonderful experience to see little children as small as two learning how to swim.

At Pontefract like all other towns in England, there is good well stocked library. I started visiting it for reading newspapers like *The Times* and *The Guardian*. I found them very informative and developed a taste for reading articles on current issues—political and scientific. The library had very liberal rules for membership. I had to fill up a simple form and give proof of residence and identity. For identity I showed my passport and for proof of residence a recent telephone bill of Anil sufficed. It was so simple and I was issued a membership card within no time. During my stay at Pontefract I borrowed many books from the library mostly on British history and on both the World Wars. I also read books on their educational system.

United Kingdom consists of countries of England, Wales, Scotland, Northern Island and British Territory of Gibraltar. Education in the U.K. is a devolved matter with each of the countries having separate systems under government, the U.K. Government is responsible for England; whilst the Scottish Government, the Welsh Government and the Northern Ireland Executive are responsible for Scotland, Wales and Northern Ireland, respectively.

In each country there are five stages of education: early years, primary, secondary, further education and higher education. The law states that full-time education is compulsory for all children between the age of 5 (4 in Northern Ireland) and 16, the Compulsory School Age (CSA). In England, compulsory education or training has been extended to 18 for those born after 1 September 1997. This full time education does not need to be at a school and a number of parents choose to home educate. Before they reach compulsory school age, children can be educated at nursery if parents wish though there is only limited government funding for such places. Further Education is non-compulsory, and covers non-advanced education which can be taken at Further Education Colleges (FEC's) and Higher Education Institutions (HEI's). The fifth stage, Higher Education, is study beyond "A" levels or BTEC's (and their equivalent) which, for most full-time students, takes place in universities and other Higher Education Institution and colleges. During my stay at Pontefract I visited two colleges namely Park Lane College at Leeds and Coventry College at Coventry. It gave me an opportunity to see their working. I found many foreign students most of them Chinese enrolled in these colleges. I was told by the managements that Chinese mostly came to learn English language. The Chinese authorities, it seemed were eager that their nationals learn the international language to forward their trade and commerce in other countries of the world. Both Leeds and Coventry are lovely cities and there are many worth seeing places and monuments. The Church at Coventry destroyed by German bombers has been preserved as such as a reminder of the horrors of Second World War.

During our stay at Pontefract we discovered many commonalities between England and Kashmir. Beside similar climate fauna and flora also resemble to a great extent. Most fruit trees like Apple, Pear, Cherry, Plum, Peach, Apricot and Mulberry are found in plenty in England like in Kashmir. I found some common birds like sparrows, swallows, herons, crows, kites, ring doves, starlings, pigeons and water birds like ducks, swans, moorhen, coots and grebes as in Kashmir. Many herbs found in Kashmir like dandelion, common purslane. sorrel, mallow, rhubarb, small medick, buttercup, amaranth, medicago, spurge, calendula, etc. grow wild aplenty in England. There are also resemblances in trees like poplars, willows, pines, birches, oaks, junipers, hazels and maples. The last one namely maple (*Acer*) is more or less like a Chinar (*Platanus*) having similar leaves but they belong to different orders and families. The red deer of England has a close resemblance with Hangul of Kashmir. Similarly foxes, wild cats and jackals are also found in both the places.

England, Wales and Scotland have many interesting tourist spots. Except Wales which was comparatively a long distance away, we visited most places in Scotland and England. We started with tourist spots of interest in the vicinity of Pontefract followed by a visit to Edinburgh. The places close to Pontefract that we were taken by Anil and Tina on weekends included Wakefield, Leeds, Huddersfield, Doncaster, York and Hull. All these places have their own special Characteristics and tourist attractions like Cathedrals, museums and parks. Wakefield has a sizable population of Indians and Pakistanis. Leeds is also a well-known educational centre. Many of my teachers and well-known academicians of Jammu and Kashmir had studied here. It still attracts a large number of students from India.

York city's greatest attraction is National Railway Museum displaying earliest locomotives to the latest ones. York Castle and York Minster where Archbishop stays are other attractions. Visit to the old city centre and Jarvis Viking Centre was also memorable. In the old city, there are small houses with narrow stair cases leading to showrooms. These buildings reminded me of our own Zainakadal and Bohrikadal houses with narrow stairs leading to showrooms of handicrafts, shawls and carpets. Jarvik Viking centre gives tourists a chance to revisit the site of the last great Viking battle fought on English soil, where a King was slain and an extraordinary act of courage saw a lone warrior hold an entire army at bay! England was continuously attacked by Vikings—Scandinavian raiders and pirates from 8th to 11th century.

Huddersfield town is situated near the confluence of the River Colne and River Holme. It is a large market town being 11th largest town in the U.K. with a sizable population. It is known for the sport Rugby. There are two good colleges and a university at Huddersfield. Hull is situated on both banks of the River Hull in east Yorkshire. Some of the tourist attractions here are Streetlife Museum of Transport, the Humber Bridge (the longest suspension bridge in the world), Holy Trinity Church, Hull's Old Town, Hull Museum and Hull Maritime Museum. Hull is a university town and a popular cultural destination.

For a visit to Scotland we had to reserve hotel rooms at Edinburgh because of the tourist rush. Edinburgh and Glasgow are two major cities of Scotland and well-worth visiting. There are other places like Dumfries that are worth a visit. Edinburgh can be divided into two parts—the old town and the new town. The once old town was full of trade, over-crowded, with poor sanitation and dark history, yet rich in culture and neo-classical architecture. You can even find an underground city here as Edinburgh was built on top of itself. The new town stands in contrast with the old with its wide streets and neoclassical architecture.

The most prominent mark of Edinburgh is the Castle which sits on an extinct volcano. It dominates the Edinburgh's skyline and holds military and royal history. Holyrood Palace is another place of interest. The Queen resides in this palace when visiting Scotland. The palace also holds dark history of the murder of Mary Queen of Scots by her jealous husband Lord Darnlay. St. Giles Cathedral has been a place of worship since 854 A.D., however, most of today's building is less than 200 years old. Next to the St. Giles sits the old Scottish Parliament (1639 to 1707).

The Royal mile is a street in the heart of Edinburgh's medieval history. It is a must see because it is full of character and contains many attractions of the old town. It was a place where people lived, worked and traded and also a place of hangings and dark history. Another attraction is Carlton Hill. Edinburgh's most iconic views are seen here. It gives a clear view of Edinburgh castle and Arthur's seat dominating the skyline. Here one can also see one of Edinburgh's most iconic views where contrasting old town sits next to the new town boasting of Scottish's golden age. The time of the Scottish enlightenment which brought about neo-classical architecture and great thinkers like Adam Smith, father of economics, Alexander Graham Bell, inventor of the telephone, James Hutton father of geology and Sir Walter Scott the inventor of the novel whose monument can be seen from Carlton Hill, the largest ever built in honour of a writer.

The Edinburgh's new town came about due to poor sanitation and overcrowding in the old town. The new town was designed by a young architect James Craig in 1766. The main street of the new town is the George street with St. Andrews Square at one side and Charlotte Square at the other. St. Andrews Square is one of the most fashionable residential areas of Edinburgh.

One other attraction of Edinburgh is the National Museum of Scotland. This museum takes you through Scotland's early beginnings to the present day. There is much to learn about Science and Technology, Animal Kingdom and the Extinct remains from dinosaur period. Edinburgh University is one of the best universities of the United Kingdom and worth visiting.

Glasgow is number two city of Scotland. Set in a beautiful location like Edinburgh it is a hub of educational activity. Some of the attractions of this beautiful city are Kalvingrove Art Gallery and Museum, Glasgow Cathedral, Glasgow School of Art, Botanical Garden, Kalvingrove Park, Glasgow Science Centre, House for an Art Lover, Glasgow Green and Scottish Football Museum, etc.

It was during our stay at Pontefract that attacks on Twin Towers in New York took place on September 11, 2001. We had gone out for morning walk and on our return Anil gave us the heart breaking news. B.B.C. was beaming pictures of the attack on the Twin Towers and the chaos around them. Details of the attacks in New York city and on Pentagon in Washington D.C. started pouring in the day. The heart rending scenes beamed on the T.V. screens made one think about the ugly face of terrorism. If a powerful country like U.S.A. could be attacked like this what was in store for other secular states disliked by terrorist organizations like al-Qaeda, ISIS, Lashkar-e-Taiba, Hizb-ul-Mujahideen and Taliban. India was already at the receiving end from the terrorist organizations active in Pakistan. It was the terrorist organizations operating from Pakistan that had forced out the Hindus from Kashmir and made them refugees in their own country. By evening it was clear that the attacks were coordinated by terrorist group al-Qaeda on the United States on the morning of Tuesday, Sept. 11, 2001. The attacks consisted of suicide attacks used to target symbolic U.S. land marks.

Four passenger airliners—which all departed from Airports on the U.S. East Coast bound for California—were hijacked by 19 al-Qaeda terrorists to be flown into buildings. Two of the planes, American Airlines flight 11 and United Airlines flight 175, were crashed into the North and South towers, respectively, of the World Trade Centre Complex in New York City. Within an hour and 42 minutes, both 110-storey towers collapsed, with debris and the resulting fires causing partial or complete collapse of all other buildings in the World Trade Centre Complex, including the 47-storey 7 World Trade Centre tower, as well as significant damage to ten other large surrounding structures. A third plane, American Airlines flight 77, was crashed into the Pentagon (the HQ of the U.S. Department of Defense) in Arlington county Virginia leading to a partial collapse in the Pentagon's Western side. The fourth plane, United Airlines flight 93, initially was steered toward Washington, D.C. but crashed into a field near Shanksville, Pennsylvania, after its passengers tried to overpower the hijackers. In total, the attacks claimed 2,996 people (including 19 hijackers) and caused at least $10 billion loss in property and infrastructure damage and $3 trillion in total costs. It was the deadliest incident for firefighters and law enforcement officers in the history of the U.S. with 343 and 72 killed respectively.

Suspicion for the attacks quickly fell on al-Qaeda. The United States responded to the attacks by launching the War on Terror and invading Afghanistan to depose the Taliban, which had harbored al-Qaeda. Although, al-Qaeda's leader, Osama bin Laden, initially denied any involvement, in 2004, he claimed responsibility for the attacks. Al-Qaeda and Osama bin Laden cited U.S. support to Israel, the presence of U.S. troops in Saudi Arabia, and sanctions against Iraq as motives. Having evaded capture for almost a decade, Bin Laden was located in Abbottabed Pakistan and killed by members of American Special Force on 2 May 2011. Pakistan on its part had expressed complete ignorance about the whereabouts of Bin Laden.

*****

In the month of October 2001, Anil and Tina suggested that we should go on a European tour by coach and find out the best possible packages from local tour agencies. There were a few tour agencies at Pontefract and I contacted one of them. Many tour package by coach were available with some well-known tourist companies of London and I collected literature for discussion at home. Going through the various packages available we narrowed down to a 7 nights 8 days package offered by COSMOS of London for 750 Pound Sterling per head. It included our travel, stay in 3 or 4 star hotels, breakfast, dinner and transfers.

Next day we again visited the tour agency and they gave us a form to fill up and checked our documents. We were told that a coach would pick us up from Wakefield on 12 October

2001. We paid 1500 Pound Sterling against a receipt and two tickets. A couple of days later we received a phone call from COSMOS London expressing regret that they would not be able to pick us up from Wakefield due to some reason and that we would have to go to London to join the tour party on the fixed day. They also said that we would receive a refund of 50 Pound Sterling each if we agreed otherwise the whole amount paid would be refunded. I told them to give me a day to find out whether a morning train from Wakefield to London was available and call me again the next day.

A morning train from Wakefield was indeed available which would take us to London on 12 October. So we booked two return rail tickets from Wakefield to London for 12 October and from London to Wakefield for 19 October 2001. COSMOS called the next day and I agreed to their proposal. So our European tour was fixed now. The package that we had chosen included the European countries of Brazil, Luxembourg, Switzerland and France.

On the morning of 12 Oct. 2001, Anil dropped us at Wakefield Railway Station some 20 kms. away from Pontefract. The train left at 6.30 a.m. and we reached King's Cross Railway Station London at 8.15 a.m. It took us just fifteen minutes by taxi to reach the COSMOS office where coaches for different destinations were waiting. At the counter we were allotted a coach which would take us to Dover Ferry Port in South East England. Our coach left at 9 a.m. and within an hour we were at Dover. At the port our passports were checked and we were taken to the ferry that would take us across the English Channel to Calais in France. We were accompanied from London by a tour guide who organized everything for us including transfer of our baggage. We did not get time to see Dover except in passing. The White Cliffs of Dover, however, made their lasting impression on our minds. There was a pleasant surprise waiting for us as we met a Delhi based Kashmiri Pandit couple (Surname Bazaz) on the ferry who like us also belonged to Nai Sarak mohalla, at Srinagar. They too were on a European tour though on a different coach with a different package.

The ferry crossing lasted for an hour and half. On the other side of the channel was the Calais town of France. Calais overlooks the Strait of Dover, the narrowest point in the English Channel, which is only 34 km. wide here, and is the closest French town to England. The White Cliffs of Dover were visible from here as it happened to be a clear day. Calais is a major port for ferries between France and England, and since 1994, the Channel tunnel has linked the two countries by rail. The ferry crossing reminded me of *A Tale of Two Cities* a novel by Charles Dickens which was the English text in my B.Sc. class. The story is set in London and Paris before and during the French revolution.

At Calais we were received by a young French lady who spoke fluent English and introduced herself as Ms. Katherine our Coach Director. The Driver was an Albanian Muslim Abdyl who did not speak English. The Luxury coach which would carry us to different destinations in Europe had wide and comfortable seats. We were a party of 24 people including the driver and tour Director and would be together for eight days and seven nights. After formalities of checking our passports at Calais we were allowed to proceed on a very memorable tour of Europe.

From Calais we proceeded to Brussels in Belgium, at about 1 p.m. The scenery of the Countryside of both France and Belgium was quite picturesque. The climate was quite good and unusually pleasant for the month of October. The distance of about 200 km. from Calais in France to Brussels in Belgium was covered by the coach in about three hours including a stop over at Bruges a halfway point for refreshment and buying white Chocolate. At Brussels we were accommodated at Hotel IBIS, a three star hotel. After resting for an hour we were taken on a round of the city in the evening. Brussels is famous for its night lights. It is said that these light are so bright that they can been seen from the outer space. The language spoken in Belgium, Luxembourg and Netherlands is called Benelux.

We visited the following places of interest in Brussels:

1. Atomium is an impressive structure originally constructed for Expo 58, the 1958 Brussels World

Fair. Designed by the engineer Andre Waterkeyn and architects Andre and Jean Polak it stands 102 m tall and consists of stainless atom particles connected by escalators with exhibitions and views from 92 m. It was so close to our hotel that we went walking to see it.

2. Manneken Pis is a landmark small bronze sculpture, depicting a naked little boy urinating into a fountain's basin. It was designed by Hieronymus Duquesnoy the Elder and put in place in 1618.
3. Musical Instruction Museum is a music museum is central Brussels. It is renowned for its collection of over 8000 instruments. We saw it from outside only.
4. Cathedral of St. Michael and St. Gudula is a Roman Catholic Church in Brussels.
5. Brussels Town Hall is a Gothic building from the middle ages. It is located on the famous Grand place in Brussels.
6. Place Royale is a historic square near the center of Brussels.
7. The Belgian Comic Strip center Chronicles the history of Belgian Comics.
8. Parliamentarium is the European Parliament's visitor centre in Brussels. After a whorlwind visit of these sites we returned to our hotel where dinner was served. In the column of food preferences in the original booking application we had mentioned non-vegetarian but "no beef please". So during our entire visit, which included breakfast and dinner, beef was not served to the entire group. May be some others had also shown this preference. Our group included people of different nationalities. There were New Zealanders, Australians, Japanese, Thais, Americans including a couple of Indian origin and two of us Indians. The group included a newly married Thai couple on their honeymoon. In due course bonding developed amongst us despite the fact that we were

of different age groups ranging from 25 to 75 years and of different nationalities.

On 13 October 2001 an early morning knock on the door reminded us that we had to get ready for onward journey. After a wash and a self prepared morning cup of tea we went to the dining room where breakfast was served. By 9 a.m. we were ready to leave for our next destination Luxembourg city. The distance of over 170 km. was covered by our coach in about two and half hours. The scenic drive through the green hills of Belgian Ardennes was an enchanting experience.

The Luxembourg city is the capital of the Grand Duchy of Luxembourg a landlocked country in Northern Europe. It stands at the confluence of the Alzette and Petrusse Rivers in Southern Luxembourg. The city contains the Luxembourg castle, the Gothic Revival Cathedral of Notre Dame, AM Tunnel (underground art gallery), the Grand Ducel Palace, the Adolphe Bridge, the City Hall, Fort Thungen, the University of Luxembourg and Second World War American Cemetery and Memorial. The cemetery is the final resting place of 5,076 American military dead, including General George S. Patton. There is also memorial to 371 Americans whose remains were never recovered or identified.

Our stay at Luxembourg as per our itinerary was short and after visiting the land marks mentioned we proceeded to Switzerland. The distance from Luxembourg city to border of France and Switzerland was more than 470 kms. The coach passed through the main French cities of Metz, Nancy, Strasbourg and Mulhouse before touching Basel in Switzerland. The countryside of Eastern France is beautiful with large farms cultivating grape vines. France is famous for its wine industry.

From Basel we went to Zurich and then to the first stop in Switzerland namely village Sisikon in the Canton of Uri. Switzerland republic is a federation of 26 cantons. In Switzerland four languages are spoken. These are Roman, German, French and Italian. The currency used is Euro. By the time we reached our Hotel Eden it was late in the evening. We must have travelled more than 700 km. that day, most of it through plains but partly through mountains. There are wide four lane roads even in the mountains and traffic moves smoothly. There is also a network of railways and tunnels in Switzerland. We were received warmly at the hotel. After settling down in our rooms we were invited to have our dinner in a well decorated dining hall and served hot food including duck meat.

For the three days of our stay at Sisikon we had a hectic schedule. The Hotel Eden was our base from where we visited the most beautiful mountain locations of Switzerland. Sisikon is a beautiful village situated on the shore of lake Lucerne (Luzerne). It is dominated by the characteristic pre-Alpine peaks. It is an ideal departure point for hikes around the Urnersee. Sisikon has several history-steeped spots: on the lake shore 3 kms. South of the village is the Tell Chapel the place where legendary William Tell is reputed to have saved himself by leaping from the boat of Gessler the provincial Governor.

During our 3 day stay at Sisikon we were taken to a number of places including Lucerne city in Central Switzerland, a cruise of Lake Lucerne and a visit to the top of Mount Titlis. The Lake Lucerne is located at an elevation of 433 m. and has an area of 113.6 sq.km. It has crystal clear water and is very beautiful. All Lakes of Switzerland are clean and free from pollution. Mount Titlis Engelberg is at an elevation of 3,228 m. situated in the Alps. It is reached by cable-car and is the loftiest peak exuding a Snow and ice spectacular that is visually stunning. An Indian Restaurant atop served us hot and tasty Masala Dosa and Coffee. In Lucerne city there are some memorable spots like the Dying Lion Monument an awesome beautiful carving on stone, Glacier Garden, Lucerne culture and convention centre etc.

Our next destination was Vevey in Switzerland. Enroute we were shown Castle of Chillon on the shore of Lake Geneva with its frightening dungeons. We were also taken to cheese factory at Gruyere and saw how cheese is made. The beauty of Switzerland quite matches the beauty of Kashmir that is perhaps why Jammu and Kashmir is called Switzerland of India. I believe if we improve the infrastructure and provide comfort and facilities there is no reason why Jammu and Kashmir will not receive more tourists than it does now. For tourist arrivals calm and peace must prevail—unfortunately, however, some vested interests do not allow this to happen in Kashmir. The lakes and wetlands of Jammu and Kashmir are polluted and shrunk and are no match of the clean beautiful and well-maintained lakes and water bodies in Switzerland. We need to take a leaf out of their book for cleaning our lakes, increase our forest cover, create good tourist infrastructure and improve transport facilities for the sake of our own prosperity.

We reached Vevey in the afternoon of 16 October. It is a town in the Canton Vaud, in the north shore of Lake Geneva. It is a part of the French-speaking area of Switzerland and is noted for being the final home of Comedy legend Charlie Chaplin and his family from 1952 to 1977. It is also home to the world headquarters of the food giant Nestle, founded here in 1897. Milk Chocolate was invented in Vevey by Denial Peter in 1875. We stayed in the Hotel De Famille and from the window of our Hotel room we could see the lake Geneva the largest water body in Switzerland. Besides Vevey other important cities on the shores of Lake Geneva are Geneva, Lausanne, Montreux, and Saint-Gingolph. In the evening, we strolled through the town and found that there are as many as four museums and three Churches in the town. There are other land marks like the city Hall, Saint Jean Tower, La Gravette the granary, Charlie Chaplin Statue, the fountain Aile Castle and the administration and Historical Archives of Nestle. On our return we were served hot dinner as a guitarist played sweet melodies on his guitar. Our whole group which had by now become like a family enjoyed the meal as well as the music.

On 17 Ocober after a nice breakfast we boarded our coach once again for our journey to Paris. The coach took us from Vevey to Interlaken. It is a holidayer's paradise and very popular tourist destination. It comes under Bern Canton. The town is located between Lake Thun and Lake Brienz, and alongside the Aare river that flows between the two lakes. We stopped in the town for a short while but could not see the heritage sites because these were not in our tour itinerary. Our next stop was Beaune city in France where we had lunch before proceeding to Paris.

It was office closing time when we reached Paris and streets were congested with traffic. So our coach moved at proverbial snail's pace to reach Hotel IBIS situated at Porte De Montreuil, Avenue Prof. A. Lemiere, where we had to stay for one day and two nights on the last leg of our tour. After settling down in our rooms we were advised to have a look of the Avenue and nearby places and return for dinner at 8 p.m. sharp. So we stepped out of the hotel and walked some distance. I had to buy some medicines and found a chemist shop nearby. However, the French Pharmacist could not understand or speak English. I had to give him in writing the generic names of the medicines which he understood. Language barrier is one of the common problems faced by most tourists all over the world. However, it is a relief that English is understood and spoken in most tourist spots. People connected with tourist business in India, for example, do understand and speak English. Some have learnt German, French and Spanish which helps them greatly. We also visited a nearby Mall to buy yoghurt which we had not been able to take for many days. Again language was a barrier and the sales girls were not able to understand what we wanted. Fortunately we overheard two young customers in their twenties conversing in Punjabi. We spoke to them in Hindi and they helped us in finding yoghurt. They told us that they had come to France looking for work. We also found a beautiful brown coloured toy dog for Ahan which he instantly liked when we presented it to him back home. On 18 October soon after breakfast we were given a briefing by our tour director about the places that we would be visiting and cautioned us not to leave the group while going places. It was a lovely day and we boarded our coach for a very exciting sight seeing tour of Paris—the capital and most populous city of France situated on the bank of Seine River. Paris has an area of 105.4 square kilometers. The city was founded in the 3rd century B.C. by a Celtic people called Parisii, who gave the city its name. By the 12th century, Paris was the largest city in the Western world, a prosperous trading centre, and the home of the University of Paris, one of the first in Europe. In the 18th century, it was the centre stage for the French Revolution, and became an important centre of finance, commerce, fashion, science, and the arts a position it still retains today.

The places that we visited in Paris included the Louvre, the most visited art museum in the world as well as the Museum of French Impressionist Art and Museum of Modern and Contemporary art. We also visited the notable architectural landmarks of Paris namely Notre Dame Cathedral (12th century), the Sainte-Chapelle (13th century), the Eiffel Tower (1889) and the Basilica of Sacra-Coeur on Montmartre (1914). We also visited Joan of Arc Square and walked along the banks of Siene river. We took out some time to visit Rivoli Park in the heart of Paris and were astounded to see some East Europeans begging outside. While some members of the group went to see Palace of Versailles, we preferred to stay back to have a look of the city. For visiting museums we had to pay entry fee which was not included in the package. We were back in our hotel by dinner time. Since the Paris visit had been hectic we felt tired. The tour director advised us to go to bed early as we were scheduled to return to England the next day.

On 19 October after breakfast we boarded our coach for a trip from Paris to Calais. The distance was about 300 kms. and it took us about 4 hours to reach Calais. We had started at 9 a.m. and reached Calais at 1 p.m. The time to say good bye to our tour Director and coach Driver had come now. Earlier the group had decided to contribute some money for them as a token of our appreciation for making our trip so nice and comfortable. After a group photograph our charge was handed over to the guide who would help us to board the ferry to cross the English Channel and then again organize our return to London in another coach.

Both the ferry crossing and return coach travel to London were quite comfortable. After exchanging good wishes and salutation the members of the group bid good bye and went their own ways. We took taxi to King's Cross Railway Station for return journey to Wakefield. From the railway station we rang up Anil about our arrival in London. The train was due to leave at 5 p.m. As is well-known the British Railways are very efficient and trains leave and arrive on time. The return journey was full of nice memories of a trip made to four European countries. We also wanted to visit Germany, Austria, Italy and Spain but that would have to wait for some future date. At Wakefield Railway Station Anil, Tina and our dearest Ahan were waiting to receive us. Ahan was thrilled to see his stuffed brown dog. I asked him by what name he would call his dog. His immediate reply was "Timmy". Ahan is an animal lover and very fond of dogs. He wanted to have a dog which his parents resisted because they did not have time to attend to a pet. Seven years later, however, when they did get a Staffordshire bull terrier pup Ahan named him "Rocky". It has grown into a lovely dog. The two of them have developed a close bond.

The European tour left a lasting impression on our minds for a number of reasons. The cities, villages and towns are built in an orderly manner. The roads are wide and clean. There is greenery wherever you go. You will not find people throwing litter or urinating in open. Laws are strictly enforced by the authorities and obeyed by the people. There is freedom of movement and speech. The citizens mind their own business and prosperity is visible everywhere. We did not come across a single case of vandalism any where. The people are courteous, disciplined and no body tries to jump the Q. They love pets and keep them well. When walking their dogs they carry polythene bags to remove the poop of the pets immediately and dump in the nearest available dog bin. Last but not the least there are no borders between the European countries and they move about freely within the European Union. We did not have to show our passports anywhere except at Dover when going over to Calais and again on our return because United Kingdom has maintained its borders strictly. We did not encounter movement of troops anywhere in the four European countries that we visited. Second World War brought devastation in its wake and the European Nations learnt the hard way to live in peace. Can we too do it one day for peace, prosperity and development in South Asia?

Chapter 16

Britain's Own Ravana

As our first visit to Britain was coming to a close Anil and Tina suggested that all of us visit London to see some important landmarks of the great city. They took some time off from their work and on the morning of 3 November 2001 we proceeded to Wakefield Railway Station in their car. Leaving the car in the parking lot we boarded a London bound train and reached the impressive and busy King's cross Railway Station at about 10.30 a.m. After taking our breakfast at a restaurant outside the station we proceeded to Trafalgar Square. Built in 1845 Trafalgar Square is the most visited place in the Central London. At its centre is Nelsons Column, which is guarded by four Lion Statues at the base. There are a number of other statues and sculptures in the square. The square is also used for political demonstrations and community gatherings. We saw an Indian documentary maker picturising a scene at the site. There were also lots of pigeons picking food from the tourists. Some of them are so bold that they take it from your hands. Ahan was very excited to offer food to the pigeons with his own hands.

At a stone's throw from Trafalgar square is the Piccadilly Circus. It is a road junction and public space of London's West End, built in 1819, to connect Regent street with Piccadilly. It's status as a major traffic junction has made Piccadilly Circus a busy meeting place and a tourist attraction. The Circus is also famous for neon signs as well as the Shaftesbury memorial fountain and statue of Eros. It is surrounded by several notable buildings, including the London Pavilion, Criterion Theater and Burlington House which houses Royal Academy of Arts and the Linnaean Society (of which I am an elected Fellow since 2003).

From Piccadily we took a taxi to reach our hotel Holiday Inn in Russell Square which is a large Georgian square with statue of founder, the Duke of Bedford, plaza and water feature. By now we were quite tired and retired to our rooms for some rest. Later in the evening we walked around the area and discovered that the famous British Museum was very close to our hotel. There were some quite good restaurants in the area and after having our dinner in one of them, we returned to our hotel for night's sleep.

The next morning, we got ready early for a busy day. After breakfast we walked to the Russell square tube station which took us across the Thames river through the underwater tunnel. On our itinerary were a Cruise in the Thames, a visit to the famous London Tower bridge, a ride in the London Eye, and a visit to the Parliament House, Big Ben and 10 Downing Street, where the British Prime Minister lives.

Thames river cruise in without doubt one of the best ways to see London, passing through the heart of the city and past so many of its most famous attractions like the Big Ben, Tower Bridge, the Shard and HMS Belfast. The Cruise provided us an opportunity to experience the sights and splendor of the great city of London. We could also see Westminster and London eye from the cruise itself. After getting down from the cruise boat we proceeded to visit the historic London Tower Castle located on the north bank of the River Thames in central London. It was founded towards the end of 1066 A.D. as part of Norman Conquest of England. The White Tower, which gives the entire castle its name was built by William the Conqueror in 1078, and was a resented symbol of oppression, inflicted upon London by the new ruling elite. The Castle was used as a prison from 1100 A.D. until 1952 A.D. although not built for that purpose. A grand palace, it served as a Royal residence. As a whole, the Tower is a complex of several buildings set within two concentric rings of defensive walls and moat. London Tower is cared for by the charity "Historic Royal Palaces" and is protected as a World Heritage site.

The Tower Bridge crosses the River Thames close to the Tower of London and is an Iconic symbol of London. It is one of the five London Bridges now owned and maintained by the Bridge House Estates. It was built in 1886-94 and is a combined bascule and suspension bridge. The bridge consists of two bridge towers tied together at the upper level by two horizontal walkways designed to withstand the horizontal tension forces. The bridge deck is accessible to both vehicles and pedestrians.

Our next destination was the British Parliament. It is the supreme law making body in the United Kingdom, British crown dependencies and British overseas territories. It's head is the Sovereign of the United Kingdom (currently Queen Elizabeth II) and its seat is the grand palace of Westminster in Westminster, London. The U.K. Parliament and its institutions have set the patterns for many democracies throughout the world, and it has been called the mother of parliaments. Big Ben is the nickname of the Great Bell of the clock at the North end of the Palace of Westminster in London, and often extended to the clock and the clock tower. The Clock Tower (now called Elizabeth Tower) holds the second largest four-faced chiming clock in the world (Minneapolis city Hall having the largest). The tower was completed in 1858. It can be easily seen from the Westminster Bridge, a road and foot traffic bridge, over the river Thames linking Westminster on the north side and Lambath on the South side.

10 Downing street is at a walking distance from the Westminster bridge. Situated in the Downing street in the city Westminster, London, Number 10 is over three hundred years old and contains nearly one hundred rooms. The British Prime Minister lives here on the third floor. The other floors contain offices and conference, reception, sitting and dining rooms where the prime minister works and where government ministers, national leaders and foreign dignitaries are met and entertained.

The last place we visited on second day of our visit was the London eye. It is a giant and world's tallest cantilevered wheel on the South Bank of Thames river in London is 135 meters tall, and has a diameter of 120 meters. When erected in 1999 it was the World's tallest Ferris wheel but has been superseded in height by the 245 meters tall observation deck on the 72nd floor of "The Shard" which opened to the public on 1 Feb. 2013. It is the most popular paid tourist attraction and has 32 sealed and air conditioned ovoidal passenger capsules. Each capsule holds up 25 people. Also known as the Millennium wheel, London Eye receives more visitors than the Taj Mahal and the Great Pyramids of Giza annually. It offers the highest public viewing point in London and one can see up to 40 kilometers in all direction (that's as far as Windsor Castle on a clear day). At night it offers the most magnificent view of London.

London has a history dating back to over 2000 years. During this time, it has grown to become one of the most significant financial and cultural capitals of the world. It has experienced plague, devastating fire, civil war, aerial bombardment, and terrorist attacks. The historical sites in London are too many and during three days of our visit we could not visit all. We had to choose the more important ones.

So on the 5 Nov. 2001, the third day of our visit we sat down in the morning to choose the more important sites from our point of view and also visit those which would not take much of our time as we had been invited by Dr. Savitri and her husband Dr. Mike to be their guests for the night at their residence in Blackheath. It is an area of South-east London located East of the Town of Lewisham and South of the town of Greenwich.

Thus it was decided to visit Buckingham Palace, followed by visits to Madam Tussada's museum, Sherlock Holmes museum and Canary Wharf before proceeding to Blackheath. In London transport is very efficient. Taxis are available at every corner. London tube and the bus services are excellent. There are also tourist buses with guides that carry you to different interesting locations and you can even hop them. We preferred taxi because we were four adults and a little kid and it would be difficult to hop and would cost almost the same amount as the taxis. So we checked out from our hotel in Russell's square and took a taxi straight for Buckingham Palace.

The beautiful Buckingham Palace is the London residence and principal workplace of the monarch of the United Kingdom. Located in the city of Westminster, the palace is often at the centre of state occasions and royal hospitality. It was originally known as Buckingham House, the building which forms the core of today's palace was built for the Duke of Buckingham in 1703. It was subsequently acquired by King Georg III in 1761 for his queen Charlotte. During 19th century, it was enlarged and became the royal palace of the British monarch on the occasion of accession of Queen Victoria in 1837.

A visitor to the Buckingham Palace cannot escape to notice the Victoria Memorial in front of the main gates. It was created by sculptor Sir Thomas Brock in 1911 and erected in front of the main gates constructed by architect Sir Aston Webb. The visitors are allowed to see the Buckingham Palace exterior everyday between 9.30 a.m. to 6.30 p.m. They can also see the change of guard ceremony in the fore-court. The guards wearing a typical dress are called Beefeaters. The palace is also open for inside visits during summer when the queen is not in residence, for which a ticket has to be purchased. It costs the British Government Pound Sterling 15 million a year for upkeep of Buckingham Palace. From Buckingham Palace we proceeded to visit Madame Tussad's Museum which is a great tourist attraction located on Marylebone Road in Central London. It was set up by wax sculptor Marie Tussad in 1884. It is housed in the former London planetarium and is known for recreating life size Wax Models of celebrities. We took some pictures with our favorites like Indira Gandhi and Amitabh Bachchan. There are also Wax Models of Mahatma Gandhi, Jawaharlal Nehru, Rajiv Gandhi and Narsimha Rao besides celebrities from the fields of cinema, sports, politics, literature and science. We liked the models of Picasso, Madame Tussad, Charles Chaplin, Nicole Kidman, Queen Elizabeth II, Muhammed Ali, Muhammad Ali Jinnah, Benazir Bhutto, John F. Kennedy, Nelson Mandela, Martin Luther King to name a few. The attraction also houses its famous Chamber of Horrors.

Anybody visiting Buckingham Palace cannot miss the nearby large Hyde Park famous for mass demonstrations. Hyde Park is also known for its Speaker's Corner used by famous as well as by not so famous people to vent their spleen. The park is a classical example of freedom of speech and expression for which the Great Britain is well-known.

Our next place of visit was Sherlock Holmes Museum located at Baker street. Sherlock Holmes and Doctor Watson lived at this address 221B Baker street London, between 1881 and 1904 according to the stories written by Sir Arthur Conan Doyle. The house is protected by the government due to its special architectural and historical interest; while the 1st floor study overlooking Baker street is still faithfully maintained for posterity as it was kept in Victorian Times. The Museum is privately run since 1990 by Sherlock Holmes Society of England and is dedicated to the famous fictional detective Sherlock Holmes. It is in this house that Sherlock Holmes and Dr. Watson resided as tenants of Mrs. Hudson. Outside the Museum there stood a look alike of Sherlock Holmes and dressed like him. We stood with him for a photograph. By the time we left Sherlock Holmes Museum it was past 3 p.m. and felt hungry and entered the nearest McDonald's to eat something hot and crisp.

From the Baker street to Canary Wharf we took the underground train. It took us less than half an hour to reach Canary Wharf. Once outside the tube station we found ourselves among high-rise buildings and decided to Walk around the place. Canary Wharf is a major business district in Tower Hamlets east London. It is one of the U.K.'s two main financial centers along with the traditional city of London and contains many of Europe's tallest buildings, including the second tallest in Great Britain, on Canada square.

Canary Wharf is located on the West India Docks on the Isle of Dogs. From 1802 to 1939, the area was one of the busiest docks in the world. After 1960 the port industry began to decline leading to all the docks being closed in 1980. After the docks were closed the British Government adopted various policies to stimulate the redevelopment of the area, including through the creation of the London Docklands Development Corporation in 1981.

It was past 6 p.m. when we boarded the Monorail from Canary Wharf station to Blackheath station. It took us about twenty minutes to reach there. From the Rail Station we took a taxi to reach the beautiful double storey residence of Dr. Savitri and Dr. Mike. They were expecting our arrival and welcomed us warmly. Promila and myself were meeting them for the first time. Actually Dr. Savitri and Tina's mother Dr. Girija had worked together in early Sixtees in U.K. for their M.R.C.O.G. degree and became great friends. Later Dr. Savitri had married Dr. Michael Falcon and settled down in U.K. Dr. Girija had married Dr. Nasir Ahmed Shah and returned to settle down in Kashmir and both earned great reputation as outstanding doctors. During our conversation over tea Mike suggested that all of us join him to take part in the Guy Fawkes Day, Bonfire and Firework Night Celebration as it was 5th November. He also suggested that before that we settle down in our rooms on the first floor and take rest for a while.

At 7.45 p.m. sharp Mike called us downstairs. He was ready to take us to the nearby Blackheath Park where we would witness the Guy Fawkes Night Comparable to Dussehra in India. He put Ahan (they were already on friendly terms!) on his shoulders and asked us to follow him while Savitri chose to stay home to prepare dinner for us. So four of us Promila, Tina, Anil and myself followed him to the nearby Blackheath Park hardly five minutes walk from their home. There we saw assembled a large crowd of men, women and children and lots of hawkers selling candies, fruits, eatables and toys of all sorts. There were also food stalls and a bar. It was like an Indian Mela. At one end of the Park was built a tall lighted effigy which was clearly visible from where we stood. There was the usual noise that is associated with a Mela. Mike told us that the tall lighted effigy represented Guy Fawkes who was a bad man like the Indian Ravana. At exact 8 p.m. fireworks started and the whole sky shone with brilliant and colourful lights. The display of firework was notable for its beauty and variety. Unlike in India it was not noisy and there was no smoke to pollute the air. I do not know what materials they use for making them. This must have continued for about half an hour. We enjoyed it and Ahan sitting on a vantage point on the shoulders of tall Mike was ecstatic and like other kids shouted with joy. Then followed the burning of the Guy Fawke's effigy represented by the tall structure with fire crackers. The crowd made all sorts of gestures and loud cries as Guy Fawke's effigy went into flames. The scene was quite comparable to burning of effigies of the evil Ravana and his two brothers. As the effigy of Guy Fawke's burnt more fireworks started. The program then came to an end at about 9 p.m. I volunteered to carry Ahan on my shoulders back home. An Indian style dinner was waiting which Savitri had taken pains to prepare for us.

Guy Fawkes Night, also known as Guy Fawkes Day, Bonfire Night and Firework Night is an annual Commemoration observed on 5th November, primarily in Great Britain. Its history begins with the events of 5 November 1605, when Guy Fawkes, a member of the gunpowder plot, was arrested while guarding explosives the plotters had placed beneath the house of lords. Celebrating the fact that King James I had survived the attempt on his life, people lit bonfires around London, and months later the introduction of the observance of 5th November Act enforced an annual public day of thanksgiving for the plot's failure. Guy Fawkes is a symbol of evil and wrong doing and so is Ravana. Dussehra in India is celebrated as the victory of truth and righteousness over evil.

Within a few decades gunpowder Treason Day, as it was known, became the predominant English commemoration, but it carried strong religious overtones. It also became a focus for anti-Catholic sentiment. Towards the end of the 18th century reports appear of children begging for money with effigies of Guy Fawkes and 5 November gradually became known as Guy Fawkes Day. By 20th century Guy Fawkes Day had became an enjoyable social commemoration. The present day Guy Fawkes Night is usually celebrated at large organized events, centered on a bonfire and extravagant firework displays.

Guy Fawkes Night originates from the gunpowder plot of 1605, a failed conspiracy by a group of provincial Catholics to assassinate King James I of England and replace him with a Catholic head of state. The failed conspirators including Guy Fawkes were executed and the Parliament passed the observance of 5th November Act, Commonly known as the "Thanksgiving Act".

On the morning of 6 November 2001, after breakfast we took leave of our hosts at Blackheath and travelled by Monorail to Canary Wharf from where we travelled by tube rail to King's Cross where from we had already booked our return tickets to Wakefield. After paying at the parking meter for parking of our car Anil drove us back to Pontefract. The visit to London was a memorable one and we had enjoyed it the most. We saw many other parts of the great city of London during our subsequent visits and every time discovered something new and interesting. For example during a visit to the Regent Park in London we climbed to the top of the small hill and could see most of the land marks of London from there. Effigy of Guy Fawkes the Ravana of the Great Britain continues to be burnt on 5th November every year in London and other towns as we do on Dussehra to commemorate what is seen as victory of good over evil having universal appeal.

Chapter 17

Unification of Jammu, Kashmir and Ladakh

Credit for unification of disparate regions with diverse ethnicities, religions, languages, cultures and history into the Princely State of Jammu and Kashmir goes to the Dogra rulers. The state was constituted between 1820 and 1858 and was somewhat artificial in composition. It combined different regions, religious and ethinic groups: to the east, Ladakh was ethnically and culturally Tibetan and its inhabitants mostly practiced Budhism; to the south, Jammu had a mixed population of Hindus, Muslims and Sikhs; in the heavily populated Kashmir valley, the population was overwhelmingly Sunni Muslim and a small population of Hindus and Sikhs; to the northeast, sparsely populated Baltistan had a population ethnically related to Ladakh, but which practiced Shia Islam; to the north, also sparsely populated, Gilgit Agency, was an area of diverse, mostly Shia groups; and to the West, Poonch was Muslim, but of different ethnicity than that of the Kashmir valley.

The Princely State of Jammu and Kashmir with a total area of 84,471 sq. miles extended from $32^{0}\ 17^{\prime}$ to $36^{0}\ 58^{\prime}$ N. and from $73^{0}\ 26^{\prime}$ to $80^{0}\ 30^{\prime}$ E. Jammu the southern most part of the state was adjacent to the Punjab districts of Jhelum, Gujarat, Sialkot and Gurdaspur. There is a small level land along the Punjab frontier, bordered by sparsely wooded, broken and irregular low hilly area called Kandi. It is home to the Chibs and Dogras. In the north is a range of mountains some 8000 ft.

high with temperate climate and forests of oak, rhododendron and chestnut and higher up of deodar and pine. There lie the beautiful uplands Bhaderwah and Kishtwar. The mighty Chenab drains these mountainous areas. Further up are the Pir Panjal mountains leading to the Kashmir valley drained by the Jhelum river.

Further up lie steeper Himalyas leading to Astore and Baltistan on the North and to Ladakh on the east, a tract drained by the great river Indus. Far away to the north-west lies Gilgit, west and north of the Indus, the whole area shadowed by a wall of giant mountains which run east from the Mintaka passes of the Hindukush, leading to the Pamirs and the Chinese dominions past Rakaposhi (25,561 ft.), along the Muztagh range past K_2 Gadwin—Austen (28,265 ft.), Gasherbrum (28,100 ft.) and Masherbrum (28,561 ft.) to the Karakoram range which merges with Kunlun Mountains. West ward of the northern angle above Hunza-Nagar the mighty maze of mountains and glaciers trends a little south of east along the Hindukush range bordering Chitral, and so on into the limit of Afghan territory.

History

Jammu and Ladakh

Many historians and locals believe that Jammu was founded by Raja Jamboolochan in 14th century. During one of his hunting campaigns he reached the Tawi river where he saw a Goat and Lion drinking water at the same place. The king was impressed and decided to set up a town after his name as Jamboo. With the passage of time the name was corrupted to Jammu.

The descendents of Jamboolochan continued to rule Jammu till 1780. However, after the death of Ranjit Deo the kingdom of Jammu was captured by the forces of Ranjit Singh of Lahore and it became a tributary of Sikh power. After the death of Raja of Jammu, Kishore Singh, his son Gulab Singh was recognized by the Sikhs as his heir in 1820 for rendering distinguished services in Sikh campaigns especially the annexation of the

Kashmir valley by Sikh army in 1819. He then, initially under the Sikhs, began expanding his Kingdom.

As Raja of Jammu, Gulab Singh conquered Bhaderwah after a slight resistance and then annexed Kishtwar after the minister, Wazir Lakhpat, quarreled with the ruler and sought assistance of Gulab Singh. The Raja of Kishtwar surrendered without fighting Gulab Singh's forces when they arrived. The conquest of Kishtwar allowed Gulab Singh control of the roads leading into Ladakh which then led to conquest of that territory. Although there were huge difficulties, due to the mountainous terrain and glaciers, the brave Dogras under General Zorawar Singh conquered the whole of Ladakh in two campaigns.

A few years later, in 1840, General Zorawar Singh invaded Baltistan, captured the Raja of Skardu, who had sided with Ladakhis, and annexed his territory. The following year Zorawar Singh, while invading Tibet, was overtaken by winter, and being attacked when his troops were disabled by cold, perished with nearly all his army. The Tibetan forces were so impressed with his bravery that they raised a memorial in his honour at the place where he died. The memorial exists there to this day. By 1840 whether it was by policy or by accident Gulab Singh had encircled Kashmir.

In the winter of 1845 War broke out between the British and the Sikhs. Gulab Singh remained neutral until the battle of Sobraon in 1846, when he appeared as a useful mediator and the trusted advisor of Sir Henry Lawrence. Two treaties were concluded. By the first treaty the State of Lahore handed over to the British, as equivalent to an indemnity of one crore rupees, the hill countries between the rivers Beas and the Indus: by the second the British made over to Gulab Singh for 75 lakh rupees all the hilly or mountainous country situated east of the Indus and west of the Ravi.

Kashmir did not, however, come into the Maharaja's hands without fighting. Imam-ud-din, the Sikh Governor, aided by the restless Bambas from the Jhelum valley, routed Gulab Singh's troops on the outskirts of Srinagar, killing Wazir Lakhpat. Owing, however, to the mediation of Sir Henry Lawrence, Imam-ud-din desisted from opposition and Kashmir passed without further disturbances to Gulab Singh. At Astore and Gilgit the Dogra troops relieved Nathu Shah, the Sikh Commander who took service under Gulab Singh.

Not long afterwards the Hunza Raja, attacked Gilgit territory. Nathu Shah on behalf of Gulab Singh responded by leading a force to attack the Hunza valley; he and his force were destroyed, and Gilgit fort fell into the hands of Hunza Raja, along with Punial, Yasin and Darel. The Maharaja then sent two columns, one from Astore and one from Baltistan, and after some fighting Gilgit fort was recovered. In 1852, the Dogras were annihilated by Gaur Rahman of Yasin, and for eight years the Indus formed the boundary of the Maharaja's territory.

Gulab Singh died in 1857; and when his successor, Ranbir Singh, had recovered from the strain caused by the First War of Independence, in which he had loyally sided with the British, he was determined to recover Gilgit and to expand the frontier. In 1860 a force under Devi Singh crossed the Indus and advanced on Gaur Rahman's strong fort at Gilgit. Gaur Rahman, however, had died before the arrival of the Dogras. The fort was taken and held by the Dogra until 1947.

Kashmir

According to one folk etymology, the name "Kashmir", means "dessicated land" (from the Sanskrit: Ka = water and shimeera = dessicate). According to another folk etymology, following Hindu mythology, the sage Kashyapa drained a lake to produce land now called Kashmir.

With a fertile soil and temperate climate, the valley is rich in rice, vegetables and fruits of all kinds and famous for the quality of its wool. Kashmir has been inhabited since prehistoric times, sometimes independent but at times subjugated by invaders from Bactria, Tartary, Tibet and other mountainous regions to the North and from the Indus valley and the Ganges valley to the South. At different times the dominant religions have been Hinduism, Buddhism and Islam.

The first historical account of Kashmir is the Rajatarangini (the river of kings) written by Kalhana in mid 12th century.

It is a metrical chronicle of the Kings of Kashmir from the earliest time written in Sanskrit. It is believed that the book was written sometime during 1147-49. The work generally records the heritage of Kashmir, but 120 verses of Rajatarangini describe the misrule prevailing in Kashmir during the reign of King Kalash, son of Ananta Deva. Although earlier books are far from accurate in their chronology, they still provide an invaluable source of information about early Kashmir and its neighbours. Kalhana is rightly credited as the first historian of India because none before him had given a truly chronological account of the historical events.

Starting from the history of very early times (3102 BC) the chronicle comes down to the reign of Sangrama Dave (1006 AD). The second work called Divitya Rajatarangini by Jonaraja, continues the history from where Kalhana left off, and, entering the Muslim period gives an account of reigns down to that of Zain-ul-abedin (1423-74). After the death of Jonaraja his student Srivara carried on the record from 1459-86. The fourth work, called Rajavalipataka, by Prajnia Bhatta, completes the history of the time of incorporation of Kashmir in the dominions of the Mughal emperor Akbar in 1588.

By the early 19th century, the Kashmir valley had passed from the control of the Durrani Empire of Afghanistan and four centuries of Muslim rule under the Mughals and the Afghans, to the Sikh armies. In 1846, the valley came under the control of Dogra rulers after the signing of "Treaty of Amritsar". Thus was born the Princely State of Jammu and Kashmir as it existed in August 1947 when the British freed India but not before dividing it into two countries of Pakistan and India. Thus was also born the dispute over Kashmir between the two newly born independent countries. Consequences of this dispute will be discussed in another chapter.

Kalhana states in the Rajatarangini that the valley of Kashmir was formerly a lake. This was drained by the great sage, Kashyapa, son of Marichi, son of Brahma, by cutting the gap in the hills at Baramulla (Varaha-mula). When Kashmir had been drained, Kashyapa asked Brahmans to settle there. This is still the local tradition and in the existing physical condition of the country, we may see some ground for the story which has taken this form. The name of Kashyapa is by history and tradition connected with the draining of the lake, and the chief town or collection of dwellings in the valley was called Kashyapa-pura name which has been identified with Kaspapyros, Hecataeus and Kaspatyros of Herodotus. Kashmir is also the country meant by Ptolemy's Kaspeiria.

The common belief that Kashmir was once a lake is not far from the truth. From geological evidence it is clear that Kashmir remained under the Tethys sea, an ocean that existed between the continents of Gondwana (or Pangaea) and Laurasia during much of Mesozoic era, before the opening of the Indian and Atlantic Oceans during the cretaceous period. Fossils of marine fauna in the sendimentary rocks of Carboniferous to early Jurassic age like trilobites, molluscs and fish found there prove it beyond doubt that Kashmir was under Tethys sea at one time.

About 210 million years ago the map of the world was different from what it is today. It was then that the giant continent Gondwana or Pangaea, began to disintegrate and drift apart. Where the lands separated, the waters of the ocean rushed in to form new seas. Over the next 120 million years, the massive pieces of Gondwana drifted across the oceans of the earth, taking up new positions.

North America and Europe, which had been a single land mass drifted apart, and the Atlantic Ocean spread out between them. The African continent floated lazily for millions of years, before it joined up with Asia. Gradually, the world began to assume more of its modern-day appearance. In the beginning, the land that was to become India, lay almost to the south pole of the earth, tucked in between two other land masses, that would eventually become Antarctica and Australia. When the land mass broke up in the southern region, Australia was set adrift. So, too was the triangular plate, that would eventually become India. This plate of land floated steadily north, towards the mass of land that would one day become Asia.

While the continents were adrift, the dinosaurs achieved the peak of their origin. They had ruled the earth for million years. But quite abruptly (in terms of the planet's life span) they disappeared from the face of the earth, never to be seen again.

As the floating Indian subcontinent approached Asia, the sea was forced out. Finally, about 50 million years ago, the two vast land masses met head on. As India rammed into Asia, there were terrible upheavals on both sides. On the Asian side, the land was pushed upwards, creating the high lands of Tibet, on the Indian side, two giant slabs of rock were pushed up into the sky. These were to become the mighty Himalayas—the highest mountains in the world. The force of collision of the floating land mass was so great that for millions of years, the land was in upheaval. During this time, the Himalayas were shaped. The rocks rose upwards and then tumbled aside—again and again—as fresh seismic activity shook the newly formed regions.

Finally, the force of collision of the floating land mass was exhausted. The Himalayas as we now know them, had been formed. The remnants of the pre-historic oceans, that had closed in, were lifted thousand of feet high into the mountains and became the two great watersheds of the region. Flowing to the east were the Ganges and Brahmaputra. Flowing to the west were the five rivers, which formed the basin of Indus valley. Along these river valleys, millions of years later, would grow some of the world's greatest civilizations.

The valley of Kashmir, the Panjal consisting of outer plains, the outer hills and the Middle mountains and the Zanskar and Karakorum mountains share their origin with that of the Himalayas. The oval Kashmir valley lying 1700 meters above sea level is around 140 km. long and about 40 km. wide. It was indeed a huge lake as shown by satellite pictures filled by water flowing from the melting glaciers and snow of the surrounding mountains. Remote sensing and satellite pictures also lend credence to the common belief about its origin as a lake called Satisar which was got drained out by the sage Kashyapa as a result of his penance to drive out the demon which lived in its waters.

Scientifically it can be safely presumed that at some point of time a geological upheaval created a gorge near Baramulla (Varaha-mula) which resulted in draining of the lake. The presence of Karewas (Vodur in Kashmiri) in the valley and their structure also supports the idea that Kashmir indeed was once a lake. Despite the continuous erosion since a couple of million years, about half of the valley is still occupied by Karewa sediments. These sediments are dominantly lacustrine in origin.

Partition of India

Hari Singh, who had ascended the throne of Kashmir in 1925, was the Maharaja in 1947 at the conclusion of British rule of the subcontinent and the subsequent partition of the British Indian Empire into newly independent Union of India and the Dominion of Pakistan. An internal revolt backed by Pakistan began in the Poonch Jagir against oppressive taxation by the Maharaja. The Poonch rebels consisting of serving and ex-army men supported by Muslims of Punjab and NWFP declared an independent government of "Azad" Kashmir on 24 October 1947. Two days earlier, i.e. on 22 October 1947 tribals from NWFP accompanied by Muslim deserters of Kashmir Army and supported by Pakistani regulars launched a series of surprise attacks across Jammu and Kashmir. As is well-known the Pakistani invaders quickly overwhelmed the forces of Maharaja Hari Singh. Muzaffarabad fell within a few hours of the attack and the invaders after killing Hindus and Sikhs indulged in loot, rape and arson. They then proceeded towards Baramulla, Sopore and Srinagar. At the Uri Bridge Brigadier Rajinder Singh lost his life after putting up a valiant fight. He held the invaders for two days which gave time to Maharaja to flee the valley and the Indian army to intervene on his request. The Pakistani invaders on entering Baramulla indulged in rape, murder, loot and arson. They did not spare even nuns of the Christian hospital there. One valiant young Muslim nationalist Maqbool Sherwani misdirected the invaders and delayed their march to Srinagar for which they punished and killed him mercilessly.

The tribesmen engaged in looting and killing along the way perhaps to frighten the Maharaja into submission. Instead the Maharaja appealed to Lord Mountbatten Governor-General of India for help and he agreed on the condition that the ruler accede to India. Once the Maharaja signed the Instrument of

Accession (for which he had full support of Sheikh Mohammed Abdullah) Indian soldiers entered Kashmir and drove Pakistan sponsored irregulars from all but some parts of the state namely Mirpur, Poonch Jagir, Muzaffarabad, Gilgit and Baltistan. Mirpur, Poonch Jagir and Muzaffarabad comprised the so-called "Azad Kashmir" while Gilgit and Baltistan later called Northern Areas came directly under the control of Government of Pakistan. While the Pakistan-occupied Kashmir (POK) has its own nominal government, Northern Areas are directly administered by a political agent appointed by Pakistan since November 1947. After China occupied Aksai Chin during Sino-Indian War in 1962, an adjoining region, the Trans-Karakoram tract—a 5480 sq.km. territory in Shaksgam—was illegally gifted to it by Pakistan in 1963.

Chapter 18

Kashmir Conflict: The Way Forward

The Princely State of Jammu and Kashmir as it existed in 1947 was a Muslim majority State ruled by a Hindu Maharaja. The state consisted of disparate units differing ethnically, linguistically and culturally. It goes to the credit of the Dogra rulers that despite these differences they kept the state united for over a hundred years. However, the seeds of disunity were sown when the idea of division of India on the basis of Two Nation Theory started making rounds. The population of the state of Jammu and Kashmir on the whole was divided over whether the state should join the dominion of India or Pakistan. Muslims of the state were also divided over whether the state should join the dominion of India or Pakistan. They were divided in their aspirations—many in Jammu Province and in the Gilgit Baltistan wanted to join Pakistan. Equally majority of secular-minded Muslims in the Kashmir valley, Gojars, nomadic Bakerwals, Sikhs, Hindus and Buddhists favoured to join India.

In the aftermath of the tribal attack Maharaja Hari Singh had no option left but to request India to help him resulting in accession of the state to the Indian dominion. There were two factors: one that despite a stand still agreement signed with Pakistan, the latter engineered an attack to force him to accede to it; two the muslim population of the state was divided and the Hindus, Sikhs, Buddhists, Jains, Gojars, Bakerwals and Christians were solidly behind him to join India. Besides, he had the support of secular-minded popular leader of Kashmir Sheikh Mohammed Abdullah.

Prior to partition of India polarization had started in Jammu and Kashmir as in other parts of the country. There was a Muslim uprising in Poonch. The Muslims there were Punjabi speaking and always had close affiliations with western Punjabis. They did not like dominance of Kashmiri speaking Muslims of the valley whose undisputed leader Sheikh Abdullah held secular views. When the tribals attacked the state the Muslim Ex-Army men of Poonch joined them. The Poonch Muslims favoured joining Pakistan and no sooner did the tribals attack the State than did they declare independence and formed the so-called "Azad Kashmir".

The polarization of population of J&K state resulted in that the so far passive subjects of Jammu became active some supporting and others opposing the Maharaja. These actions of the population politically and physically divided the princely state into pro-Pakistan and pro-India factions. The tribal attack added fuel to the fire resulting in communal violence in Muzaffarabad, Poonch, Kotli, Mirpur, Rajouri, Udhampur and Jammu. The Valley and Ladakh, however, remained free from communal violence. While the whole subcontinent was burning Kashmir and Ladakh remained untouched and acted as a beacon of light. It earned praise from Mahatma Gandhi who said that he could see a "ray of light" in Kashmir alone.

It is thus obvious that even prior to the partition of India the people of the princely state of Jammu and Kashmir were not unanimous in joining either India or Pakistan. The Maharaja was also not able to decide one way or the other. The simmering discontent among the Muslims of Poonch and the desire of some Muslims of Jammu on one hand favouring accession to Pakistan and Hindus, Sikhs, Buddhists, Jains, Gujars, Christians and Muslims in the valley in favour of India on the other hand must have put the Maharaja in a fix. There was a clear cut division among his subjects and he remained undecided. It is believed that he toyed with the idea of declaring his state as an independent country. Pakistan's impatience to grab Kashmir using tribal raiders as a cover changed all that forcing him to accede to India.

Kashmiris on their part following the raiders attack united and formed a people's militia to defend themselves. Young men and women united and organized themselves to defend the citizens from the invading Pakhtoons supported by regulars of Pakistan army. These raiders after looting, raping and pillaging Kashmiris wanted to capture the state for Pakistan. Had the raiders not indulged in their criminal activities and come straight to capture Srinagar they might have even succeeded in their mission but that was not to be. Majority of Kashmiris have never wanted to became a part of Pakistan—neither then nor now.

The people of the princely state of Jammu and Kashmir were politically conscious and they always wanted to determine their own future following the partition of India. True, they were not unanimous in their opinion whether to join Pakistan, India or remain independent. Given the time and choice to decide they might have even succeeded through mutual consultations and talks to come to a conclusion. However, that could not happen because of the violent interference from Pakistan side.

A precious opportunity was thus lost in 1947-48 itself and much water has flowed down the Indus, Jhelum, Chenab and Tawi rivers since then. The third option of an independent Jammu and Kashmir was lost there and then and the dispute now involves only two parties namely India and Pakistan. In 1972, Shimla Agreement clearly declared that all differences between India and Pakistan were bilateral issues. This line has been followed in India-Pakistan composite dialogue since January 2004. Even in Musharaf-Singh talks that apparently came close in 2007 to resolving the dispute did not involve the people from both sides of the divided Jammu and Kashmir. The Indian and Pakistan negotiators are not prepared to countenance the "third option" of independence of J&K. As a matter of fact the only point on which both the countries agree in their dispute over Kashmir is that neither Jammu and Kashmir nor any part of it can become independent.

The proposition of the Azadi seekers to unite the state of Jammu and Kashmir into an entity as it existed in 1947 is an impossible task. The state as it existed in 1947 is simply an imagined entity. The ceasefire of 1949 that has divided the state into parts controlled by Pakistan and India is the only reality now. Despite India's claims that Pakistan Administered Kashmir (POK) as a part of Hari Singh's J&K state belongs to it, the reality is that these cannot be reclaimed from Pakistan any more. While the Northern Areas offer India strategic opportunities in relation to China but economically backward and rabidly Islamist POK will be a liability.

Pakistan on its part has not made POK an integral part of it in the hope that one day it might succeed in obtaining more of Jammu and Kashmir particularly the Muslim majority Kashmir valley through a proxy war. This is a dream that cannot come true. Pakistan has tried to occupy Kashmir by force in 1947, 1965, 1971 and 1999 (Kargil War) and failed. The only way to end this dispute is by talks and negotiations.

The present position has been analyzed by Christopher Snedden (2013) in his well researched book *Kashmir—The Unwritten History*. I quote him—"My assertion that J&K is now an imagined entity relates to the second change in the Kashmir dispute: the former princely state is never likely to be reunified. Since 1947 the five regions of J&K have become heavily integrated with and dependent on their metropolitan powers. With the obvious exception of the disgruntled Kashmir valley, J&K's other four regions appear to be reasonably content with this arrangement. Jammu and Ladakh want to be with India; POK and Gilgit-Baltistan appear happy being with Pakistan. India and Pakistan also, do not want to lose any of the areas in J&K into which they have put substantial efforts and resources since 1947.

Equally neither nation appears to want to, and neither seek to obtain, the (potentially hostile) areas of J&K "occupied" by the other. India does not want to obtain (Muslim) POK and (Shia Muslim) Gilgit-Baltistan. Pakistan does not want to acquire (Hindu dominant) Jammu and remote (Buddhist/Shia)

Ladakh. The only area both appear to want to possess is the (Muslim) Kashmir valley where ironically, most people appear uninterested in joining either nation. Finally neither nation's military has the capability, or the will, to capture the entire state, including the hostile areas currently outside their control. To capture all of J&K is too difficult because of its size and challenging terrain, the difficulty of long and vulnerable supply lines, and the ability of entrenched incumbent forces to oppose vulnerable attacking forces. Furthermore, this task is now seemingly impossible—undesirable—given that India-Pakistan military rivalry now includes a significant nuclear dimension. A divided, dis-aggregated J&K will therefore continue".

So far so good but his assertion that the people of the divided Jammu and Kashmir alone can settle the dispute does not appear possible. The fact remains that the stakeholders are too many in number, holding divergent views and opinions with hardly any meeting ground. For example, although the majority of the people of POK and the Kashmir valley share a common religion, yet they differ linguistically and culturally. There is not much common between them. Besides, even though they share Islam as their religion, their sects like Shias, Sunnis, Ahamdias and other sects stand poles apart in their views. Then there are other stakeholders-like Kashmiri Pandits, Sikhs, Christians, Bakerwals and Gujars who are pro-India. Many Kashmiri Pandits under the banner of "Panun Kashmir" want a separate "homeland" within the valley. They are not prepared to settle for anything less after having been forced to become refugees in their own land by none other than Kashmiri Muslims. Having been embittered by the forced exodus from the valley, they justifiably want a separate "homeland" as a union territory. People of Jammu and Ladakh as Christopher Snedden himself says are pro-India. So where is the meeting ground, among the disparate populations of the erstwhile princely state of Jammu and Kashmir. Further India is in full legal control of Kashmir valley and other parts like Jammu and Ladakh whereas the areas under Pakistan are held by it illegally. They were occupied and never acceded to Pakistan. Legally these occupied territories belong to India. The United Nations resolutions about which

Pakistan and Kashmiri separatists talk so frequently require Pakistan to vacate POK. Will they do it? What about the areas of the erstwhile princely state that Pakistan has gifted to China? Under what right or authority did Pakistan do it?

India has a strong claim to retain the Kashmir valley for a number of reasons. The Maharaja legally acceded to the Indian dominion and sent her forces at the request of Hari Singh to throw out the Pakhtoon raiders and others who accompanied them. As such it is totally wrong to say that the Indian forces are "occupation forces". India is a secular democratic country with a Muslim population more than that of Pakistan. So to say that Kashmir valley on the basis of a Muslim majority should go to Pakistan is flawed. What about the Indian Muslims who are truly nationalist citizens of India? India has also spent significant effort and money to develop the Kashmir Valley and is in the process of developing it further. In contrast Pakistan has left POK totally backward and underdeveloped in all respects.

Pakistan on its part considers itself incomplete without Kashmir but majority of Kashmiris do not want to join Pakistan. Some of them want to be independent. Pakistan has tried proxy war since 1989 which has brought death and destruction to the people of the state. It has destroyed the very ethos and social fabric of Kashmir commonly known as "Kashmiriat". The harmony in which all religious groups and sects lived before has been shattered. Almost the entire population of peace—loving and harmless Kashmiri Pandits, who had lived there for over five thousand years were forced out of the valley by terrorists sent by Pakistan who indulged in brutal murder and rape of innocent people mostly Hindus and Sikhs. Most Hindu houses and shrines were set on fire and destroyed.

Vast majority of Kashmiri Muslims are followers of Sofi Islam. They dislike violence. The massacres of innocent men, women and children by the terrorists at Sangrampura, Vandahama, Chithisinghpura, Nadimarg, Prankote, Champanari and many other places shocked them. They disapproved of it and frowned upon these brutal killings. As a result of these violent actions of terrorists but for a minority of radicalised Muslims none likes Pakistan and Pakistanis in Kashmir.

As a consequence of the proxy war waged by Pakistan through the foreign militants and terrorists the Indian State machinery had to act. The para military forces, the local police and the army personal were duty bound to counter the threat of destabilization of the state and to protect the people and their properties. In a war-like situation the civilians no doubt are caught in cross-fire and some lose their precious lives. Many misguided local youth who were trained in use of arms by the Pakistanis also joined the militancy and waged a war against the State. In October 2015 former President of Pakistan Pervez Musharraf admitted that Pakistan had supported and trained insurgent groups to fight in Kashmir during 1990's resulting in ongoing insurgency. He called terrorists like Osama Bin Laden, Haqani, Maulana Azhar and Hafiz Sayed Pakistan's "heroes". Therein lies the real problem. The mindset of Pakistani Generals and rulers eulogizing terrorists as heroes is the big hurdle in solving differences between the two nations.

As the insurgents hid in thickly populated urban and rural areas that inevitably brought hardships to the people as the armed forces came looking for them. In the exchange of fire unfortunately innocent people died. This angered the local population and alienated them from India. Their anger that should have been directed against the militants hiding amongst them was cleverly deflected by their master's proganda machinery towards the armed forces and the police. Thus the Indian state came under people's wrath and anger. In such situations people lose rationale. One may ask whether men in uniform except the local police were ever seen anywhere before the proxy war started in 1989. They were confined to their barracks. Besides the Indian army is known the world over as the most disciplined force. How can any country afford to allow insurgency to destabilize it? The aim of the enemy is always to turn the peaceful population against their protectors using insurgents. On the part of the Indian Government, there is an urgent need to take steps which will ameliorate the hurt feelings of the common Kashmiri Muslims and try to end their alienation. The separatists also need to be roped in to join the mainstream politics and participate in elections. The Indian

Government may or may not talk to Pakistan on Kashmir but it does need to talk to common Kashmiris who are Indian citizens.

Dispute over Kashmir has cost both the nations dearly. It's resolution is in the interest of both the countries. Scarce national resources have been diverted from vitally—needed development and nation-building projects into creating massive and costly military equipment and nuclear capabilities. The two developing nations need to use their precious resources in nation-building and tackle the teething problems of poverty, illiteracy, food security and health care prevalent among their people.

I agree with Christopher Snedden that there is the need to give up individual egos and competing ideas of nationhood based around religion, and mutual suspicions. Many in Pakistan falsely believe that India wants to re-integrate their country. This is far from the truth. Pakistan is a separate country and nation and India cannot even think of reintegrating it. On its part India also needs to take measures to remove such false notions from the minds of Pakistanis. Creation of Bangladesh is cited by many Pakistanis as an example. However, they need to understand that creation of Bangladesh was a result of machinations of Zulfikar Ali Bhutto and Pakistan army to prevent Sheikh Mujib-ur-Rehman, a Bengali, from becoming Prime Minister of their united country. The Pakistan army indulged in genocide of Bangalis. The East Bengalis fled to India to save their souls. India on its part had to look after millions of refugees from East Pakistan. With memory of 1965 war inflicted on her fresh in mind India found an opportunity to break a belligerent and troublesome neighbour. It was Pakistan's own fault and creation.

The happenings of the past have created a serious trust deficit between the two countries resulting in hard posturing. India's superior strategic position regionally and economically makes it a bit hard for Pakistan to digest. To counter it Pakistan has found it easier to inflict a thousand cuts on India using jihadists bred in the radicalized seminaries run by dozens of organizations like LET and Jaish-e-Mohammed and others. The policy of using radicalized jihadists has now started bouncing back. Recent events of suicide bombers exploding themselves in churches, mosques, schools, universities and at public places to cause death and injury should open the eyes of the rulers and people of Pakistan. It should be understood that terrorists have no religion. They are mad fanatic men ready to kill and get killed with a false notion of landing in heaven. *Jihadists with a false notion of reaching heaven create hell on this earth.* As Prime Minister Modi at a recently held conference on terrorism organized by President Obama in the US rightly said, "Don't think that his terrorist is not my terrorist". *Terrorism is a scourge* and threat to the whole mankind and needs to be tackled internationally as a human problem.

Partition in 1947 resulted in untold miseries, death and destruction to the people on both sides of the divide. As rightly pointed out by Christopher Snedden and I feel inclined to agree with him that, "neither India nor Pakistan engaged in any type of healing touch to acknowledge what the division had meant to the dislocated and distraught people. None tried to reconcile and heal the sorrow and sadness that resulted from the trauma of the division. With the passage of time the two nations should have tried to give peace a chance but instead indulged in hostilities. To it added the closed nature of the borders between them. Had there been a free flow the people would have shared their grief and partition stories and learnt from them that the partition had inflicted wounds equally on all religions and communities. Grieving together over the death and destruction would have helped them come closer emotionally". After all they had been living together as good neighbours for centuries. Keeping them apart did not help.

In order to come closer there is a need of showing generosity and honest cooperation, initiated by the Prime Ministers, of the two nations. The past experience of not talking to each other frankly and in a spirit of give and take has subjected the people of the two countries, especially those living on the borders, to hardships and sufferings since 1947. The people living on the two sides of the ceasefire line in J&K are often dislocated by unprovoked exchange of fire. The anti-Indian uprising in Kashmir valley since 1989 has resulted in the exodus and trauma of Kashmiri Pandits from the valley and they have been forced ever since to live as refugees in their own land. They have suffered a lot physically, mentally and psychologically. The uprising in Kashmir has compelled the Indian armed forces to suppress the Pakistan supported militancy and insurgency resulting in loss of lives. The armed forces too have suffered losses of men and materials as a result of attacks by armed insurgents.

It goes to the credit of Prime Ministers Narendra Modi and Nawaz Sharif that they want to improve relations between the two countries step by step so that peace prevails in the region. The two nations have fought four wars after 1947 and gained nothing except destruction. Despite sharing so much history, geography, language, culture and ethnicity ordinary Indians and Pakistanis rarely meet. Travel between the two countries is not easy due to which people of the two sides are ill informed or even ignorant about each other. They are not only ill informed but also fed with false information and propaganda by radical elements resulting in hatred for each other.

The atmosphere of hostility and hatred needs to change. The two nations need to learn a lesson from the Europeans. After the conclusion of Second World War the Europeans understood the futility of fighting which resulted only in death and destruction. It took them a long time to recover from the large after effects of the war which had impoverished them. They understood that peace alone leads to prosperity and development. Today all the Europeans have come under the umbrella of the European Union. They have a common currency (Euro) and they can travel freely within the Union. Trade and commerce has expanded and affluence is visible everywhere. South Asia is a large subcontinent. There is no reason why SAARC countries cannot emulate the European experience and help each other in development of their countries. It requires will and grit on the part of the leadership to say good bye to the old animosities and egos. We need to look forward for the progress of our nations and people.

The Way Forward

The Kashmir dispute has indeed come in the way of normalization of relations between India and Pakistan. While India legitimately considers Jammu and Kashmir as its integral part, Pakistan thinks it is incomplete without the Kashmir valley. Pakistan's interest lies more in water that flows from the state to it than in Kashmiris even though "Indus water treaty" is more favourable to Pakistan than to India and yet it grumbles. It has objected time and again against the legitimate use of our rivers for hydroelectric projects. It has objected to use of Jhelum waters for navigation purposes in the valley. It has raised water issue in every meeting and called for World Bank arbitration on one disputed dam and taken another to International Court of Arbitration at Hague. Kashmiris are intelligent enough to understand what attracts Pakistan to annex their motherland to it. They do not want to join Pakistan and instead want 'Azadi'.

'Azadi' (freedom) of Kashmir valley is not an option though either for India or for Pakistan and the reason is simple. Both the countries understand the strategic importance of Kashmir and would not like it to become a hotbed of international intrigue and trouble. Furthermore, Kashmir valley as an independent entity cannot sustain itself economically. The Indian part of J&K state has always been dependent on its survival on the liberal Central Government assistance and funds. It is not even self sufficient in food grain production and depends on the Union Government for their supply. The only point on which India and Pakistan agree totally is that 'Azadi' of Kashmir valley is not an option at all (Christopher Snedden).

Dialogue between the two neighbours is the only option to solve their disputes. It may be a slow process but there is nothing that cannot be settled by sitting across the negotiating table in a spirit of friendship and give and take. Despite occasional hiccups the dialogue process is on. Peace has to be maintained for the sake of the region and the world. The first and the foremost task is to start with taking confidence building measures. Our past experience has been that during talks when ever India raises the issue of confidence building Pakistan wants to put cart before the horse. A complex problem requires patience and we have to start somewhere.

Pakistan needs to understand that it is currently facing internal and foreign issues. It has to tackle unstable border with Afghanistan. Pakistan's relations with Iran also border on hostility. There is also domestic violence and instability in Pakistan caused by home grown armed groups who terrorize civilians as well as armed forces alike. India also has its own share of problems especially that of Naxals in some states.

Besides these issues confronting the two nations poverty caused by inequalities between rich and poor is a major problem and Kashmir is no longer the priority that it once was. With the hardened attitudes of the two nations on the issue the wider populations on both sides of the divide are no longer interested in Kashmir. Perhaps this is the best time to work out a solution. The present day Prime Ministers of both the countries want to tackle the issue seriously and they need to be supported. If the two countries talk seriously the non-state actors would get a clear signal that they are irrelevant and peace will get a chance. On his part Prime Minister Modi has set his priorities about Kashmir and peace process with Pakistan. Prime Minister Nawaz Sharief also needs to do the same.

There is a problem, though, in negotiating a peace process. In Pakistan army has a role in politics; this is not so in India. If there has to be peace in the subcontinent the meddling of the Pakistan army has to stop. To tackle militancy and insurgency in Kashmir the Indian armed forced have had to act tough. In Pakistan army created extremist and terrorist groups to inflict wounds on its neighbours. These groups are perhaps no longer in its control now. The proverbial 'djin' (demon) is out of the bottle invisible and uncontrollable. If Pakistan army resolves to control these Kashmir—sympathizing armed jihadists, lasting peace between the two countries can be achieved. The moot question remains whether Pakistan army has the will to control the Jihadists and stop meddling in politics.

Recently Dr. Farooq Abdullah had suggested that the LOC should be converted into an International Border. It has also been suggested before by many intellectuals and political thinkers of India. It is indeed a good suggestion and perhaps the only one possible solution for peace to return to the subcontinent. Although India rightly claims that the whole princely state of Jammu and Kashmir has legally acceded to it, yet the reality is that large chunks of land are in the control of Pakistan. It is not possible to wrest these parts of the state from Pakistan without a war. Pakistan waged four wars with India to wrest Kashmir but failed. POK and Gilgit-Baltistan are do facto parts of Pakistan now. If LOC is converted into an international border these become dejure parts of Pakistan. Likewise the parts of Jammu and Kashmir with India are fully integrated with it. People of Jammu and Ladakh are happily integrated with India. Before Pakistan sponsored militancy the valley Kashmir was as peaceful as any other part of the country. The alienation of the people of Kashmir started only after the militancy. Once the LOC is converted into international border and interference from Pakistan stops the people of Kashmir will settle their grievances with the Indian Union on their own. Although most Indians would wish that the state of Jammu and Kashmir stays united in its present shape, yet there can be many options like trifurcation of the state, grant of greater autonomy to the valley with provision of "home land" for displaced Pandits within it having Union territory status. Or a solution like that of Northern Ireland in the Great Britain among many others. For all this to happen peace is the pre-condition. Terrorist attacks and stone pelting must come to an end in the valley. It has helped none and has brought only misery to the common man.

There is also need of reviving spirit of reconciliation between Muslims of Kashmir and the dislocated Hindus currently living in exile. When peace prevails the dislocated Kashmiri Pandits will find it safe to return to the valley and start living there as before with Kashmiri Muslim as good neighbours. Kashmir's future with a secular India is safe and prosperity will reign again. If peace prevails using words of Shri Narasimha Rao, sky in the limit, for the growth and prosperity of the people of Jammu and Kashmir. Once LOC is converted into an international border the two neighbours can concentrate on the welfare of their people.

They will divert precious funds from purchase of arms to their nation building and prosperity will reign the subcontinent. All that is needed is a STRONG POLITICAL WILL on both the sides. Like in the European Union we can also make travel easier between the SAARC countries. This will allow greater people to people contacts and better understanding of each other.

Let us hope wisdom prevails in the two countries and leaders shed their egos and resolve differences amicably and peacefully. When peace prevails our subcontinent will become envy of others. I want Kashmir of my childhood and youth to return to its old glory and regain the title of the "Valley of Rishis" represented by Lal Ded and Nund Rishi. Let it become the "Happy Valley" of my childhood and youth once again and attract tourists and pilgrims alike. Peace needs to prevail for growth and prosperity of the Jammu and Kashmir State.

EPILOGUE

In the last chapter, I had advocated peace between India and Pakistan and resolution of the Kashmir Issue as a result of good relationship and bonhomie that had developed between Mr. Narendra Modi and Mr. Nawaz Sharif. One wished that the two neighbours come to terms and live in peace so that both register growth, development and progress for the good of their people. After all the two nations share a lot between them in their ways of life, culture, languages, food-habits so on and so forth.

On 14 July 2015, Nawaz Sharif and Narender Modi met on side lines at Ufa in Russia, attending the Shanghai Cooperation Organization (SCO) Summit. The foreign secretaries of India and Pakistan. S. Jaishankar and Aijaz Ahmad Choudhary issued a joint statement after the bilateral meeting between the two prime ministers. According to the joint statement the prime ministers met in a cordial atmosphere and exchanged views on issues of bilateral and regional interest.

They agreed that India and Pakistan have a collective responsibility to ensure peace and promote development. To do so, they are prepared to discuss all outstanding issues. Both leaders condemned terrorism in all its forms and agreed to cooperate with each other to eliminate this menace from South Asia.

They also agreed on the following steps to be taken by the two sides:

1. A meeting in New Delhi between the two NSA's to discuss all issues connected with terrorism.

2. Early meeting of DGBSF and DG Pakistan Rangers followed by that of the DGMO's.
3. Decision to release fishermen in each other's custody, along with their boats, within a period of 15 days.
4. Mechanism for facilitating religious tourism.
5. Both sides agreed to discuss ways and means to expedite the Mumbai case trial, including additional information like providing voice samples.

Prime Minister Nawaz Sharif reiterated his invitation to Prime Minister Modi to visit Pakistan for the SAARC summit in 2016. Prime Minister Modi accepted the invitation. However, subsequently the SAARC summit 2016 to be held in Pakistan was cancelled due to worsening of the relations between Pakistan and India. The other neighbours of the two countries also expressed inability to attend following the announcement by India to boycott the conference.

Before the ink on the agreement arrived at Ufa between India and Pakistan had hardly dried three heavily armed gunmen dressed in army uniforms infiltrated international border and opened fire on 27 July 2015 on a bus and then attacked Dina Nagar police station in Gurdaspur district in Punjab. Ten people died in the attack including the Gurdaspur S.P., 3 police men, 3 civilians and the three terrorists. Hadn't the Punjab Roadways bus driver shown presence of mind and not stopped when asked by the terrorists to do so the number of civilian causalities would have been much more. From the dead terrorists 3AK-47 rifles, grenades and GPS and Night vision devices, etc. were recovered. The attack again strained relations between the two countries.

The NH-44 the main artery that connects Punjab and Jammu and Kashmir and runs parallel to the international border has become a favourite route for cross border attacks by the Pakistani terrorists. It has come to be known as "highway of terror".

Although a large portion of the India-Pak border on the 553 km. Gurdaspur-Jammu sector is fenced, there are several gaps caused by the Ravi river and seasonal rivulets that cut into the international boundary. Gurdaspur shares a long zig-zag border with Pakistan. It is easy to infiltrate from this stretch as compared to the heavily mined and guarded Line of Control (LoC) as well as the International Border in neighbouring Jammu and Kashmir. The enemy even dug underground tunnels to infiltrate; these were discovered by chance by BSF Jawans. A dense fog in winter makes border surveillance an added challenge.

As the border terrain is broken and forested the rivulet beds provide an ideal cover for terrorists who can sneak in and reach the busy NH-44 highway that runs along the border. This enables terrorists to hijack vehicles and mount rapid strikes. In almost all terror attacks, terrorists used snatched vehicles to attack the intended targets-defence installations, cantonments, air force base, army camps, police stations and ammunition dumps. The highway also witnesses heavy movement of army convoys and movement of pilgrims to Mata Vaishno Devi and Amarnath Shrines and these become easy targets for the Jihadi terrorists.

Following the Gurdaspur attack the relations between India and Pakistan had cooled again. However, in November that year, Modi once again met his counterpart in Paris on the side lines of the 2015 United Nations climate change conference. This was the first the two leaders would meet after the July Ufa meeting. This brief meet was followed by talks between the national security advisors in Bangkok where they discussed terrorism, Jammu and Kashmir and a range of bilateral issues. The Bangkok meeting was followed by talks between External Affairs Minister Sushma Swaraj and her counterpart in Islamabad.

On December 25, 2015 Modi surprised all when he landed at Lahore on way to New Delhi from Kabul where he had gone on a visit. He stopped over at Lahore to wish Pakistani PM Nawaz Sharif on his birthday and to take part in the Marriage ceremony of his granddaughter. He also paid respects to Nawaz Sharif's aging father. Although everybody in India was surprised by this move of Modi because for months he had been saying that talks and terrorism cannot go together, yet many hoped that his bold move would pave way for improving the strained relations between the two countries.

Hardly within a week of PM Modi's Lahore visit a group of heavily armed terrorists infiltrated and attacked Pathankot Air Force Base which is part of the Western Air Command of the Indian Air Force on 2 January 2016. Four attackers and two security forces personnel were killed in the initial battle with an additional security force member dying from injuries later. The gun battle and the subsequent combing operation lasted for about seventeen hours.

A further three soldiers died after being admitted to hospital, raising the death toll to six soldiers, fresh gun shots were heard and another security officer was killed by an IED explosion. The operation continued on 4th January and a 5th attacker was confirmed dead. Not until a final 6th terrorist was reported killed on 5th January was the anti-terrorist operation declared over, though further searches continued for some more time. The terrorist attack received international media coverage and was widely condemned.

The attack led to breakdown of India-Pakistan relations. It is believed that the attack was carried out by terrorist outfit Jaish-e-Mohammad, an Islamist group of Pakistan. As per the several pieces of evidence collected it was an attempt by ISI to derail a fragile peace process meant to further destablise the deteriorated relations between India and Pakistan.

Even before the gunfire had died down at Pathankot air base, people across India began asking the inevitable question: would this brazen terror attack neutralize the bonhomie and gains generated by PM Modi's surprise visit to Lahore? The question was not surprising, given the cycle that has accompanied almost every recent effort by India and Pakistan leaders to engage and move ahead with the fraught peace—a grand gesture or a visit or some forward movement and an outrageous terror attack meant to inflame and incite public opinion.

There were several attacks carried out by the Pakistani terrorists before the 2 January 2016 which are definitely a cause of concern. Besides the Gurdaspur attack, a BSF convoy was attacked near Udhampur that resulted in the death of several personnel. One of the two terrorists was killed and another one was captured alive by civilians. These intruders were trained and sent by Lashker-e-Taiba as per the statement of the captured terrorist and the evidence gathered by Indian intelligence agencies from the GPS devices used by the terrorists.

As usual India protested to Pakistan following the attack on Pathankot Air Base. As expected Pakistan denied any connection with the attack. They suggested that a joint fact finding team should visit Pathankot. India assented and a Joint Inspection Team (JIT) visited Pathankot. The Pakistan team included an ISI man also. After their return Pakistani newspapers quoted the members of the Pakistani team saying that there was no evidence of Pakistan's involvement in the Pathankot attack and that attack was a drama staged by India to malign Pakistan. Those who believed in India that Pakistani's would own up their involvement in the attack must have lived in a fool's paradise. Pakistan has always been in denial mode. What did they do after the 26 Nov. 2008 Mumbai attack by ten Pakistani terrorists in which 166 people including some foreigners died. One of the terrorists Ajmal Kasab was caught alive. He gave details of the planning made in Pakistan. Despite all the evidence including the tapes of conversation between the terrorists and their mentors in Karachi provided by India the perpetrators of the attack are roaming free in Pakistan. The Pakistani courts have not been able to punish the guilty despite clearcut evidence provided by India because the Pakistani establishment and ISI do not want jihadists to be punished. Using terror is a part of Pakistan's state policy against India.

In the summer of 2016 Kashmir was apparently peaceful and life was going on as usual. The valley was teeming with tourists and Amarnath pilgrims upto July 8, 2016, when Burhan Wani, a local militant commander of Hijbul Mujahideen was killed by the Indian security forces. Over a million tourists had visited the valley till then as against 550,000 in 2015.

After his killing anti India protests started in all 10 districts of Kashmir valley. Curfew was imposed in all the districts of the valley but protesters defied curfew with attacks on security forces and police properties. On 15 July 2016 the mobile services were suspended by the government. Kashmir valley remained under 53 days of consecutive curfew which was then lifted. Separatists have been issuing calendars of shutdown but these have not been so effective. At the time of writing the situation in the valley has improved. Schools, Colleges and offices have started working, public and private transport is plying as usual and other business activities have largely resumed. Attendance in 10th and 12th class examinations of J&K Board of School Education was over ninty-five per cent. The near five month shutdown enforced by the separatist elements has ruined the economy of the valley. At the peak of tourist season, when Burhan Wani was killed on 8th July the shutdowns brought every activity to a stop in the valley. The livelihood of thousands of house boat owners, hotels, boatmen, taxi owners, and small entrepreneurs, shop owners and daily wagers came to a stop. Almost five months of education of students were wasted. One may ask who has gained by all this forced shutdown by separatists? Thank heavens life is returning to normal. Except for a few pockets of Srinagar city writ of the separatists does not run. People have understood the plan of Pakistan to ruin them. It may be no surprise that as a result of demonetization announced by the PM Modi on the evening of 8th Nov. 2016 stone pelting by miscreants came to a stop because the hawala currency and fake notes of ` 500 and ` 1000 that were paid to them suddenly became illegal tender.

Pakistan's P.M. Nawaz Sharif while addressing the 71st session of the UN General Assembly on Wednesday night on September 22, 2016 harped on Pakistan's pet theme of Kashmir and India baiting. He described the killed Burhan Wani (a terrorist) as a young Kashmiri Leader thereby legitimizing terrorism. Anyone who raises a gun against the state is a terrorist. He described him as a symbol of Kashmiri Intifida, a peaceful freedom movement. Indian Foreign Minister Sushma Swaraj in her address to UNGA on 26 September 2016 rebutted all the allegations of Pakistan P.M. against human rights violations in Kashmir and told the International community how his country was exporting terror not only to India but to other countries also, thereby fomenting trouble everywhere including Kashmir. She referred to Uri attack by Pakistani terrorists. She described the terrorism as a scourge and mentioned terrorist attacks this year alone in Kabul, Dhaka, Istanbul, Mogadishu, Brussels, Bangkok, Paris, Pathankot and Uri as well as daily barbaric tragedies in Syria and Iraq. She said that terrorism is undoubtedly the biggest violation of human rights. It targets the innocent and kills indiscriminately.

As I have stated earlier "peace" is the only alternative between the two neighbouring countries to look forward to for the sake of development and progress of their people. Hostilities will not bear any fruit. Modiji soon after becoming Prime Minister tried to extend a hand of friendship to Nawaz Sharif who seemed to reciprocate. Unfortunately ISI and the non-state actors do not seem to be inclined to allow improvement of relations between the two countries. Whenever the two countries try to hold talks terrorist attacks take place to stall these. It cannot be a mere coincidence that terror attacks happen when the two countries try to come closer.

During 2016 many terrorist attacks were carried out on Army camps, Air Force station, CRPF and BSF. Pathankot attack was a terrorist attack committed on 2 January 2016 at the Pathankot Air Force station, part of the western Air Command of the Indian Air Force and we lost six soldiers and an officer. On September 18 terrorists of the Pakistan backed Jaish-e-Mohammed mounted a deadly attack on an Indian Army Camp in Uri killing 20 of its soldiers and injuring many others. On the midnight of 2nd and 3rd of October 2016 militants attacked a camp of the Indian Army's 46 Rashtriya Rifles in Baramulla killing one officer and injuring a number of soldiers. Another attempt to storm a RR Camp was foiled on 6th October when security men gunned down three militants after an exchange of fire in the Langate area of Handwara in North Kashmir.

The latest attack was carried out on 29th November 2016 in which two officers and five Jawans were killed. The massive terror attack took place in an army base near Jammu at Nagrota, the headquarters of the Army's 16 corps. The terrorists dressed in police uniform stormed the base camp. All the three were liquidated in the encounter.

On the same day, BSF killed three terrorists who had succeeded in entering Indian territory using 80 meter long 2×2 meter underground tunnel at International Border at Chamliyal in Ramgarh sector of Samba district. The tunnel had been dug using Chinese technology. They had planned to carry out sensational attacks on trains along Jammu-Pathankot National Highway using liquid explosive trinitroglycerine filled in plastic bottles. Had the terrorists not been eliminated they would have played havoc with innocent lives travelling in trains using Chain IEDs to blow up rail tracks and hit running trains. The terrorists who had attacked a bus and police station at Dina Nagar in Gurdaspur in Punjab on 27 July 2015 had planted similar five chain devices on the Amritsar-Pathankot line near Parmanand Railway Station, 5 kms. from the site of the attack. It is due to detection of the five IEDs by an alert railway track man while patrolling along the railway track between Dina Nagar and Jhakhori Railway Stations that a disaster was averted. The IEDs had been wired to a small bridge just before a passenger train was due to cross the bridge. The list of earlier terror attacks is long but I will mention just a few. On February 10, 2000 infiltrating militants triggered blasts in Shalimar Express Train at Satwal in Kathua District killing five persons. Militants crossed IB and triggered bomb blasts on Jammu Railway Station on August 7, 2001 killing 12 people and injuring 29 innocents. Similarly, infiltrating militants blew up a railway track in Samba on October 26, 2003.

Following the terrible terrorist attack on an army unit at Uri on 18 Sept. 2016 sleeping soldiers with lethal weapons resulting in death of 20 Jawans mostly as a result of the fire that engulfed their quarters. The three terrorists involved were also liquidated. This shocking attack angered the whole Indian Nation and the people started to question whether the policy of extending hand of friendship to Pakistan was a wise one. How could we talk to a nation that inflicts injury to our civilians and armed forces by sending in terrorists? After all these terrorists do not fall from the sky. They are pushed in to harm us. Three days after the attack, Indian foreign secretary summoned Pakistan High Commissioner and shared evidence of Pakistani involvement in the Uri attack, which Islamabad as expected rejected. On September 22 Pakistani P.M. Nawaz Sharif delivered provocative speech at the UN General Assembly, hailing the Hizbul Commandar Burhan Wani.

The Nationwide anger was so strong that Prime Minister Modi had to issue a statement that the perpetrators of these heinous attacks by terrorists from launching pads across the LoC would not go unpunished. The Defense Minister Parikar also stated that our armed forces would react appropriately at a place and time of their choosing.

In the wee hours of 29 September, the Indian army conducted a surgical strike on terror launch pads along the LoC, announced DGMO Ranbir Singh, reading from a prepared statement at a press conference. He was accompanied by Vikas Swaroop from the Ministry of External Affairs. This operation was in response to the strikes on Indian soil including the ones in Poonch and Uri on 11 and 18 September respectively according to the Indian DGMO. This announcement triggered a euphoric phase among Indians who were desperately seeking vengeance for the killing of our jawans and wanting to give a clear message to Pakistan. The DGMO also said that the action was limited to terrorist launching pads and not Pakistani Armed outposts.

Pakistan denied that any special strikes occurred. Pakistan's foreign office rejected the Indian claim as "baseless" and said India was 'deliberately' escalating conflict. The Pakistan army said that there had only been "cross border firing". Pakistan warned that it would respond militarily should a surgical strike actually occur. It claimed that two of their soldiers were killed in the firing.

After the Indian "surgical strike" across the LoC hostilities between the armed forces of the two countries increased and right through the months of October and November heavy artillery on each other has resulted in death of soldiers and civilians on both sides. Villages close to the border came under heavy fire on the Indian side causing large number of civilian causalities and injuries. Thousands of villagers had to desert their homes for safety and suffered losses. They had to leave standing crops in their fields. This is what we have seen on our side and can visualize similar civilians causalities and losses on the other side also. Who benefits from such hostilities? Do the two nations really have to follow a path leading to death and destruction?

After taking over as army chief of Pakistan on 29 November 2016 General Qamar Javed Bajwa had stated that there would be peace on our borders. Indeed after his taking over our borders had become silent and firing was stopped. It may be a beginning of a period of cessation of hostilities on the borders; but going by past history of Pakistani generals only time will tell. One would wish that no more militants are pushed across the border to start a new cycle of hostilities. It is also good that Mr. Sartaj Aziz advisor to Pakistan P.M. on foreign affairs attended the "Heart of Asia Istanbul Process Conference" at Amritsar on 3 and 4 December 2016.

As Afghanistan faces the resurgence of Taliban, the conference of major regional and global powers attains importance. The conference attended by nearly 40 countries and leading groupings like the European Union deliberated on various challenges facing Afghanistan including revival of a peace process in the conflict-ridden country. At the end of conference a declaration was issued which called for immediate elimination of terrorism to help the war-ravaged country in its political and economic transition. Recognizing once again that terrorism, violent extremism, separatism and sectarianism and linkages among them are gravest challenges that the Heart of Asia region and the rest of international community face, and these problems would continue to pose a severe threat to the sovereignty, territorial integrity, economic development and bilateral and regional cooperation. The participating countries reiterated a strong commitment to strengthening comprehensive cooperation among the Heart of Asia countries and intensify their efforts to combat terrorism in all its forms and manifestations through solidarity and collective action.

The conference reaffirmed the reorganization made in Islamabad in 2015 that violent extremism facilitates, exchanges and justifies act of terrorism and violence and hoped to undertake and introduce measures to curb the spread of violent extremism and terrorism. The declaration also recognized the necessity of taking serious measures to address the recruitment of youth to extremist and terrorist networks.

There was hope in some quarters that with the arrival of Sartaj Aziz in Amritsar to attend the "Heart of Asia" conference there might be some activity on the side lines. Except for exchange of pleasantries between P.M. Modi and Sartaj Aziz at Amritsar nothing of the sort happened. The principled Indian stand that no talks can be held until terrorist activities against it do not come to an end is a right one. Meaningful talks between the two countries is the only way to solve all the outstanding issues between them but peace is a precondition. How can any country hold talks with another country that holds terrorism as part of state policy to deal with her neighbors? It is high time that Pakistan bans all well-known terrorist organizations in that country and throws their leaders behind bars to stop them from recruiting and training terrorists. Only after terror attacks against India come to an end meaningful talk with Pakistan can be resumed. Pakistan must also stop meddling in Kashmir if it wants to hold fruitful discussions and talks with India.

Indian position in Jammu and Kashmir is clear. It is legally an integral part of India. True there is unrest in Kashmir—a creation of Pakistan. State of Jammu and Kashmir does not comprise of the valley alone. There are other stakeholders and the Indian state is open to hold talks with all of them. It is also true that Kashmiris are angry not only because of Wani's killing but because the trust between the valley and New Delhi has been eroded over the years. Kashmiris are also radicalized to a large extent which should be a matter of worry. The unprincipled and opportunistic polices of the valley leaders are further adding to the problem. Out of power their language changes suddenly and everything turns wrong and the centre is responsible for it. As a matter of fact Kashmir's political class has failed to engage with its own people. Verily they are a part of the problem.

The Indian Government at the centre has to talk to the Kashmiris and get them to their side. It is a political problem and should be dealt with politically. The Kashmiris, no doubt are angry and there is a trust deficit. The centre has to win back their trust, hearts and minds. For achieving this the agenda of alliance between P.D.P. and B.J.P. must be implemented in right earnest. The common man has to be reached out in all possible ways. P.M. Narsimha Rao had promised to the people of Kashmir 20 years ago that "sky is the limit" for their welfare. Mr. Ram Madhav has reiterated the same thing. This promise must be kept by the present NDA Government at the centre. We must also remember that P.M. Vajpayee was very popular among the people of Kashmir because he had touched the cords of their hearts. His approach needs to be repeated to earn goodwill of the people in Kashmir.

"With some imagination ways can be found to grant greater autonomy with no threat to India's sovereignty. This was the case upto 1953 after which State's autonomy was continuously diluted. The time has come to go to the next level in Kashmir, which is bleeding India, tarnishing its image both internally and externally, providing ammunition to Pakistan and alienating a whole generation in the state. A government that cares for its people will have to 'walk the talk" (Chanakya, Sunday, *Hindustan Times*, Sept. 04, 2006). In my opinion too it is high time to move forward and deal with our own people in the best possible way.

With the change of Army chief in Pakistan we might see a change coming on the LoC. It may be interesting to note here C Christaine fair's remark, "Pakistanis and analysts of Pakistan have long remarked with more truth than hyperbole, that while generally countries have armies, in Pakistan the army has the country". Nevertheless according to Lt. Gen. (Retd.) Syed Ata Hasnain, "General Bajwa comes at a time when equations and axes are also changing. First the Chinese are now increasingly looking at the China Pakistan Economic Corridor (CPEC) with a more serious intent. They would not want Gilgit-Baltistan in greater tension, neither Balochistan. But if the current tension with India only gets worse India is going to play both cards: diluting of tension in J&K is therefore in Pakistan's interest. Secondly, the US appears to be ignoring Pakistan as its strategic interests shift. With President Elect Trump's likely isolationist policy Pakistan's significance will further dilute. It is only nations with whom economics and business will be strong, that US is likely to strengthen relations and India is one of them. Pakistan's relationship with Afghanistan is not improving and the Taliban in Afghanistan are under no one's control. That means continuation of Pakistan's dwindling strategic space and India's continuing influence. Thirdly, the positive on the horizon is the improving relationship with the Russians and feasibility of getting weapons and equipment from that source. The Russians too may not be too happy to see their weapons in use against India with whom it still has a strong strategic relationship.

Thus from every count an improvement in relationship with India is called for. It won't happen with loss of any pride to Pakistan Army. Gen. Bajwa may after initial briefings and unbiased review realize the above. If offered tactical escape routes without loss of pride we could yet see the LoC tension drawing down. The need may be to reduce rhetoric from our side to allow this to take place" (*Daily Excelsior* 29, Nov. 2016).

Bibliography

Abdullah, Sheikh Mohemmed. *Aatish-e-Chinar*. Ali Mohemmed and Sons, Srinagar, 1985.

Akbar, M.J. *Byline*, September 29, 1991.

Ali, Muddasir. J K Government slept over repeated warnings, Greater Kashmir, Oct. 9, 2014.

Beg, Saleem. Face Book—INTACH Kashmir Chapter.

Bhat, Chander M. *Vitasta—A Part of Our Identity*. http:/ikashmir.net/chanderbhat/docs/Vitasta. pdf., 2009.

Bose, Sumentra. *Kashmir: Roots to Conflict, Paths of Peace*. Harvard Univ. Press, 2003.

Chanakya, "Kashmir after Burhan Wani Killing," Sunday, *Hindustan Times*, Sept. 04, 2016.

Ganhar, J.N. *Amarnath: The Shrine Celestial*. The Jammu and Kashmir Dharmarth Trust, 1984.

Gupta, Bal K. "Forgotten Atrocities: Memoirs of a Survivor of the 1947 Partition of India", Lulu. Com. 2012. Reviewed in *Daily Excelsior* Magazine, Oct. 26, 2014.

Hasnain, Lt. General Syed Ata (Retd), Gen. Qamar Javed Bajwa: Man, for the new season. *Daily Excelsior*. Nov. 29, 2016.

Jagmohan, *My Frozen Turbulence*, Allied Publishers, New Delhi, 1991.

Kapoor, Pramod. *Witness to Life and Freedom: Margaret Bourke—White in India and Pakistan*. New Delhi: Lustre Press, Roli Books, 2010.

Kaul, B.L. "Save The Himalayas", *The Hindu*, June 9, 1991.

Khan, Major General Mohd. Akbar. In *Defence Journal,* Karachi, (June-July 1985).

Kudaisya, Gyanesh. *History Today.* Vol. 64, Issue 5, 2014.

Lal, Pyare. *Mahatma Gandhi The Last Phase,* Vol. 11. Navjivan Ahmadabad, 1958.

Madhok, Balraj. *Jammu, Kashmir and Ladakh: Problem and Solution,* New Delhi, 1987.

———. *Kashmir: The Storm Center of the World,* A. Ghosh, 1992.

Mahajan, Mehr Chand. *Looking Back.* Asia Publishing House, Bombay, 1963.

Malik, Mohammad Syed. "1947 Tribal Invasion: Jinah's feat or folly?" *Kashmir Times,* April 4, 2010.

Margaret, Burke White. (American Journalist in Kashmir in 1947). *Half way to Freedom: A Report on the New India in the Words and Photographs.* Simon and Schuster, New York, 1949.

Mohibbul, Hasan. *Kashmir under the Sultans,* Aakar Books, Delhi, 2005.

Pandita, Rahul. *Our Moon has Blood Clots: The Exodus of Kashmiri Pandits,* Vintage Books, 2013.

Panikar, K.M. *Gulab Singh 1792-1858.* Read Books, 2007.

Peer, Giasuddin. *Understanding Kashmir Insurgency.* Light and Life Publishers, Delhi, 1992.

Puri, Balraj. *Kashmir Towards Insurgency,* Orient Longman, 1993.

Sher, R.K. Kashmir: A Valley in Tears. Kashmir Sentinel. September 15-October 15, 1995.

Singh, Col. J.P. (Retd). "Saviour of Kashmir". Brig. Rajinder Singh, *Daily Excelsior* Magazine, Oct. 26, 2014.

Sinha, Lt. General S.K. (Retd.), Accession, Azadi, Autonomy and National Integrity, News Point Jammu, Dec. 6, 2010.

Snedden, Christopher. *Kashmir: The Unwritten History.* Harper Collins, India, 2013.

Tickoo, Col. Tej K. (Retd), *Kashmir: Its Aborgines and their Exodus,* Lancer Publishers, 2012.

———. "Kashmir: Pandits offered three choices by Radical Islamists", *Indian Defence Review,* 26 Oct., 2014.

Ved Kumari. The Nilamata Purana, Vol. 1, J & K Academy of Art, Culture and Languages, Srinagar/Jammu, 1988.

Wadia, D.N. *Geology of India,* 3rd Edition, McGraw Hill, London, 1961.

https://en.m.wikipedia.org./Jammu and Kashmir Princely State.

https://en.m.wikipedia.org./Jammu and Kashmir-History.

https://en.m.wikipedia.org./History of Kashmir.

Index

B

C

H

I

J

K

M

S

T